IMAGES
of America

MULVANE

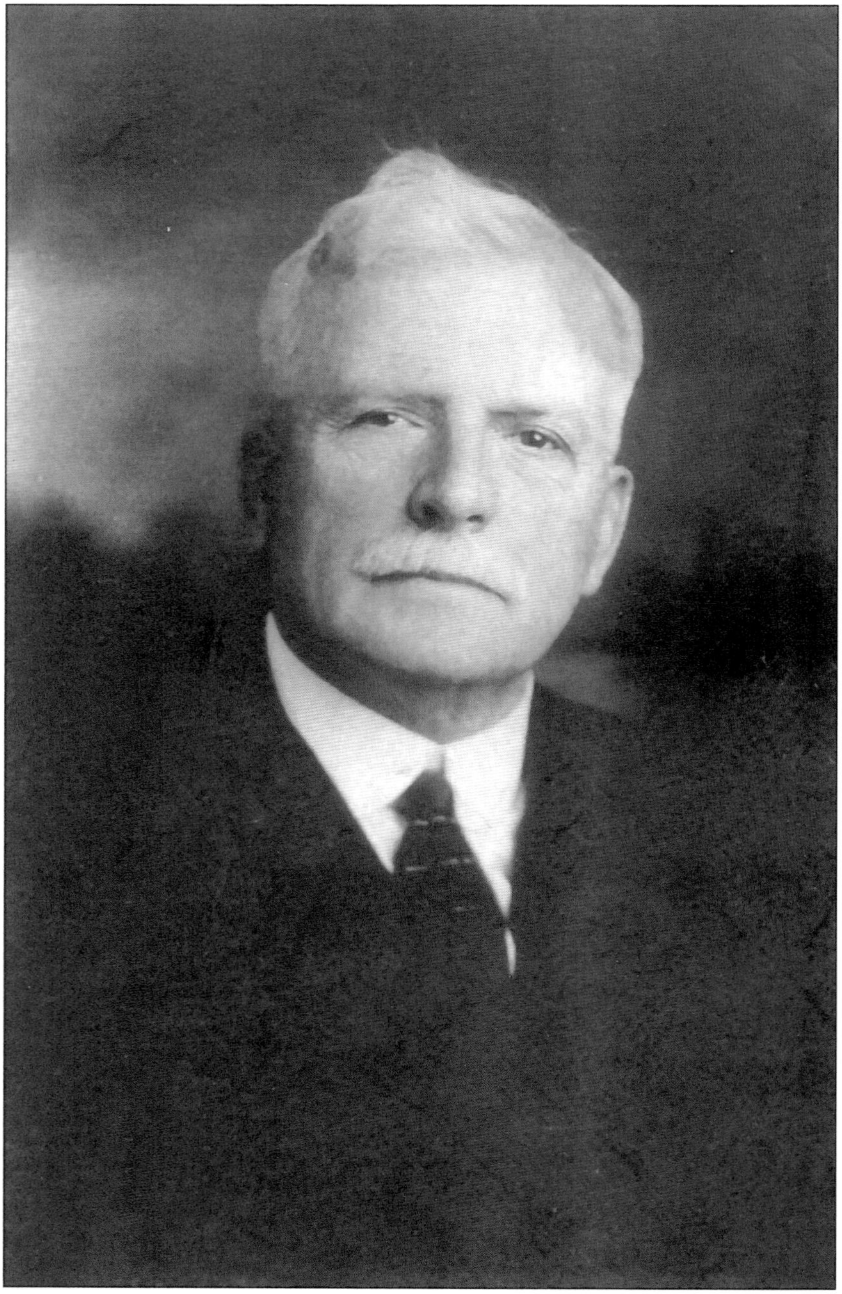

Joab Mulvane was the president of at least nine railroads and was responsible for locating towns on the Santa Fe line south from Wichita. Because he played such a prominent role in establishing the railroad settlement at its current location, the town was named for him. (Courtesy of the Mulvane Historical Museum.)

ON THE COVER: Downtown Mulvane is seen on a typical Saturday afternoon in 1947. It was a busy place where people shopped, socialized, and enjoyed life in small-town style. The old fountain that was used to water horses was still in place, and the theater showed Randolph Scott in *Badman's Territory*. (Courtesy of the Mulvane Historical Museum.)

IMAGES
of America

MULVANE

Gerald McCoy

ARCADIA
PUBLISHING

ISBN 978-0-7385-9871-0

Published by Arcadia Publishing
Charleston, South Carolina

Printed in the United States of America

Library of Congress Control Number: 2012949168

For all general information, please contact Arcadia Publishing:
Telephone 843-853-2070
Fax 843-853-0044
E-mail sales@arcadiapublishing.com
For customer service and orders:
Toll-Free 1-888-313-2665

Visit us on the Internet at www.arcadiapublishing.com

To my dad, my sisters, and the memory of my mother. I couldn't have asked for a better family; I hope I made you proud.

CONTENTS

ACKNOWLEDGMENTS

I would like to thank the Mulvane Historical Museum's curator, Vickie Lee, for her invaluable help in preparing this book. Not only was she a source of photographs and information, she was a cheerleader who provided me with encouragement and confidence when I felt overwhelmed. Vickie granted me unlimited access to files, photographs, and books that are irreplaceable. The trust that she placed in me is something that I will always remember and always cherish.

I would also like to thank Ron Dunlap and his entire family. Ron has a generous heart and is a very active member of the community. He is a longtime Mulvane businessman, and his love for the town and its people is contagious; I enjoy his friendship and benefit from his support.

Last but not least, I would like to thank Simone Monet-Williams and everyone at Arcadia Publishing. They took a chance on a photographer who had never written anything but a thank-you note and asked him to prepare a book about Mulvane, Kansas, for its Images of America series. The books help illustrate and preserve the heritage of communities all over the United States. These towns and their people are the core of our country and the source of its greatness. I am honored to play a role in telling this story.

Introduction

On January 29, 1861, Kansas became the 34th state to join the union. During the 1860s and 1870s, the land south of Wichita was primarily grassland. The Arkansas River provided water to the wildlife and to the people who settled the region.

Joab Mulvane was a prominent Topeka businessman with the Santa Fe Railroad. He was the president of at least nine rail lines and had other business interests, including the Edison Electric Light Company of Topeka, the Shawnee Fire Insurance Company, and the Kansas Salt Company. In addition to those ventures, he had a financial interest in numerous other businesses and towns across the state. He envisioned Kansas as a central distribution point for all of North America, and he had the authority to create lines and establish stops for Santa Fe throughout the state.

Ten miles south of Wichita, there was a small settlement adjacent to the river on the Sedgwick-Sumner County Line. In August 1879, local property owners H.C. Helbert and J.D. Loper agreed to donate land to the Santa Fe Company for the purposes of establishing a railroad on their properties. They also agreed to donate land for the purpose of creating a town that would serve as a rail stop on the line. Joab Mulvane played a prominent role in those proceedings, and at the suggestion of Mrs. H.C. Helbert, the town was named in his honor.

The Certificate of Incorporation for Mulvane, Kansas, was filed on September 20, 1879. Its first post office was established in October 1879. On July 15, 1886 (after two earlier banks had failed), the Mulvane State Bank opened its doors. It still operates today under the name of Carson Bank.

At some point in 1900 (the exact date is unknown), electricity came to Mulvane. Churches and businesses were the first to receive service, and the rates were very expensive. The initial fee was 50¢ for each 30 days of service, but the rate soon doubled to $1 per month.

On July 30, 1903, the first issue of the *Mulvane News* was published. Earlier attempts at newspaper publishing had not met with long-term success, but over 100 years later, the *News* is still in circulation.

On December 1, 1905, after devastating fires in 1891, 1893, and 1905, the City of Mulvane purchased fire protection equipment. On July 22, 1918, the Mulvane Volunteer Fire Department was formed.

The 20th century brought our country the Roaring Twenties and the Great Depression. Bracketing those events were two world wars. Mulvane lived through that period and developed its own identity. As the aircraft industry boomed during and after World War II, many Mulvane residents made the daily commute to the factories of Boeing, Cessna, Beech, or Learjet. They helped make Wichita "The Air Capital of the World."

Mulvane also enjoys a rich history in sports and athletics. The high school has produced several regional and state championships in girls' and boys' sports. It has been a football power and a baseball hotbed. Mulvane was the boyhood home of Carl Mays, a major-league pitcher with Hall of Fame statistics and the author of baseball's greatest tragedy.

Each year, the town hosts the annual Old Settlers Days celebration, which takes place during the third weekend of August. It began in 1873 (six years before the town was established). Jessie Bowles invited his friends and neighbors to a picnic in the walnut grove on his farm. The picnic became an annual event, with a different farmer serving as host each year. It continued to grow, and the 1904 get-together had over 5,000 guests. Today, Old Settlers Days features a parade, a street carnival, sporting events, an antique car show, musical performances by area entertainers, and a rodeo. It is attended by thousands of people from throughout the region.

Mulvane is also the birthplace of the Patriot Guard Motorcycle Club, created in 2005 by military veterans at Mulvane American Legion Post 136. The original mission of the group was to serve as a funeral escort for American servicemen and servicewomen who died in battle while serving our country in the Persian Gulf wars. It has since grown to include the funerals of law enforcement officers, fire department personnel, first responders, and any active duty member or veteran of the US Armed Forces. The club's charter states that it is just "a group of individuals with an unwavering respect for those who risk their lives for America's freedom and security." Membership is free, and the only stated requirement is "a deep respect for those who serve our country; military, firefighters, or law enforcement." The Patriot Guard now includes chapters all over the country and (as of 2011) has a membership of over 220,000 people.

Mulvane is home to the Kansas Star Casino, which is one of the most popular gaming facilities in Kansas. The Kansas Star opened in December 2011 and will ultimately include a hotel, restaurants, and an equestrian center. People from all over mid-America walk through its doors for fun and entertainment.

Mulvane has survived fires, floods, droughts, tornados, and blizzards. It has withstood economic prosperity and economic despair. Today, it is home to over 6,000 people, and its churches, schools, and businesses help form the fabric of America.

Some of the images have stories attached to them; some are just snapshots from a bygone era. They tell us about some of the town's good days and bad days, and in the process, they reveal a little bit about the kind of people who experienced those days. Whether you are a longtime Mulvane resident or just a passing visitor, you are invited to share in their past. Their tale is typical of small-town America, and ultimately, their story is our story.

One

Early Years

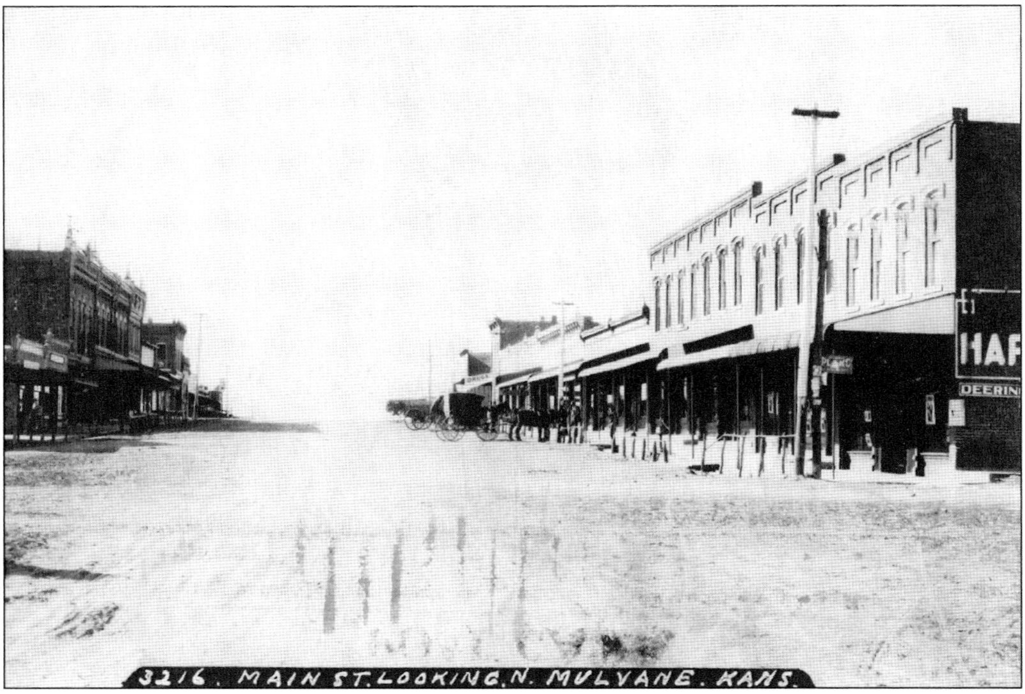

This photograph of Main Street was taken in 1906. Horse-and-buggy traffic still dominated the town, as the hitching rails indicate. Even though it was not yet 30 years old, Mulvane had developed a strong business district. (Courtesy of the Mulvane Historical Museum.)

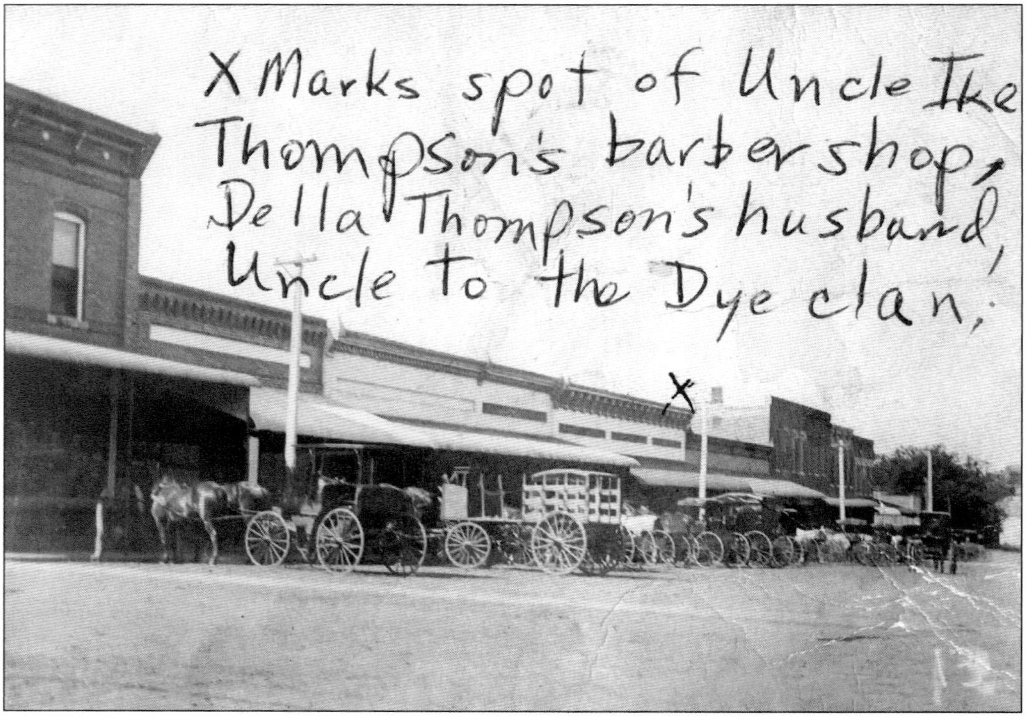

The north side of Main Street, looking east, is seen in this 1907 photograph. Ike Thompson's barbershop was located in the middle of the block. Note the utility poles that lined the streets. The horse-and-buggy era had not yet ended, but Mulvane was beginning to enter the 20th century. (Courtesy of the Mulvane Historical Museum.)

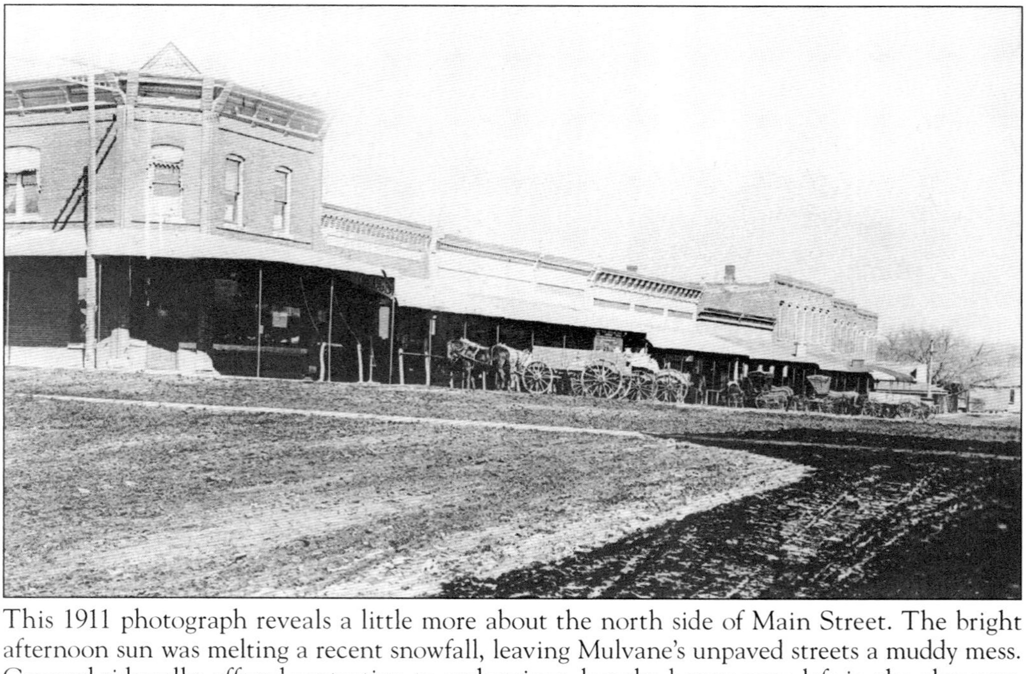

This 1911 photograph reveals a little more about the north side of Main Street. The bright afternoon sun was melting a recent snowfall, leaving Mulvane's unpaved streets a muddy mess. Covered sidewalks offered protection to pedestrians, but the horses were left in the elements. (Courtesy of the Mulvane Historical Museum.)

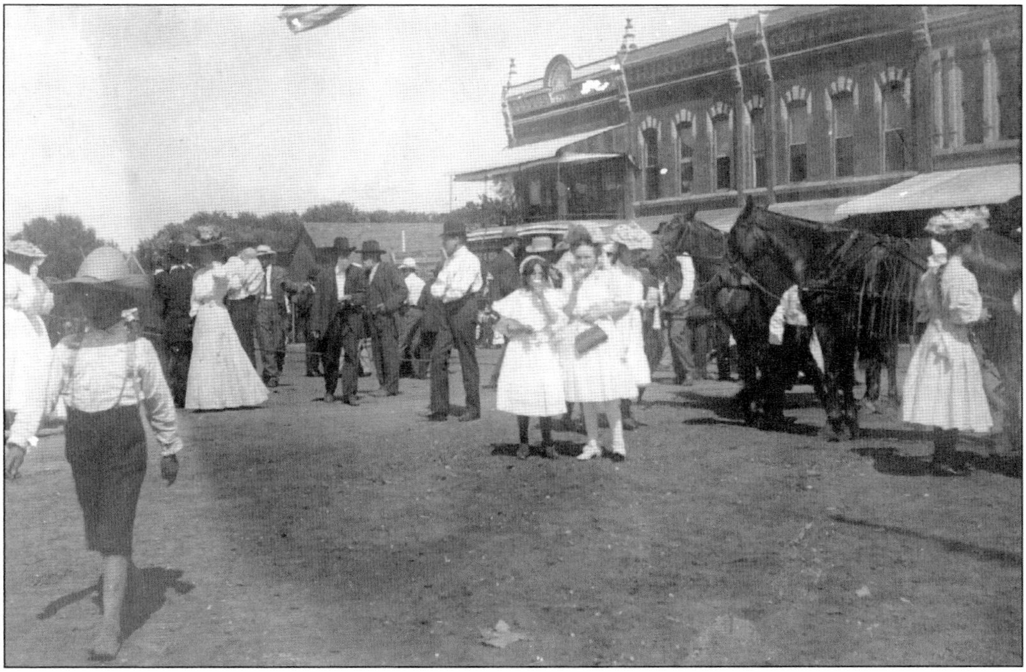

People are dressed in their finest clothes on a sunny afternoon in 1919. Although the exact nature of the event is unknown, the photograph may have been taken during a local horse show. Area residents would occasionally gather to show off their best horses. (Courtesy of the Mulvane Historical Museum.)

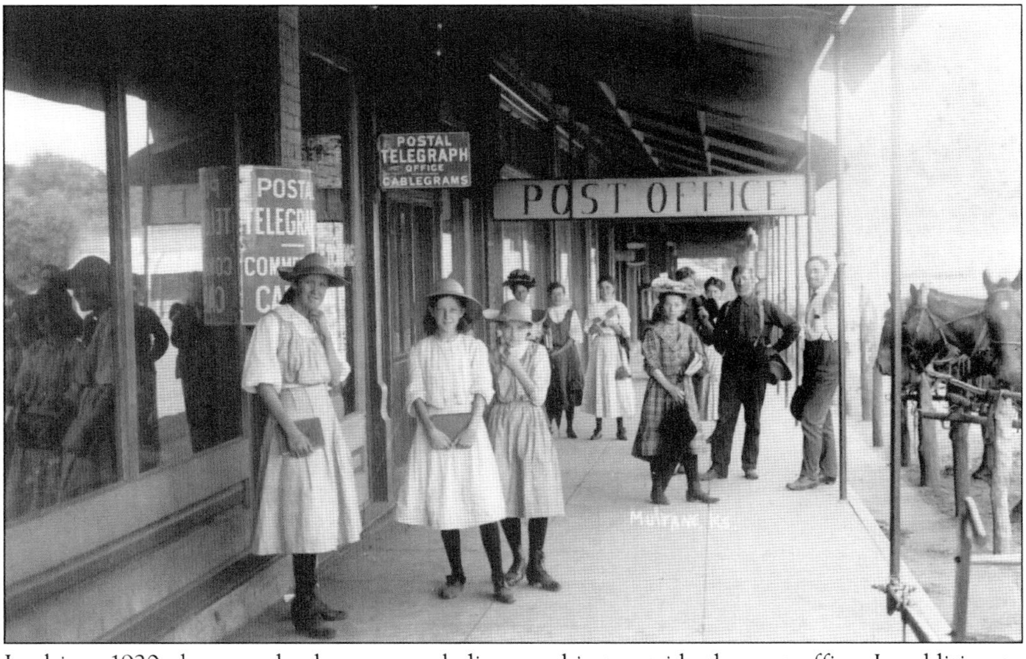

In this c. 1920 photograph, three young ladies stand just outside the post office. In addition to traditional mail service, telegraph and cablegram services were available. The horse at the extreme right seems to be very interested in the work of the photographer. (Courtesy of the Mulvane Historical Museum.)

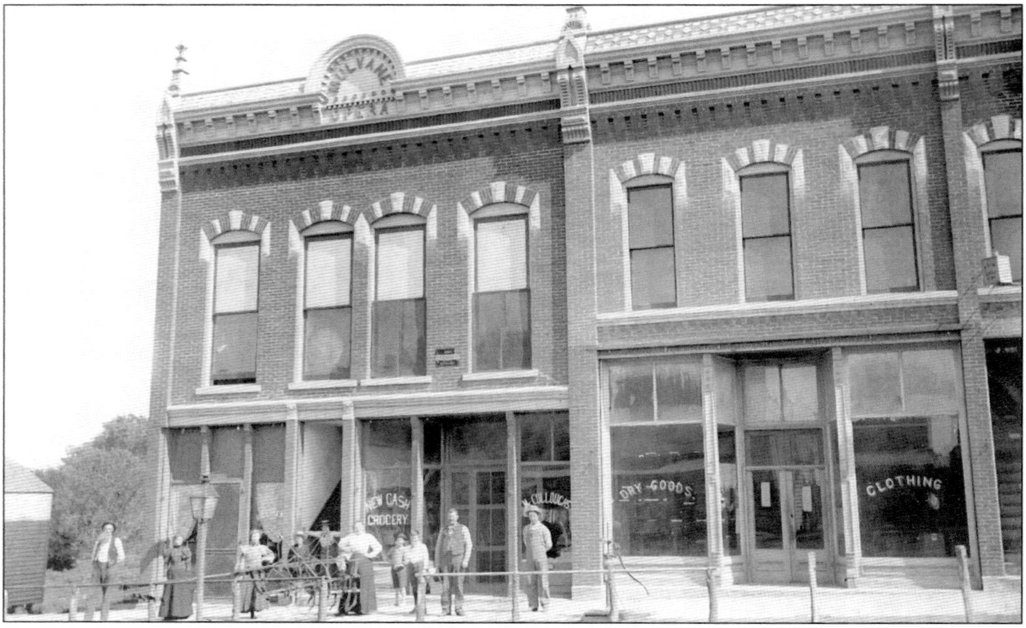

This photograph from the early 20th century shows a group of people outside a grocery store and a dry goods store. The grocery store, operated by the McCullough family, was located in Mulvane's original opera house, which was on the south side of Main Street. (Courtesy of the Mulvane Historical Museum.)

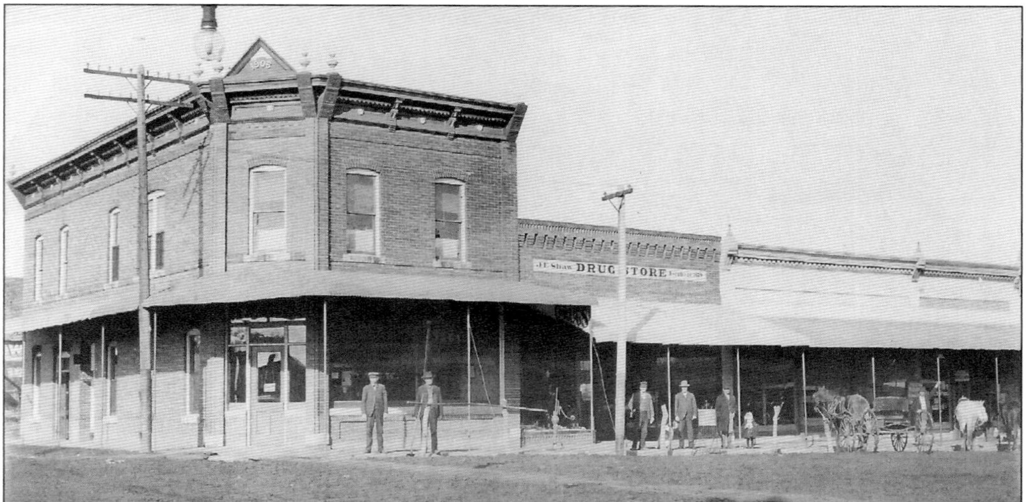

The bank building, completed in 1906, stands on the northeast corner of First and Main Streets. Next to it was Shaw's Drug Store. Founded in October 1879, just one month after the town was established, Shaw's was one of the oldest businesses in Mulvane. (Courtesy of the Mulvane Historical Museum.)

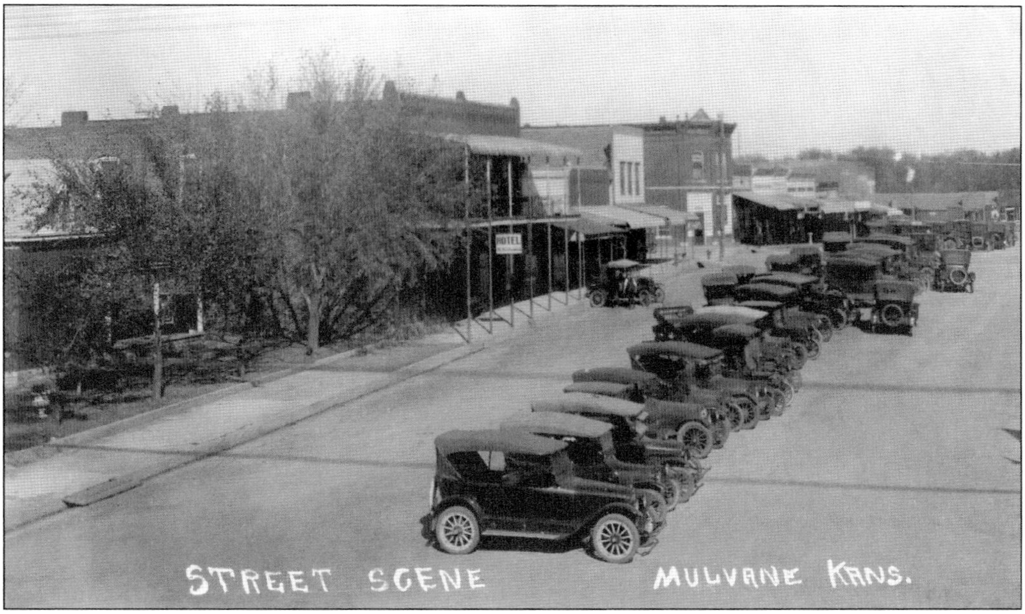

This photograph, taken from the depot in the early 1930s, shows the north side of Main Street. By then, Mulvane's downtown streets were paved, and the automobile era had arrived. The Lane Hotel sat in the middle of the block, and the bank building, on the northeast corner of First and Main Streets, was just down the street. (Courtesy of the Mulvane Historical Museum.)

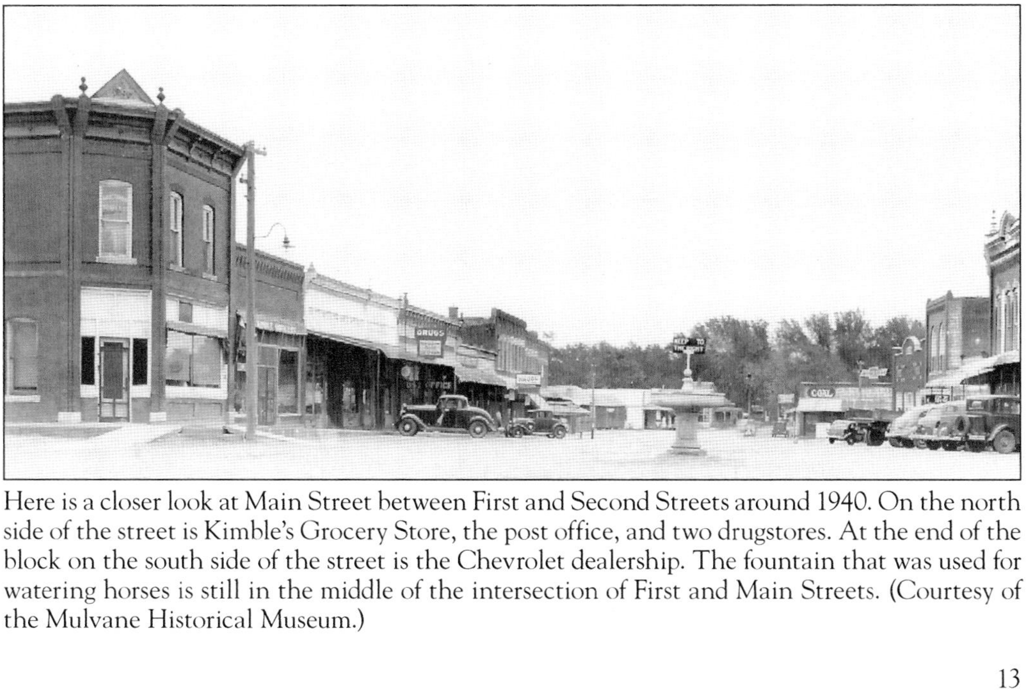

Here is a closer look at Main Street between First and Second Streets around 1940. On the north side of the street is Kimble's Grocery Store, the post office, and two drugstores. At the end of the block on the south side of the street is the Chevrolet dealership. The fountain that was used for watering horses is still in the middle of the intersection of First and Main Streets. (Courtesy of the Mulvane Historical Museum.)

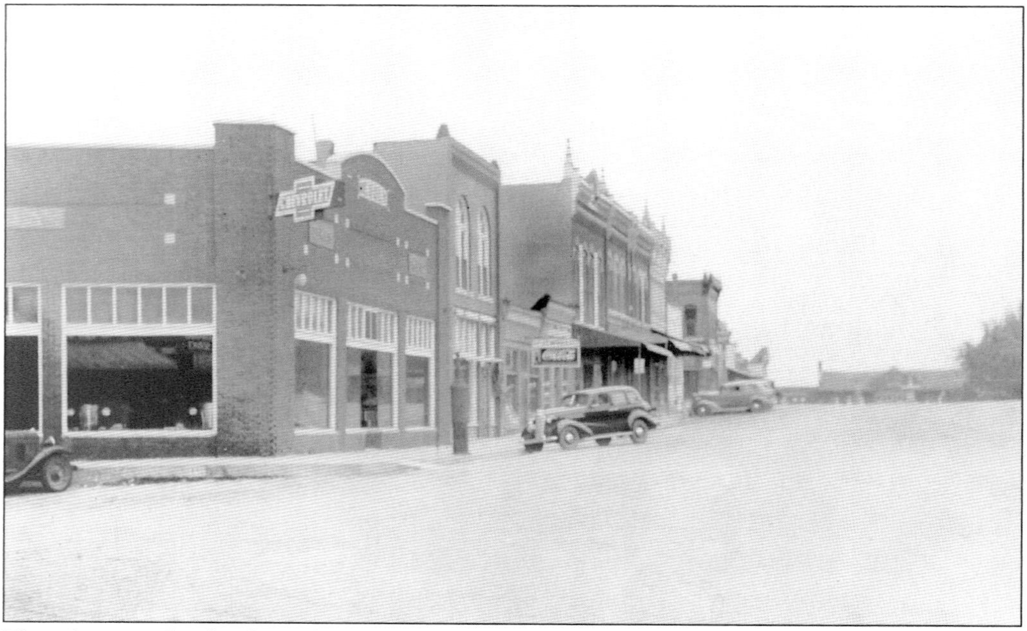

This photograph, also from about 1940, shows the south side of Main Street. The orientation is to the west, in the direction of the depot. The Chevrolet dealership was in the Nessly Building, on the southwest corner of First and Main Streets. The building would be destroyed by fire in 1999. (Courtesy of the Mulvane Historical Museum.)

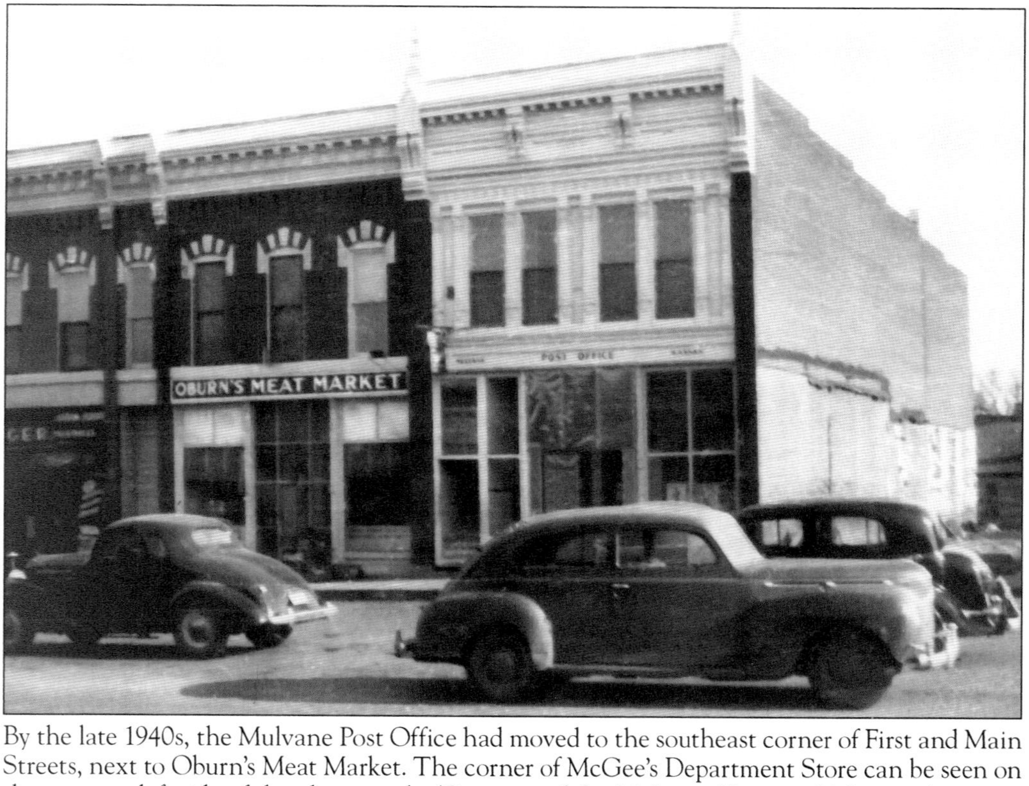

By the late 1940s, the Mulvane Post Office had moved to the southeast corner of First and Main Streets, next to Oburn's Meat Market. The corner of McGee's Department Store can be seen on the extreme left side of the photograph. (Courtesy of the Mulvane Historical Museum.)

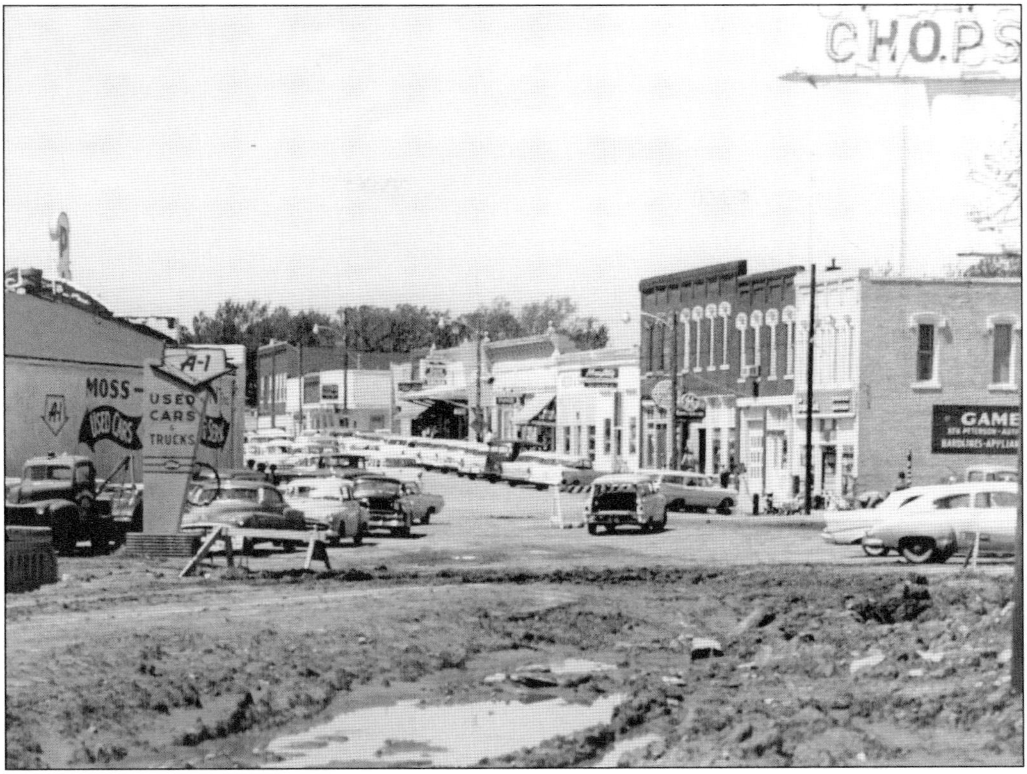

In this 1950s photograph, Mulvane begins to look like the town that it is today. The view is from east of the theater, looking west on Main Street. The traffic proves that Mulvane was a vibrant and active town. (Courtesy of the Mulvane Historical Museum.)

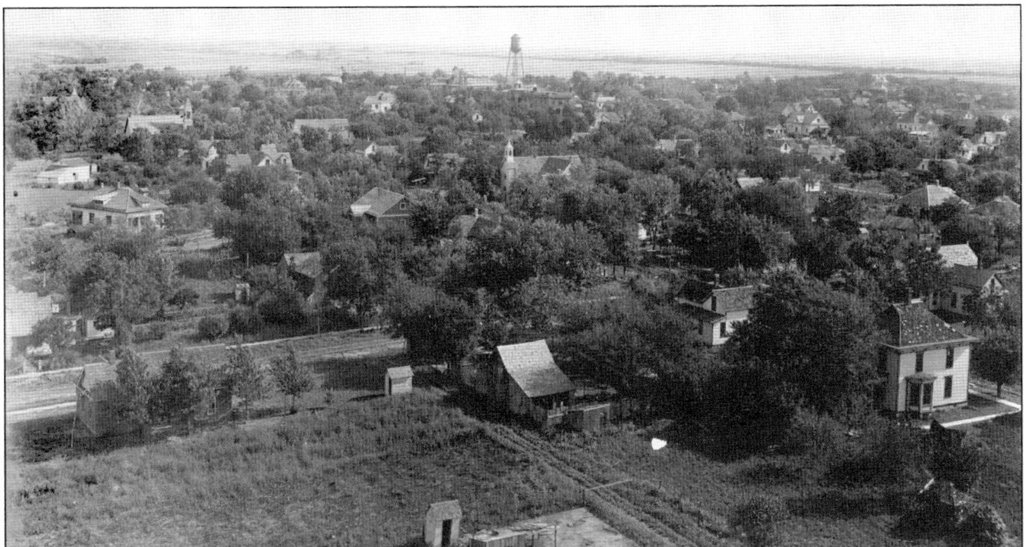
This panoramic photograph, possibly from the 1940s, is looking north and east from the top of the Mulvane Co-op. The water tower can be seen in the distance, and the grade school is next to it. The downtown area is beyond the left frame of the photograph. (Courtesy of the Mulvane Historical Museum.)

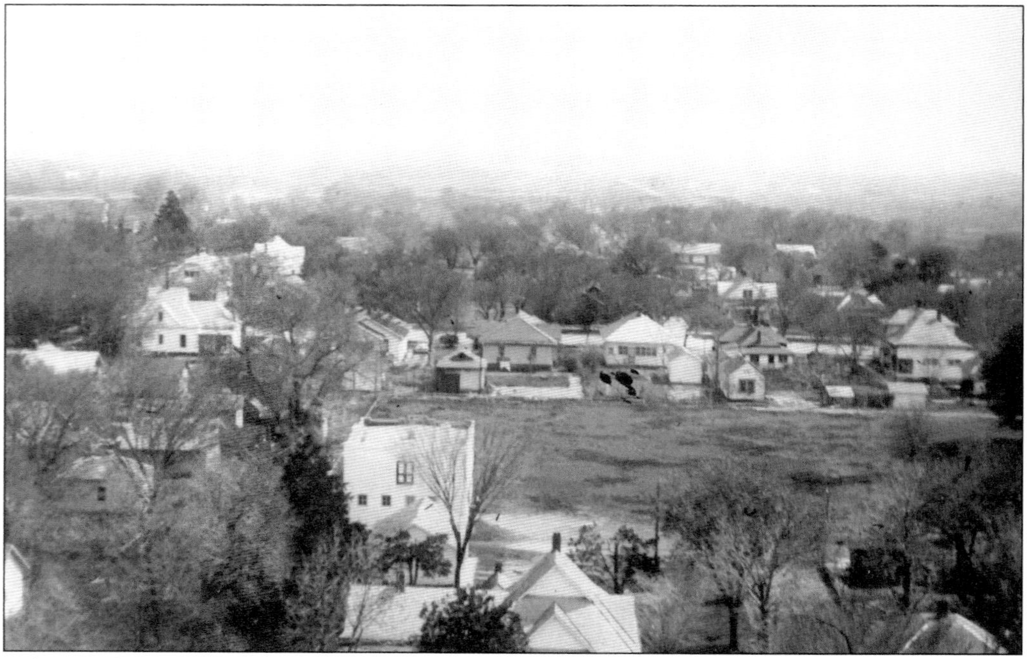

A brave photographer took this panoramic photograph (possibly in 1947) looking south from the top of the Mulvane water tower. It shows the residential area on the south side of town. Sumner County farmland lies in the distance, just beyond the trees. (Courtesy of the Mulvane Historical Museum.)

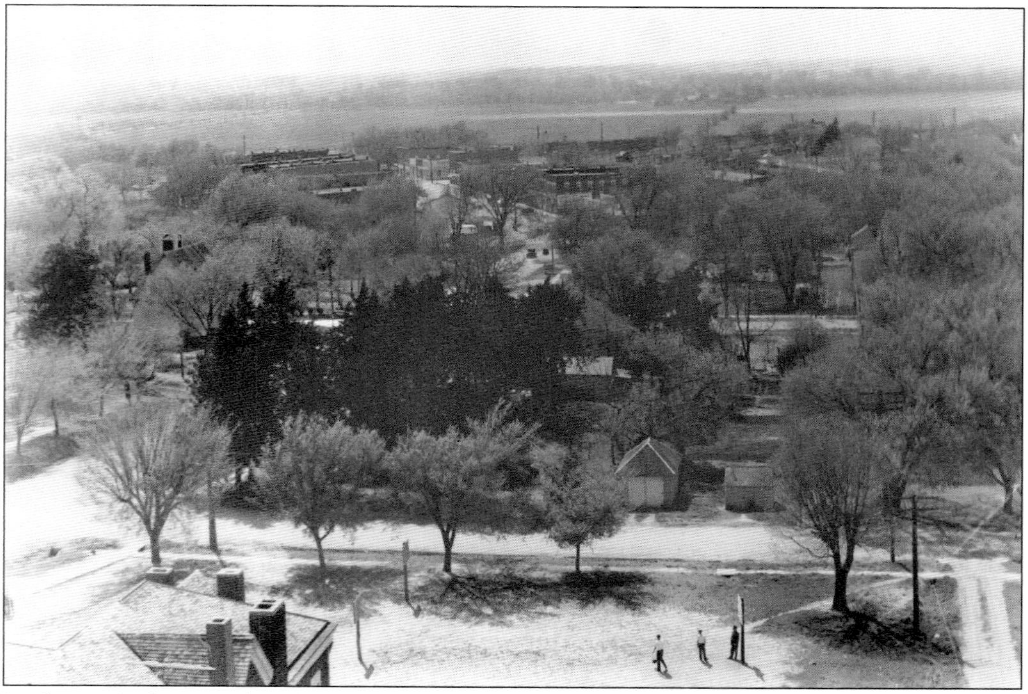

In this 1947 photograph, taken from the top of the water tower, the view is looking to the west. The grade school playground can be seen at the bottom, and downtown Mulvane is in the distance. A train can be seen at the edge of town. (Courtesy of the Mulvane Historical Museum.)

Two

Early Trains

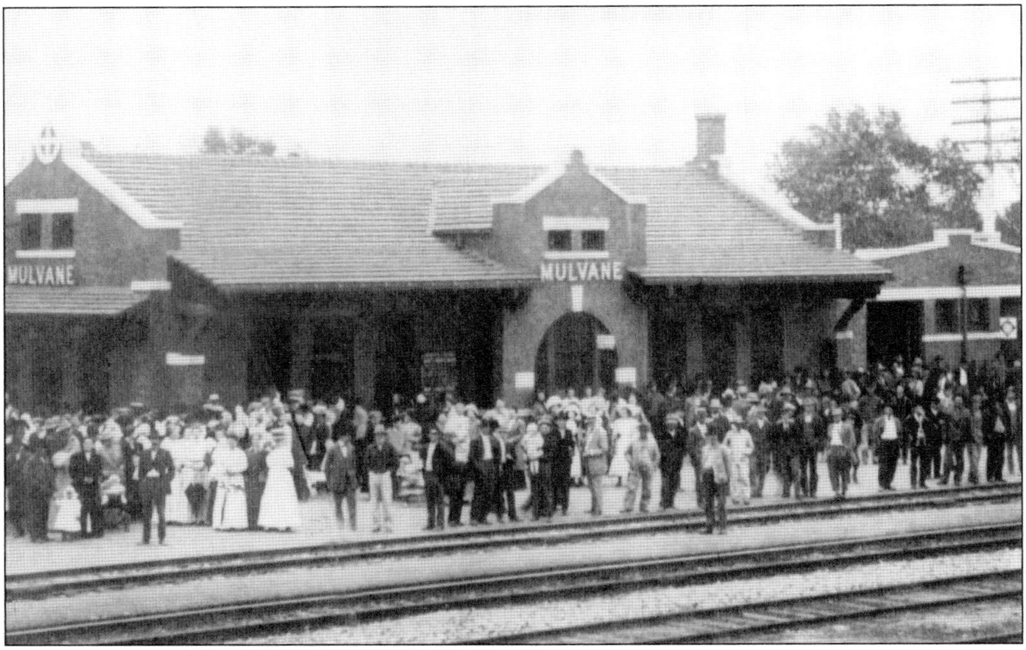

The Mulvane Depot was built in 1910. In this photograph, taken that same year, many of the town's residents gather outside of the depot. Over 100 years later, the exterior of the building looks much as it did when it was built. (Courtesy of the Mulvane Historical Museum.)

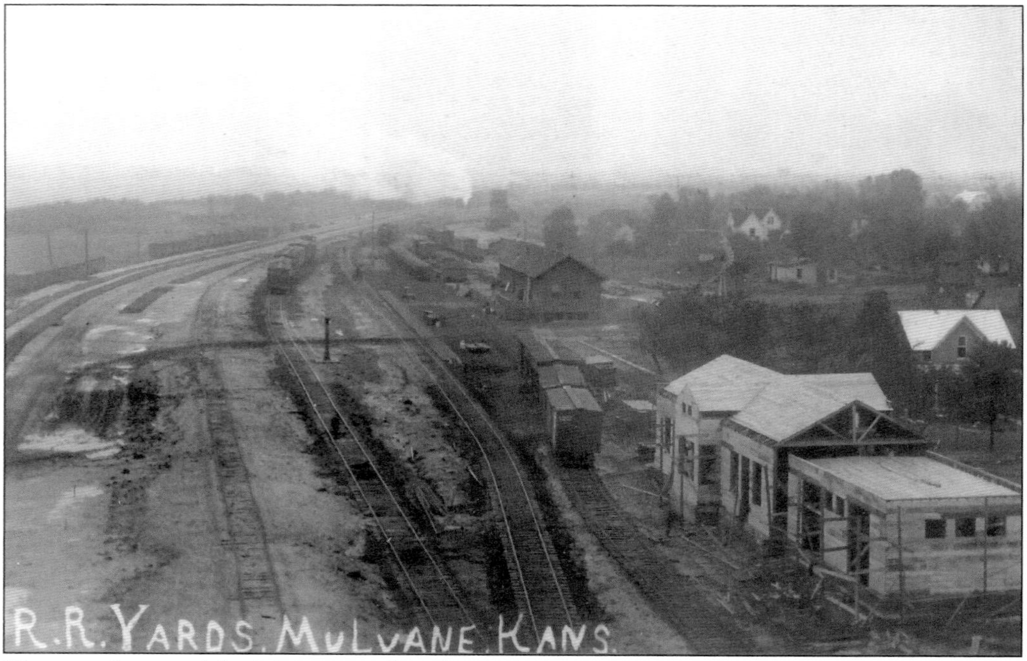

This aerial view of the Mulvane rail yard is looking north. It shows the passenger depot under construction. The freight depot can be seen in the center of the photograph, just beyond the passenger station. It had served as the passenger station prior to 1910. (Courtesy of the Mulvane Historical Museum.)

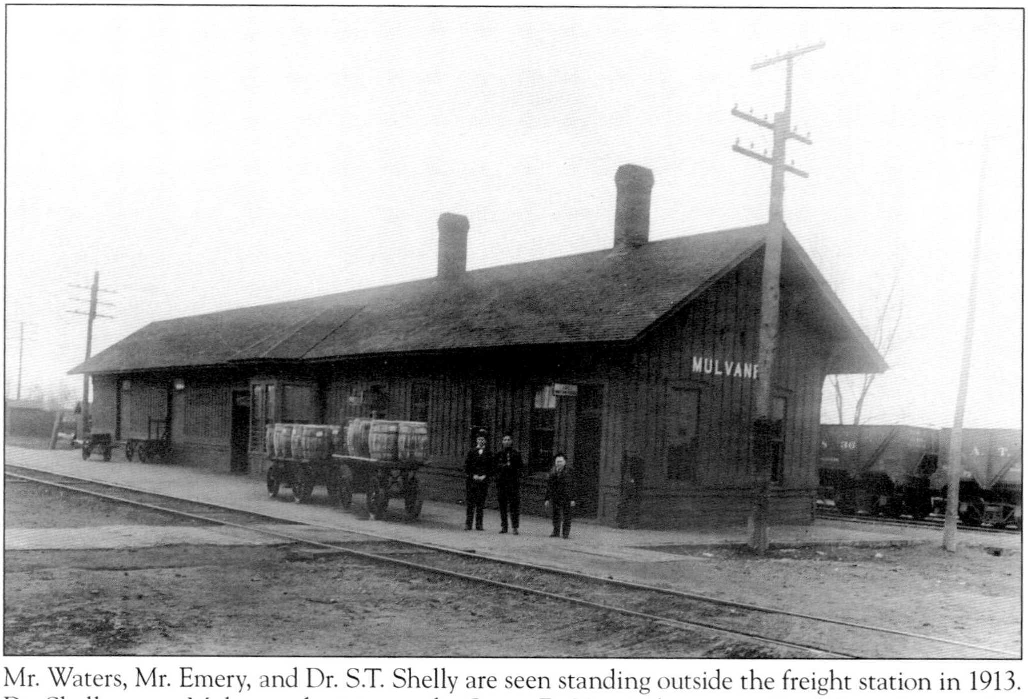

Mr. Waters, Mr. Emery, and Dr. S.T. Shelly are seen standing outside the freight station in 1913. Dr. Shelly was a Mulvane physician and a Santa Fe Hospital surgeon. He delivered more that 4,300 babies during his career, which spanned more than 45 years. (Courtesy of the Mulvane Historical Museum.)

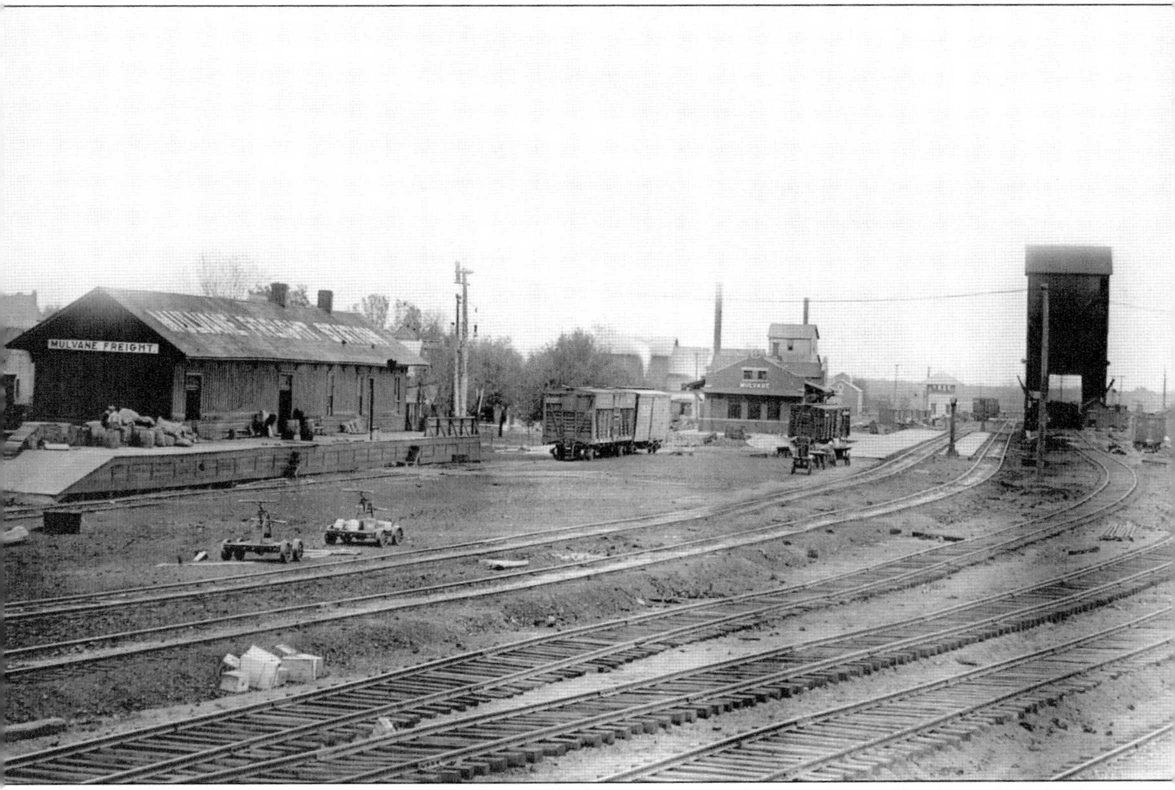

In 1916, Bob Seyfer sent this postcard to his wife, Katie, in Arkansas City. He identified the key elements of the yard and described them as follows. The Mulvane Freight Depot is clearly marked on the left side of the photograph. The passenger station is to the right of center in the photograph. The tall structure on the right side of the photograph is the coal chute. (Courtesy of the Mulvane Historical Museum.)

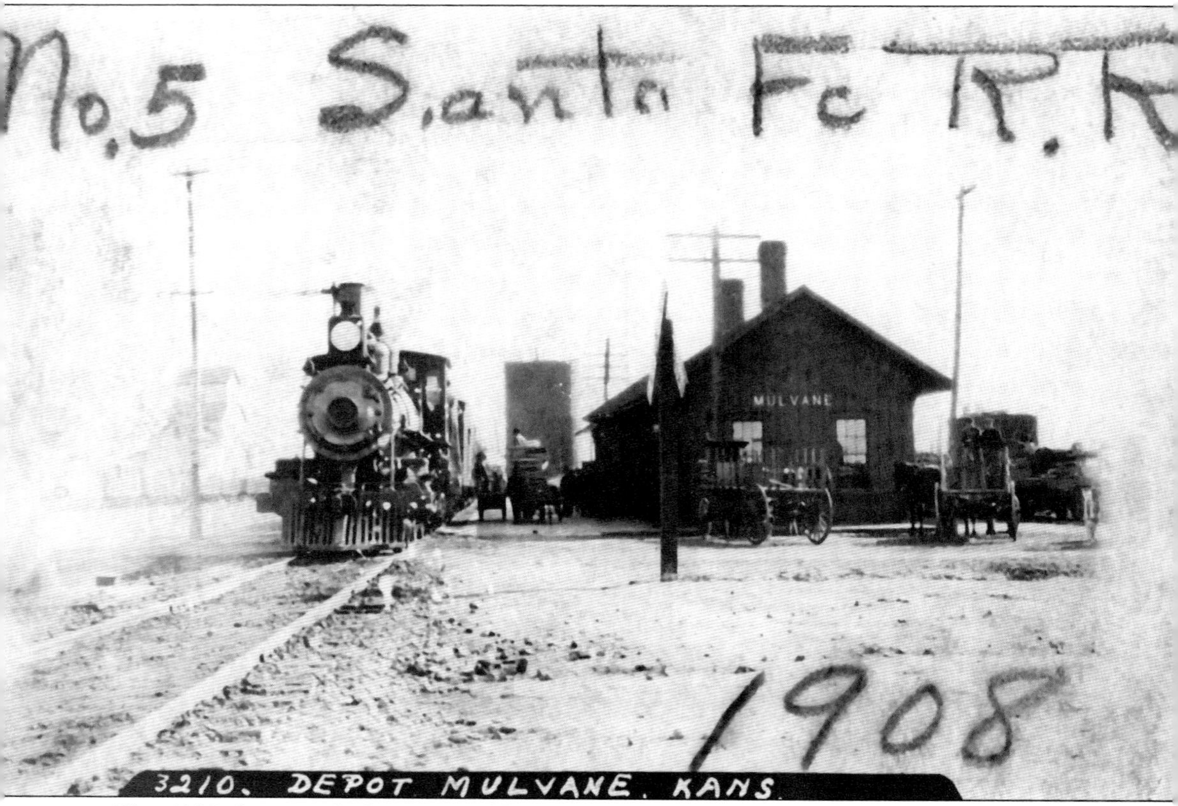

This 1908 photograph shows a southbound train sitting at the Mulvane passenger depot. Trains that originated in Wichita and points farther north regularly made a stop in Mulvane to pick up freight and passengers. Much of what is known about how the rail yard looked is from postcards that passengers would buy at the station as they were passing through town and then mail to family and friends to report on the progress of their journey. That is the case here, as a traveler was sending her love to her family in Wichita while she was on her way to Oklahoma. (Courtesy of the Mulvane Historical Museum.)

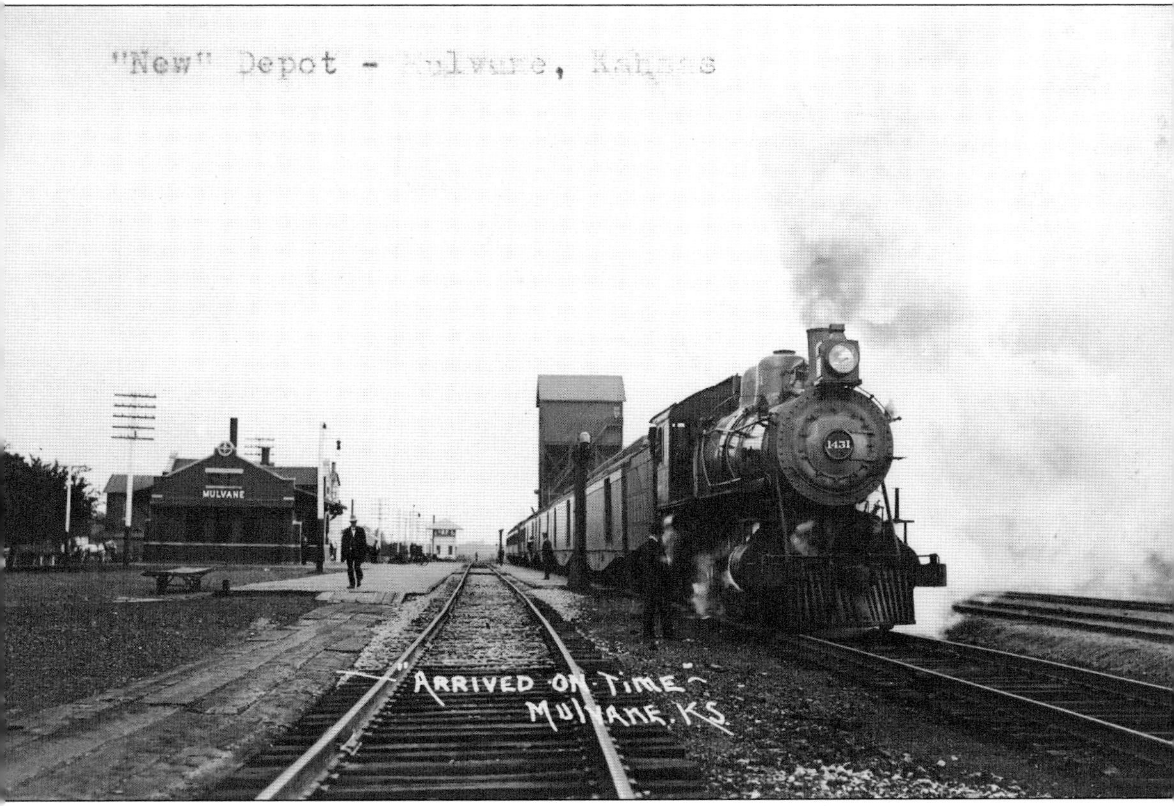

Santa Fe Engine No. 1431 builds steam as it heads north from Mulvane in this c. 1915 photograph. The train sits on the August-Wellington Line. The coal chute can be seen rising above the train on the right side of the tracks, and the switching and interlocking tower can be seen in the distance on the left side of the tracks. The passenger depot is next to the train, and the freight depot is just out of view to the left. The photograph's caption is "Arrived on time." (Courtesy of the Mulvane Historical Museum.)

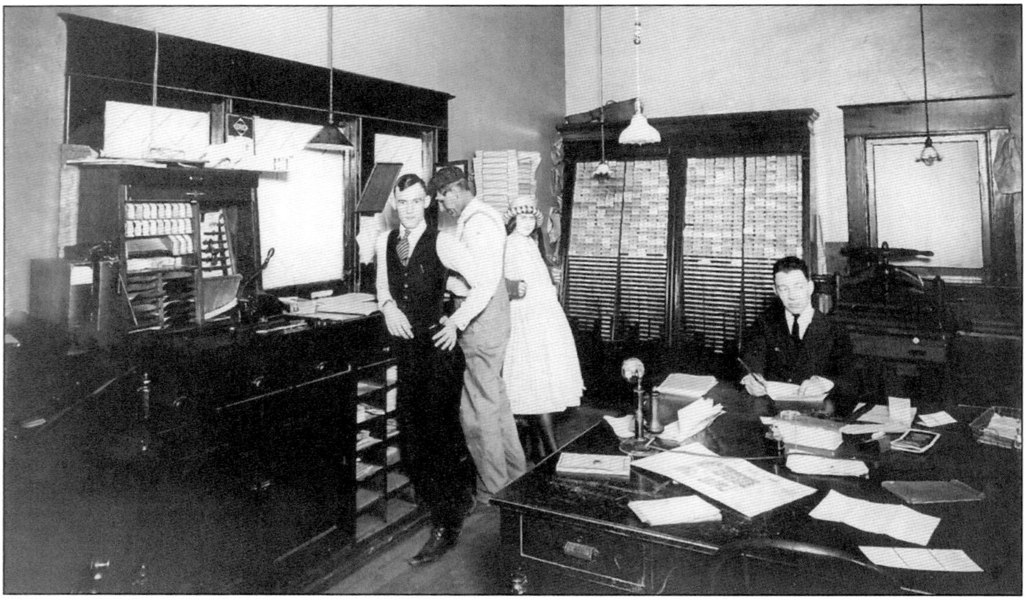

There was a lot of activity in the rail office during the mid- to late 1920s. Schedules had to be maintained, and arrivals and departures had to be tracked. The telephone had made its debut by the time this photograph was taken. (Courtesy of the Mulvane Historical Museum.)

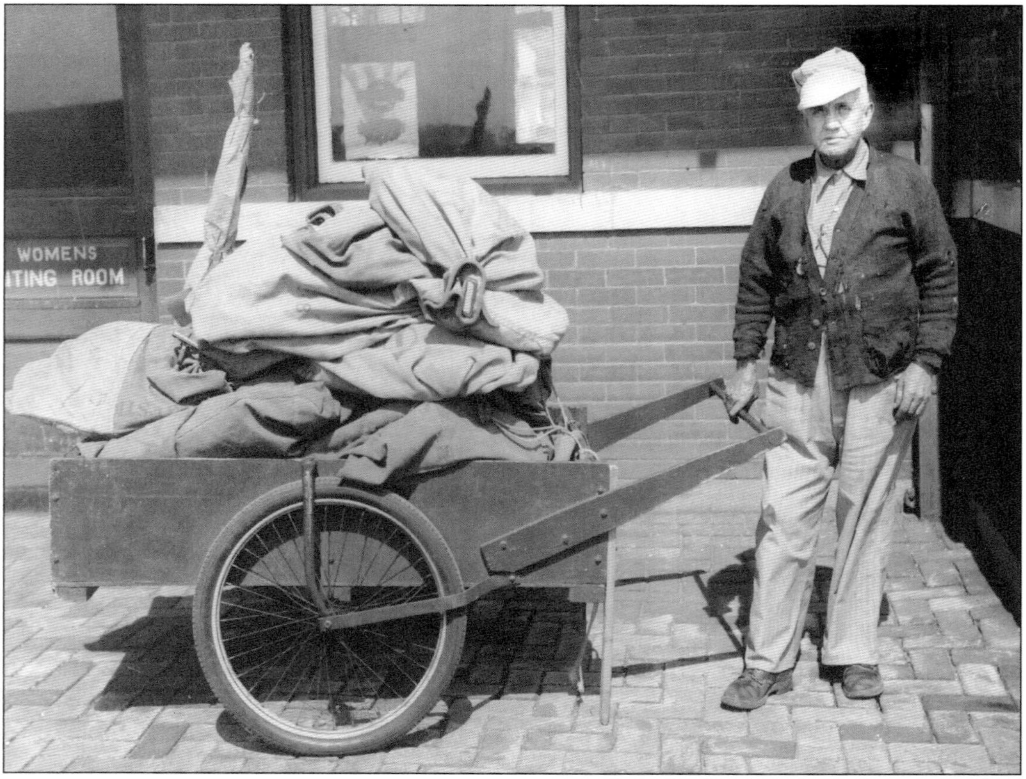

This photograph, possibly from the 1940s, shows railroad employee Abe Parker with a small cart of items to be loaded on a train. Note the sign directing ladies to the Women's Waiting Room. (Courtesy of the Mulvane Historical Museum.)

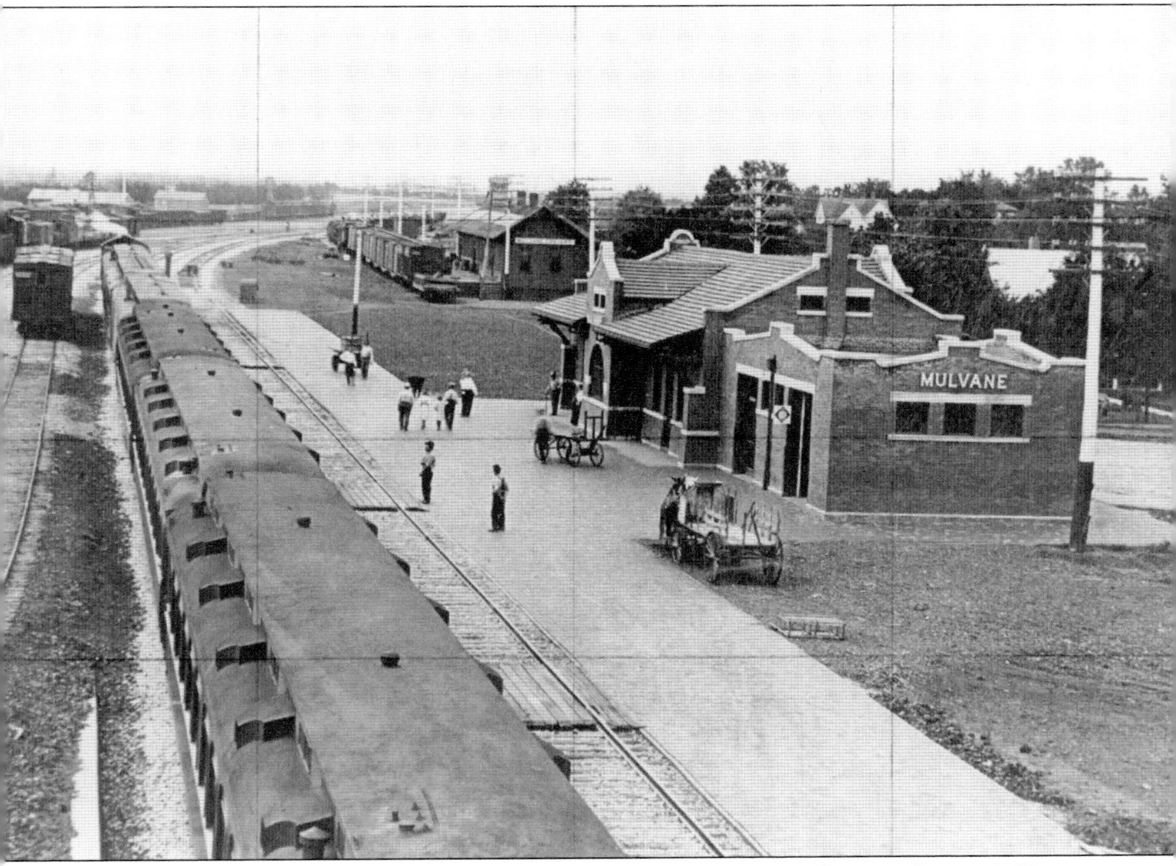

It is interesting to compare this 1920s photograph to that from 1910 at the top of page 18. Here, a northbound passenger train is seen at the Mulvane depot. Steam from the engine can be seen at the front of the train, while another train sits at the freight station. Mulvane houses can be seen just beyond the depot. Note that the rail yard is very clean. It was important that passersby had a favorable view of the city. Horse-drawn wagons were still being used to move items within the yard. (Courtesy of the Mulvane Historical Museum.)

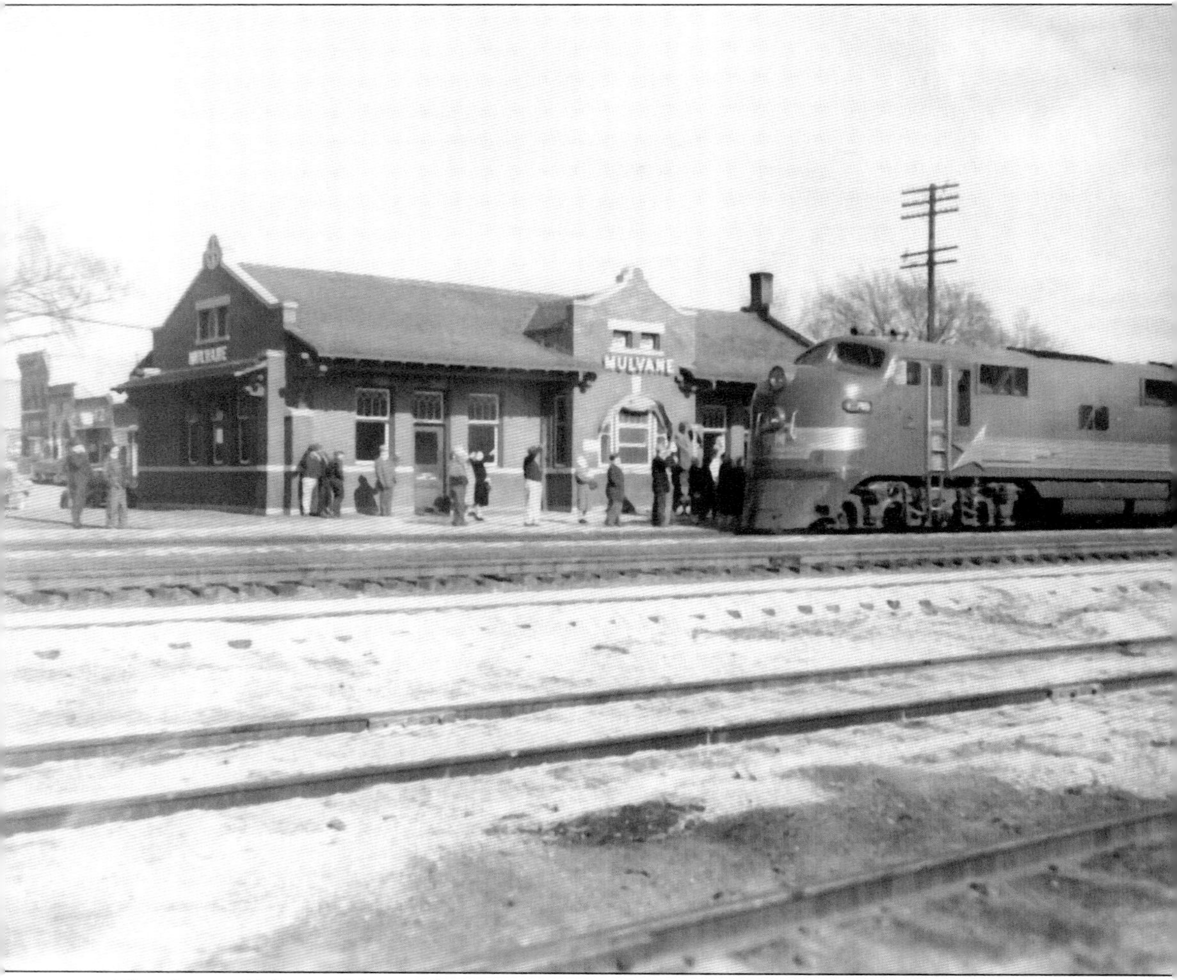

The General Motors "Train of Tomorrow" came through Mulvane in 1948. The central idea for this train originated with GM in 1944, and subsequent practical suggestions from railway officers and transportation experts were incorporated in a four-car Astra Dome train, which included a 2,000-horsepower diesel locomotive, one chair car, one sleeper car, one dining car, and one observation-lounge car. (Courtesy of the Mulvane Historical Museum.)

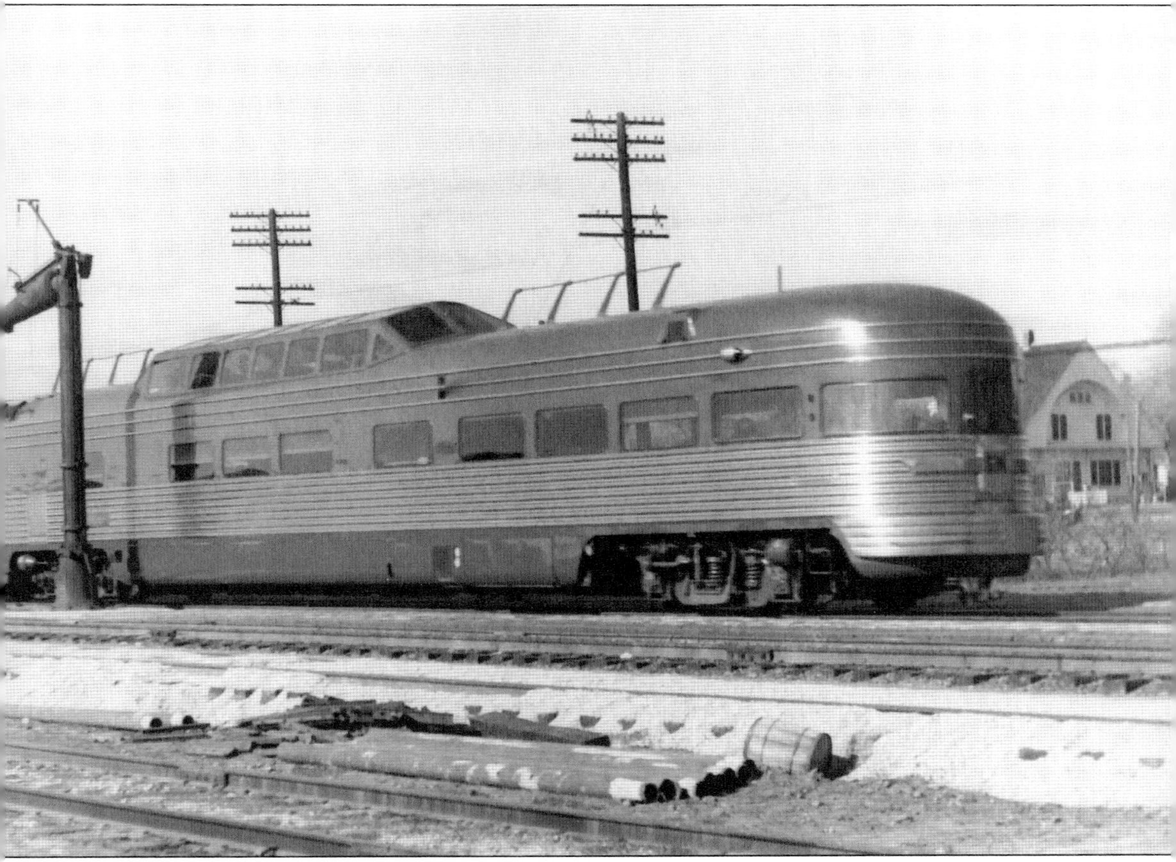

The "Train of Tomorrow" leaves Mulvane. The total length of the train, including the locomotive, was 411 feet. The car height, rail to Astra Dome roofs, was 15 feet, six inches. Each car had a capacity of 216 passengers. The Astra Dome train toured the country from 1947 until 1950 and logged over 65,000 miles. (Courtesy of the Mulvane Historical Museum.)

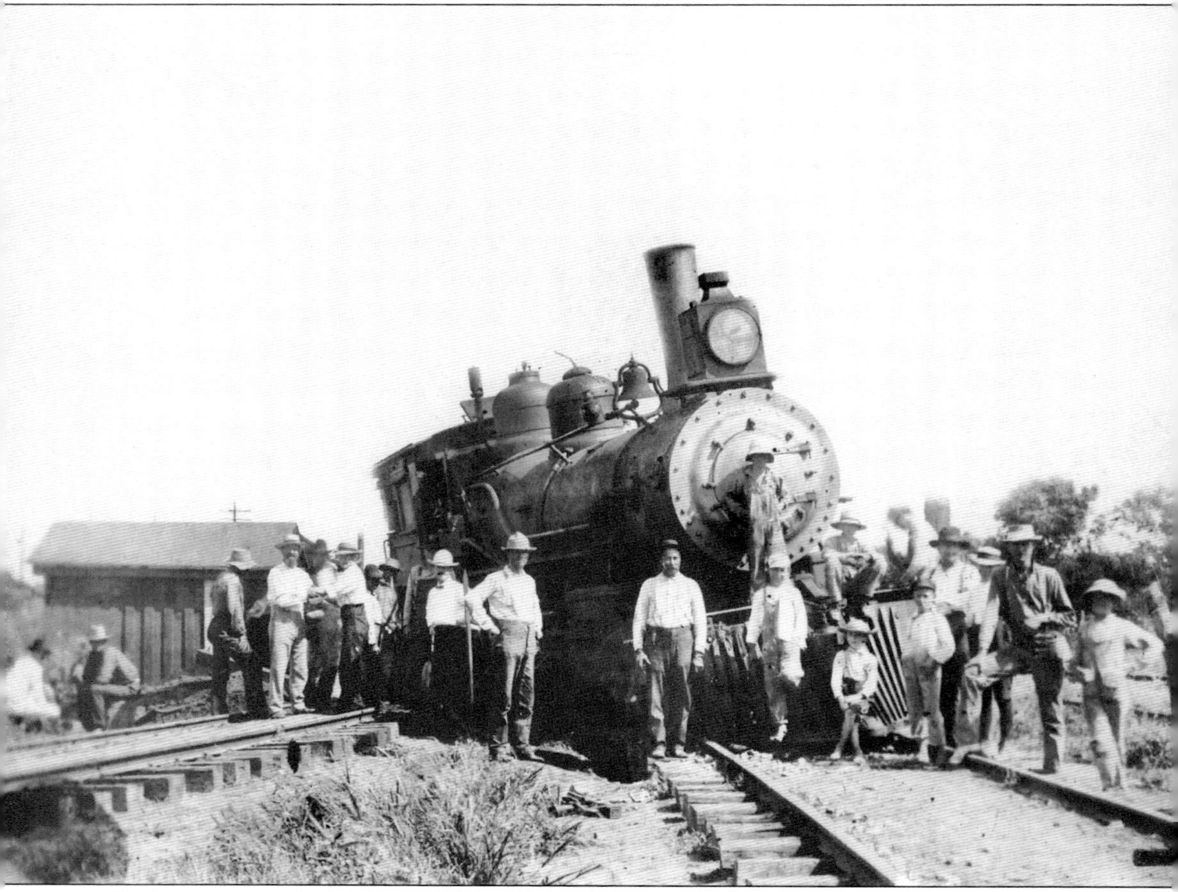

Rail accidents, though rare, did occasionally happen. Robert Seyfer took this photograph of an August 1907 derailment and mailed it to his wife, Katie, in Arkansas City. Such accidents represented huge setbacks for railroad companies. Lines could be blocked for days while debris was cleared and tracks were repaired. In an era that lacked heavy cranes and high-powered moving equipment, cleaning up train wrecks required a monumental effort and was a very dangerous job for railroad workers. Keeping trains on the rails was stressful and essential. (Courtesy of the Mulvane Historical Museum.)

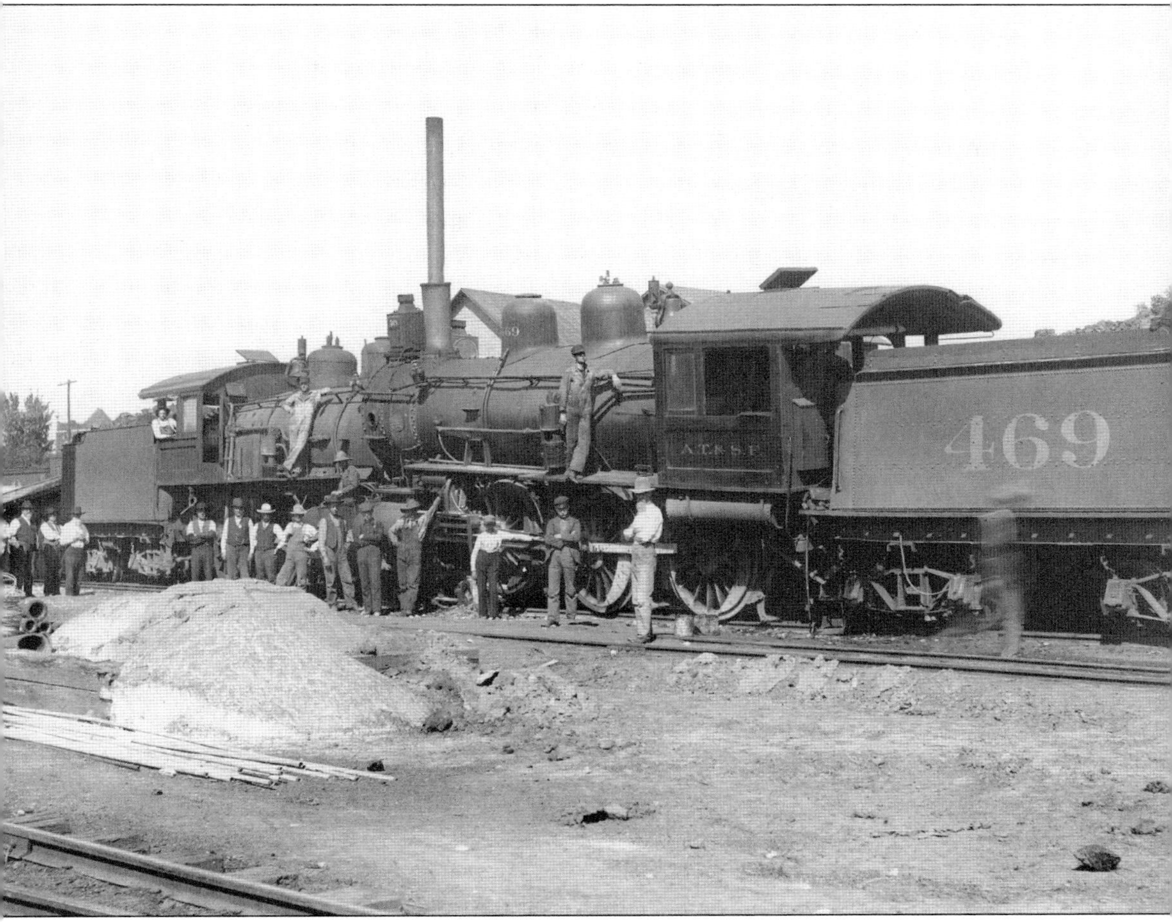

These Santa Fe engines collided in the Mulvane yard around 1910. The men on the locomotives demonstrate how massive these machines were and how difficult and dangerous it was for people to maintain them. In a situation like this, the cars would have to be disconnected from the engines, and the engines would have to be removed from the track. There were times when the rails would be damaged and repairs would have to be made to the track before traffic could resume. The cost of repairs and the loss of revenue could be very high. (Courtesy of the Mulvane Historical Museum.)

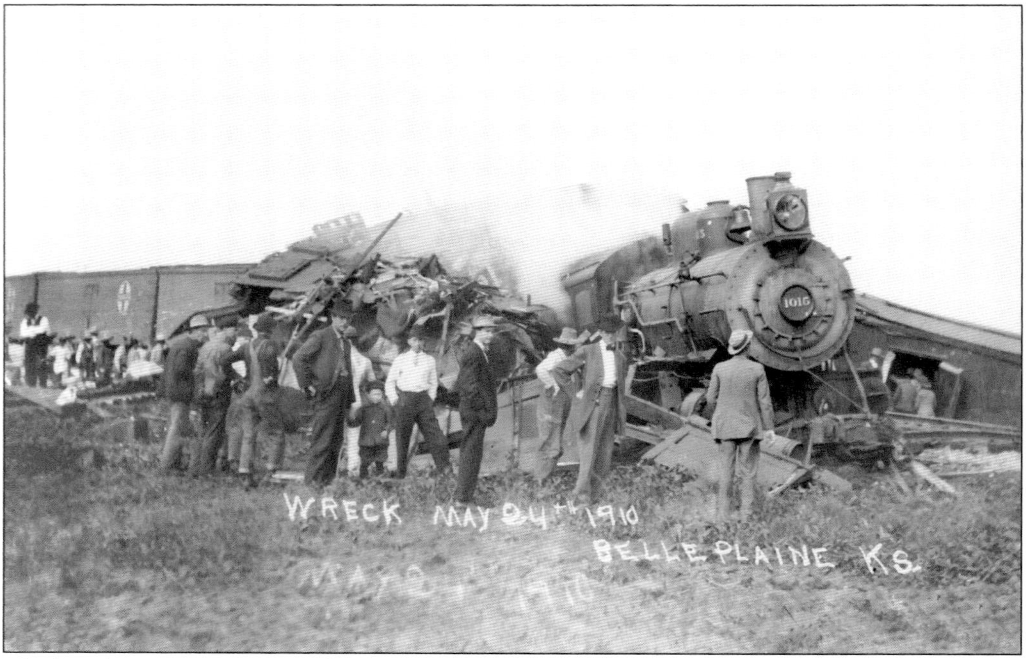

The handwritten caption on this photograph dates this train wreck to May 24, 1910, occurring near the town of Belle Plaine, which is just south of Mulvane. For hours after the accident, smoke and steam could be seen rising into the air. (Courtesy of the Mulvane Historical Museum.)

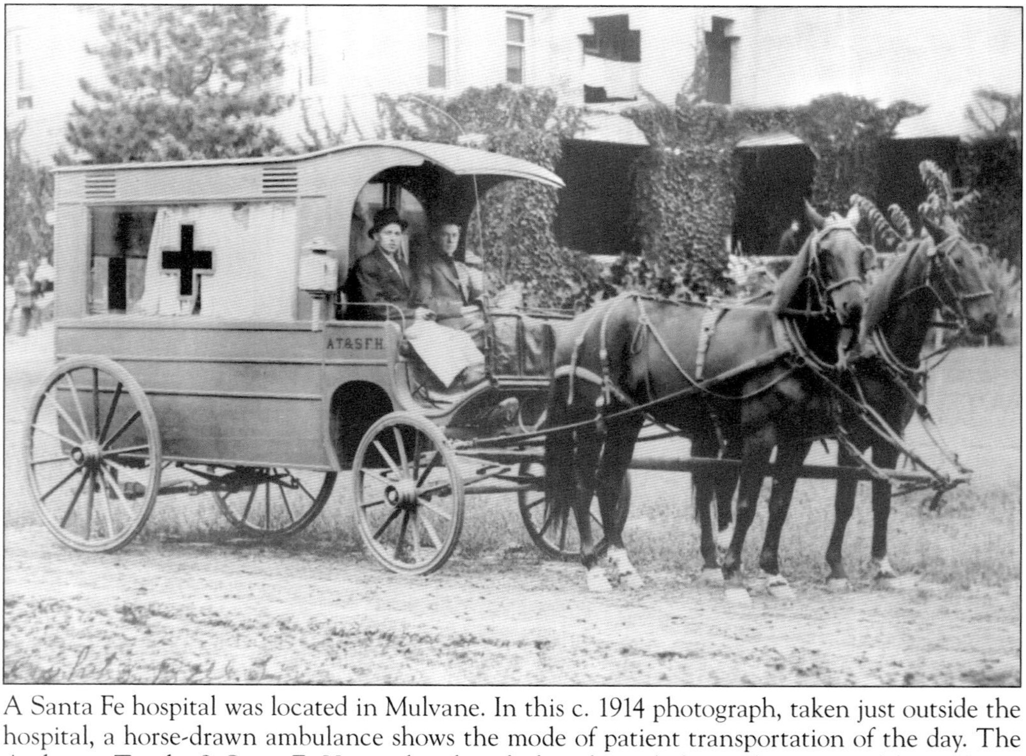

A Santa Fe hospital was located in Mulvane. In this c. 1914 photograph, taken just outside the hospital, a horse-drawn ambulance shows the mode of patient transportation of the day. The Atchison, Topeka & Santa Fe Hospital is identified on the ambulance. (Courtesy of the Mulvane Historical Museum.)

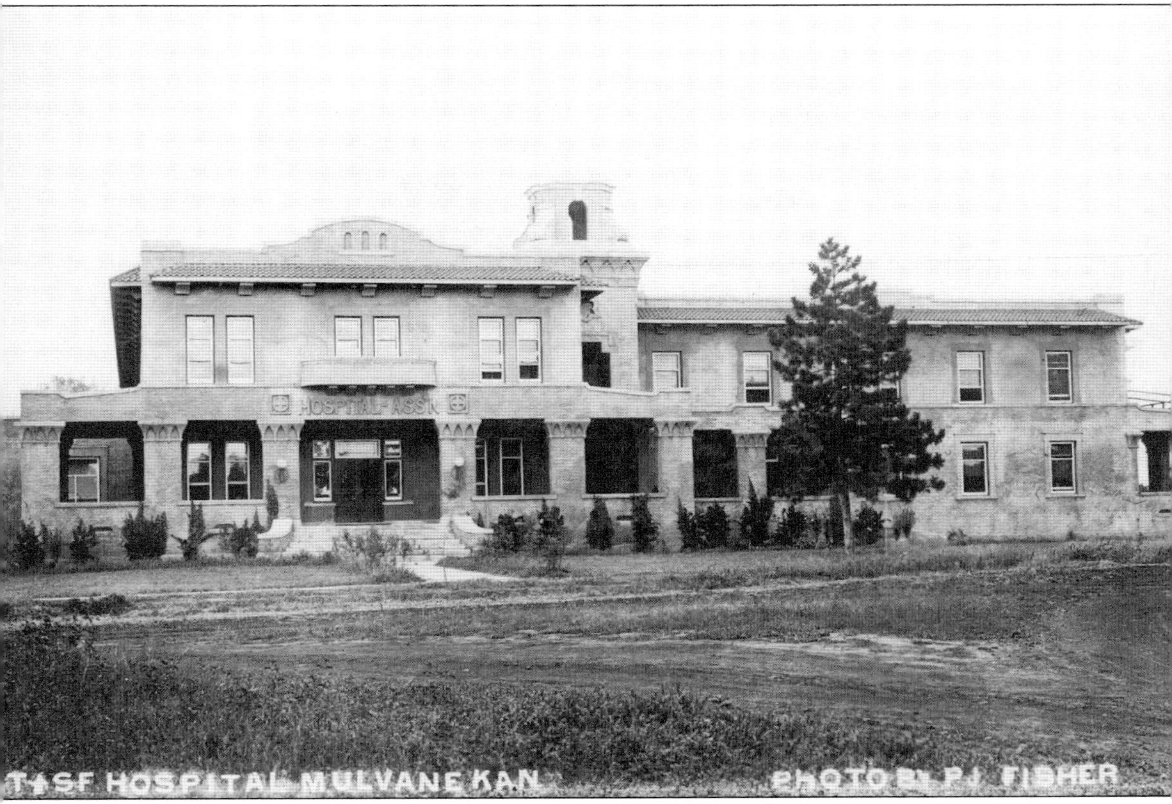

The Atchison, Topeka, & Santa Fe (AT&SF) established hospitals at rail stops along its lines so that injured employees could get medical treatment when necessary. One such hospital was built in Mulvane in 1913 and was located only four blocks from the rail yard. As was the case with the other AT&SF hospitals, this facility was staffed by local physicians and served patients throughout the area. The hospital at Mulvane had a reputation for being one of the finest in the region, and it was a landmark in the community for over 35 years. (Courtesy of the Mulvane Historical Museum.)

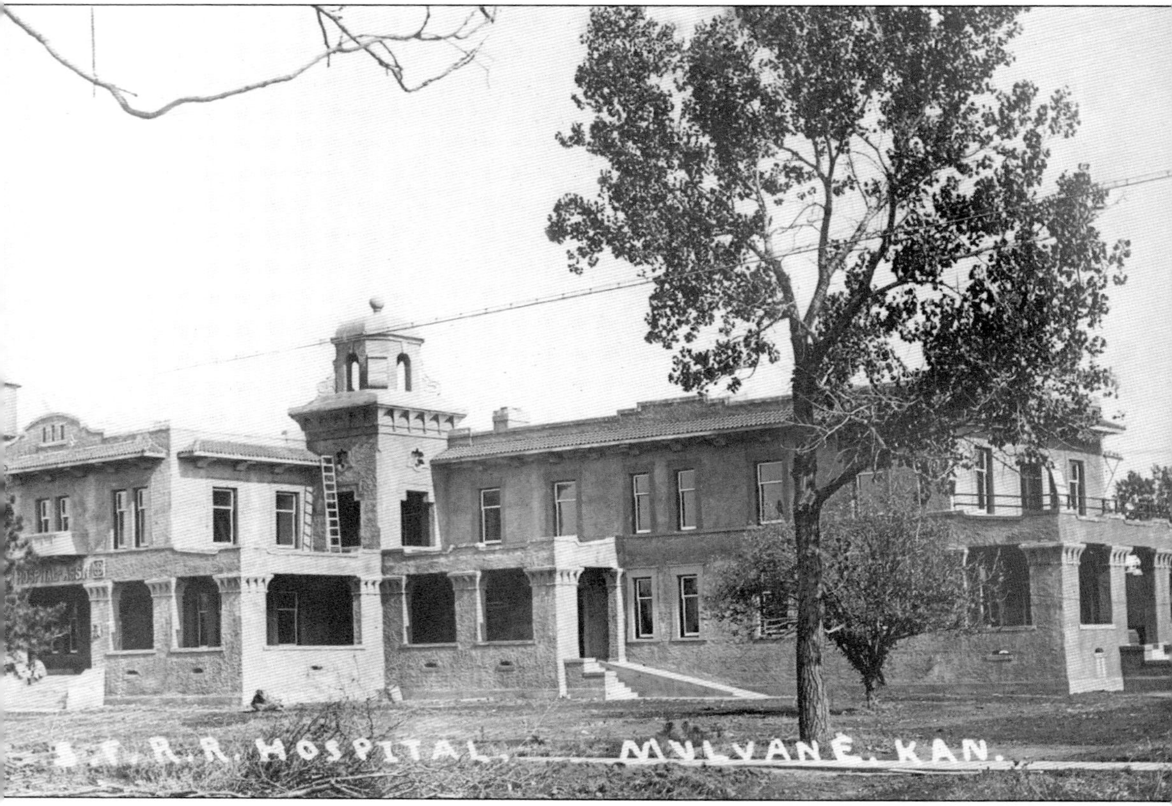

The hospital, seen here around 1920, was built in 1913 and served the area until 1949. Described as an L-shaped structure, the building was designed in a Spanish style with two stories and a basement. The hospital had 60 beds and was attended by four surgeons and 15 full-time employees. It was the largest of the Santa Fe hospitals in the region, providing treatment to patients throughout the area. It was considered to be state-of-the-art while it was in operation. (Courtesy of the Mulvane Historical Museum.)

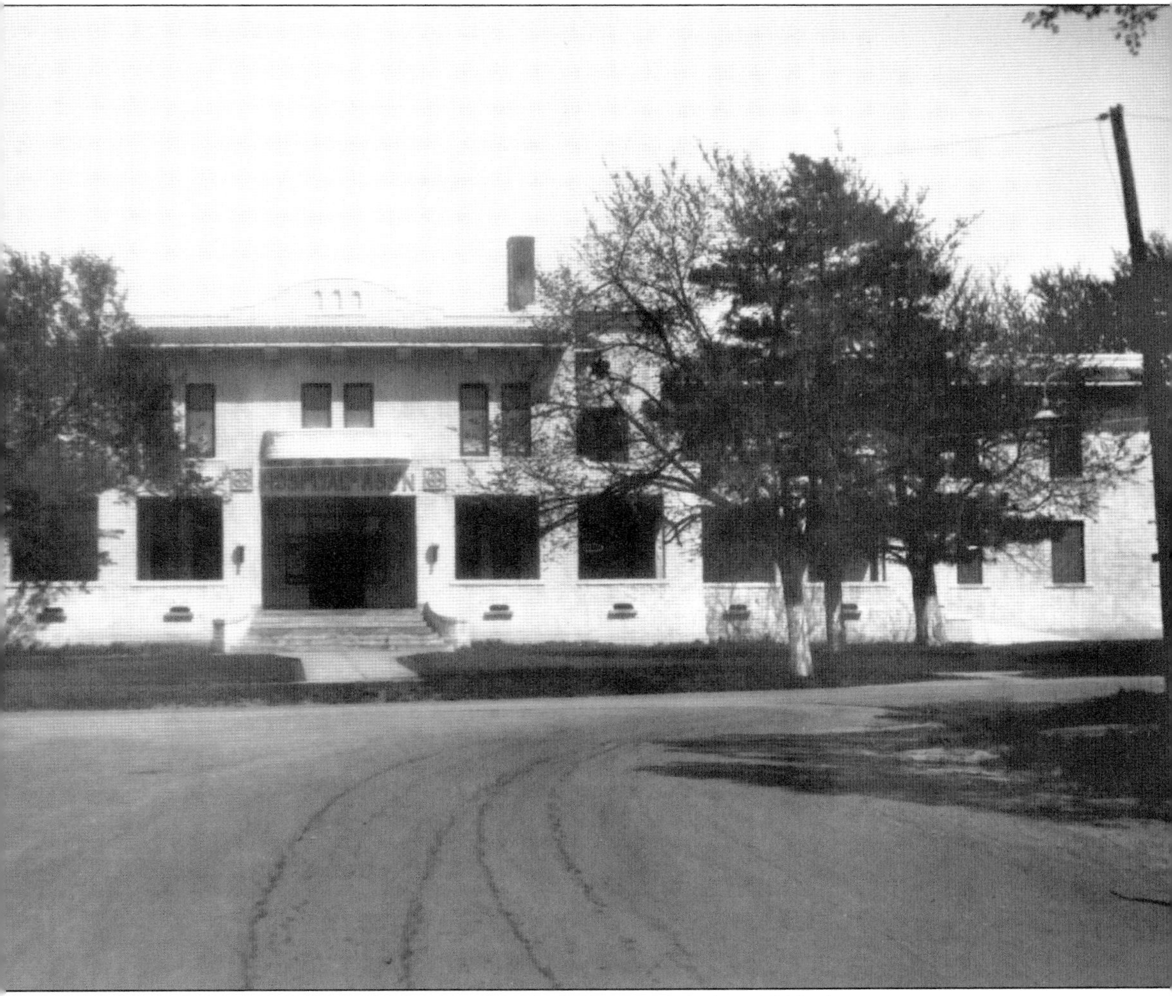

The hospital is seen here in April 1947, shortly before it closed in 1949. Among its surgeons was Dr. W.A. Heap, whose work repairing broken bones was described as miraculous. He treated two different patients who had suffered a broken leg. One was a 60-year-old man and the other was a small boy. In each case, amputation was considered to be the only course of treatment. Dr. Heap used pins, plates, and screws with both patients, each of whom made a full recovery. It was a very advanced technique for the day. (Courtesy of the Mulvane Historical Museum.)

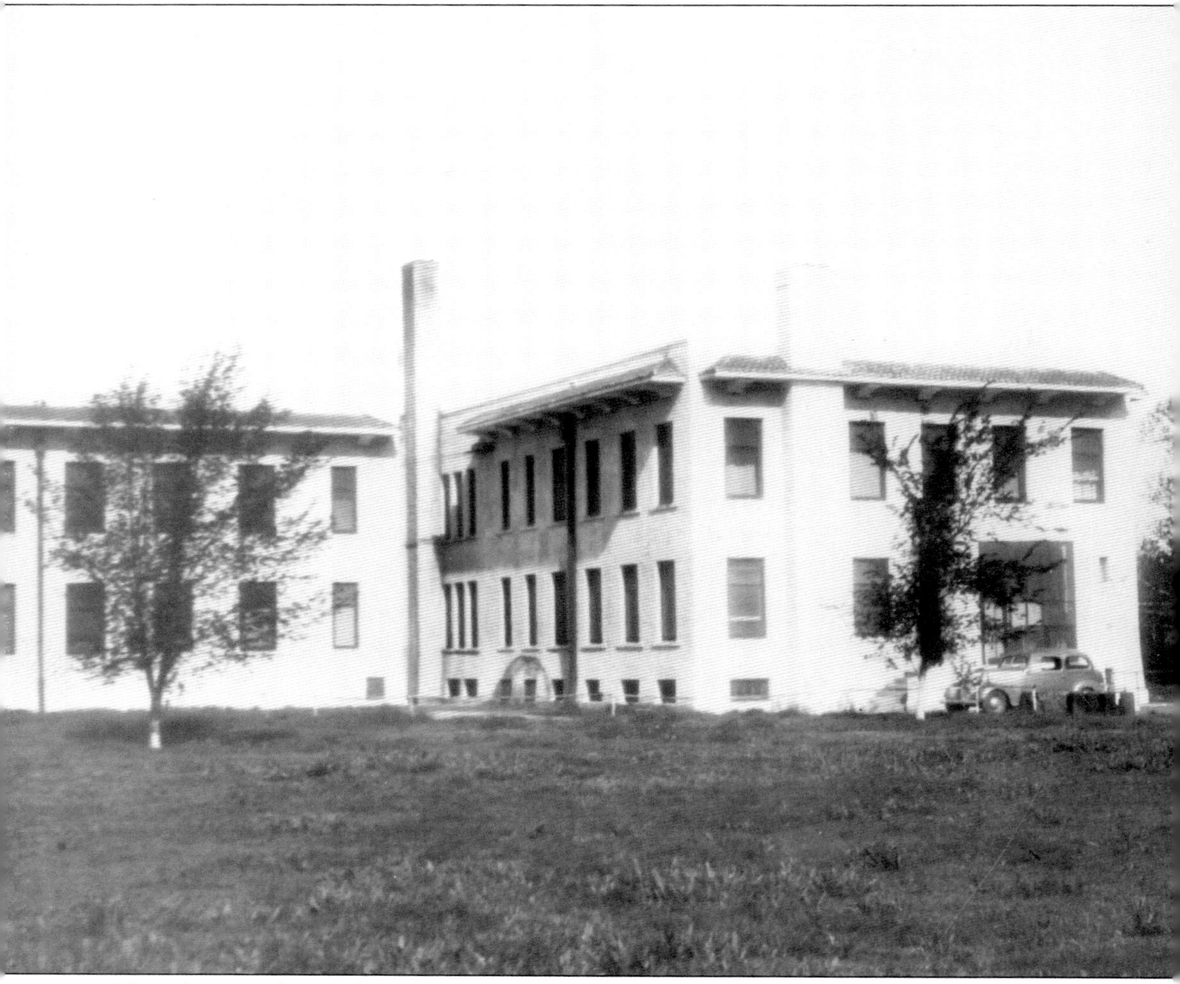

This photograph was also taken in April 1947. Another of the hospital's doctors was S.T. Shelly of Mulvane. Dr. Shelly practiced medicine for 47 years. In the 1932 Old Settlers Days Parade, he was recognized as "The Stork Doctor." He is credited with delivering over 4,300 babies during his career, a number that exceeded the population of the town when his career ended. That is an average of almost two babies per week. For nearly half a century, it was a rare Mulvane citizen who was not delivered by Dr. Shelly. (Courtesy of the Mulvane Historical Museum.)

Three

Early Work, Early Worship

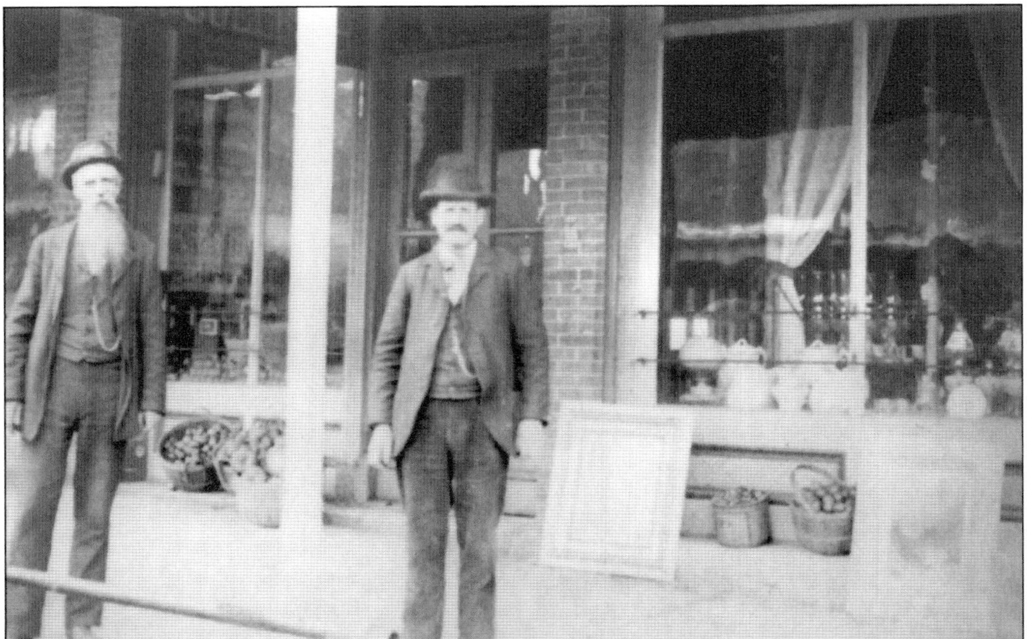

The person on the left in this 1897 photograph is C.A. Steele, who was the owner of a hardware store in Mulvane. Sam McCullough (right) owned the McCullough Grocery Store. Both men were prominent merchants in town at the end of the 19th century. (Courtesy of the Mulvane Historical Museum.)

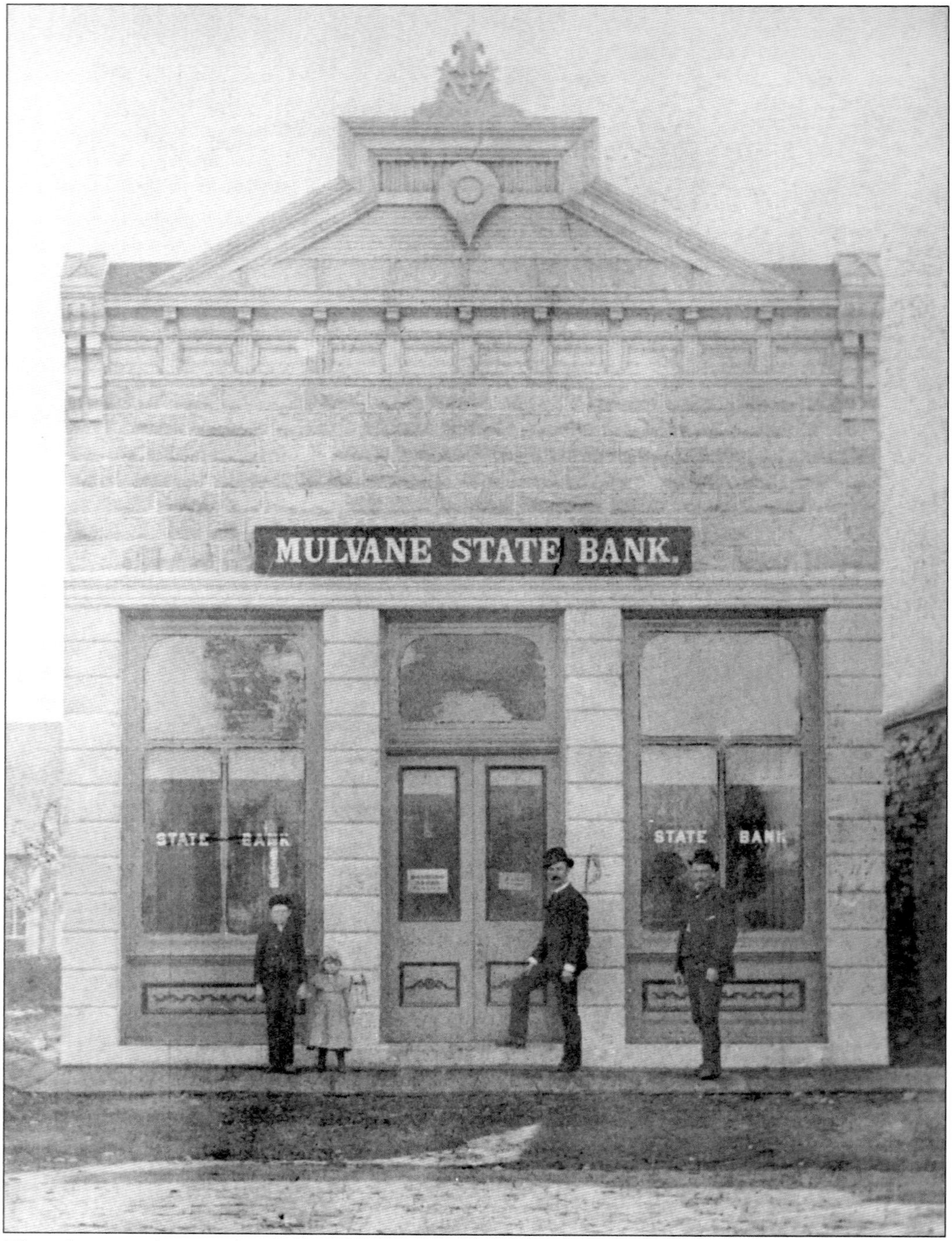

This photograph was taken in 1886, the first year of business for the Mulvane State Bank. It was the third bank to open, but the preceding institutions did not make it to the end of the 19th century. A fire on April 12, 1893, completely destroyed the building, except for the vault's stone walls. The bank was rebuilt at the same location, and today that structure houses the Heather Lane Salon (see page 120). The word "Bank" can still be seen on the front of the building. The Mulvane State Bank, operating today as the Carson Bank, has its downtown branch on the northeast corner of First and Main Streets. (Courtesy of the Mulvane Historical Museum.)

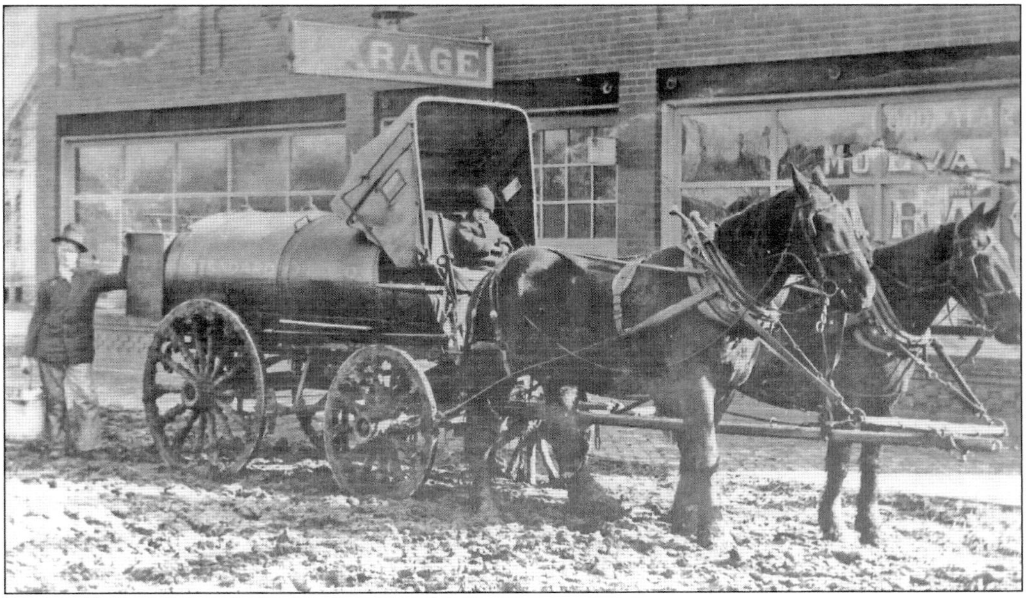

Before Mulvane's streets were paved, bad weather could render them a muddy mess. In this c. 1920 photograph, Charles Milton English and his son make the rounds to area garages with their Standard Oil wagon. The wagon was used to deliver lubricant to area garages and machine shops. (Courtesy of the Mulvane Historical Museum.)

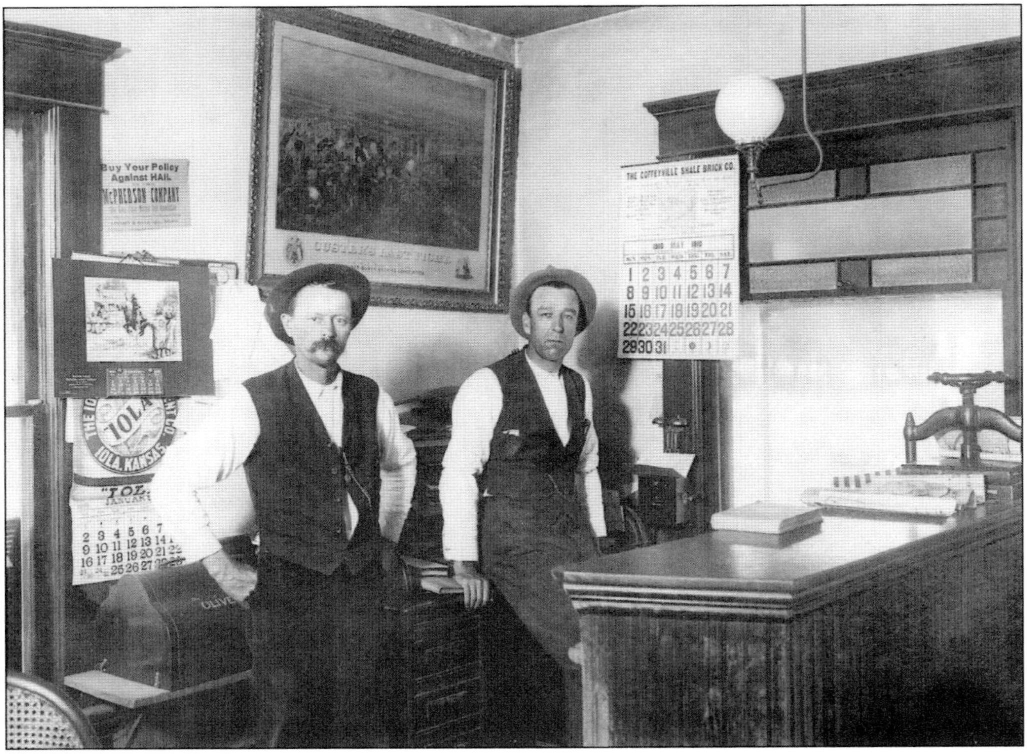

The office of the Mulvane Lumber Yard is seen in this 1910 photograph. John Citizen is on the left, and owner Charlie Canaday is on the right. It is interesting to note that over John's shoulder two calendars still show the month of January. (Courtesy of the Mulvane Historical Museum.)

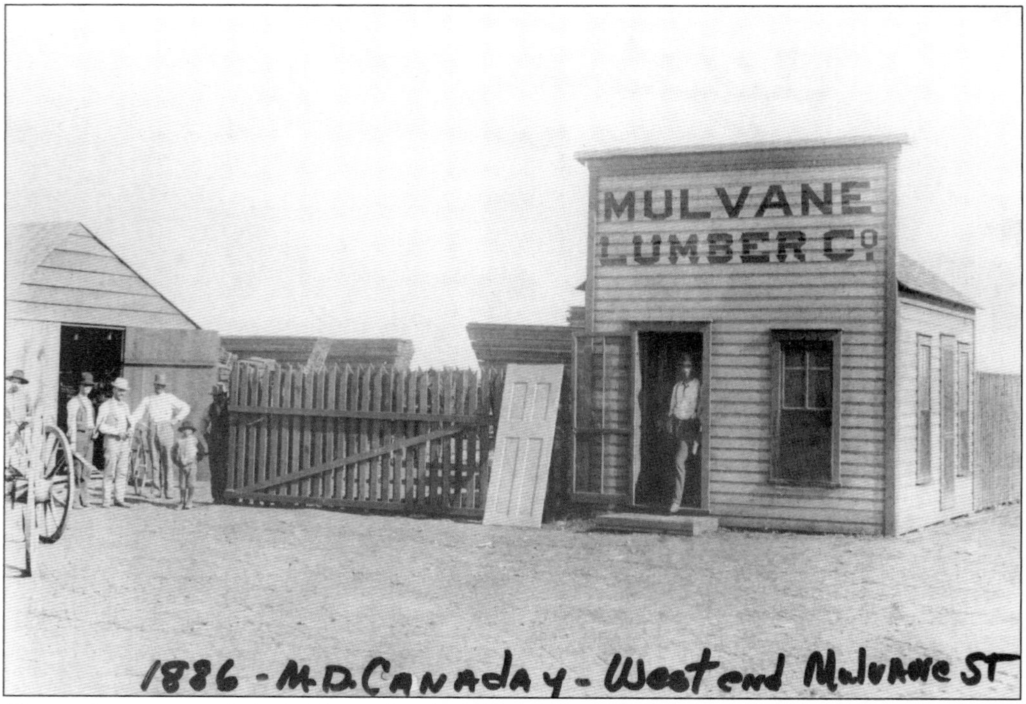

This is the exterior of the Mulvane Lumber Yard in 1886. M.D. Canaday stands in the doorway of the store, while five men and a young boy stand outside. The lumberyard was located on the west end of Main Street near the depot. (Courtesy of the Mulvane Historical Museum.)

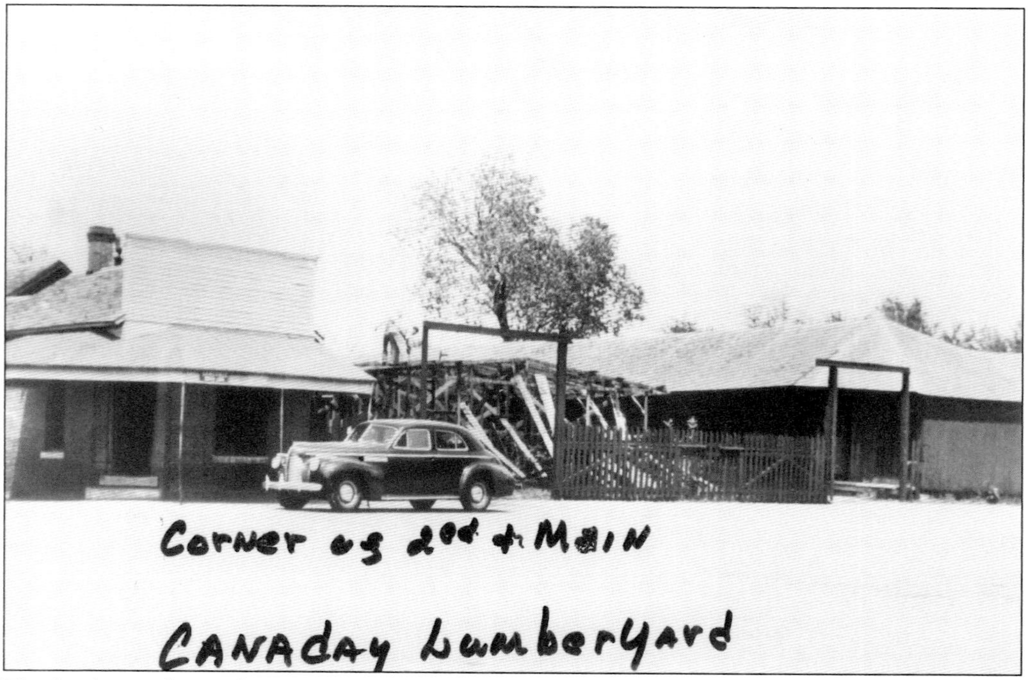

The lumberyard served customers until after World War II. In this photograph, believed to be from the early 1940s, the business has visibly grown since its early days. The lumberyard was a fixture on Main Street for many years before it closed. (Courtesy of the Mulvane Historical Museum.)

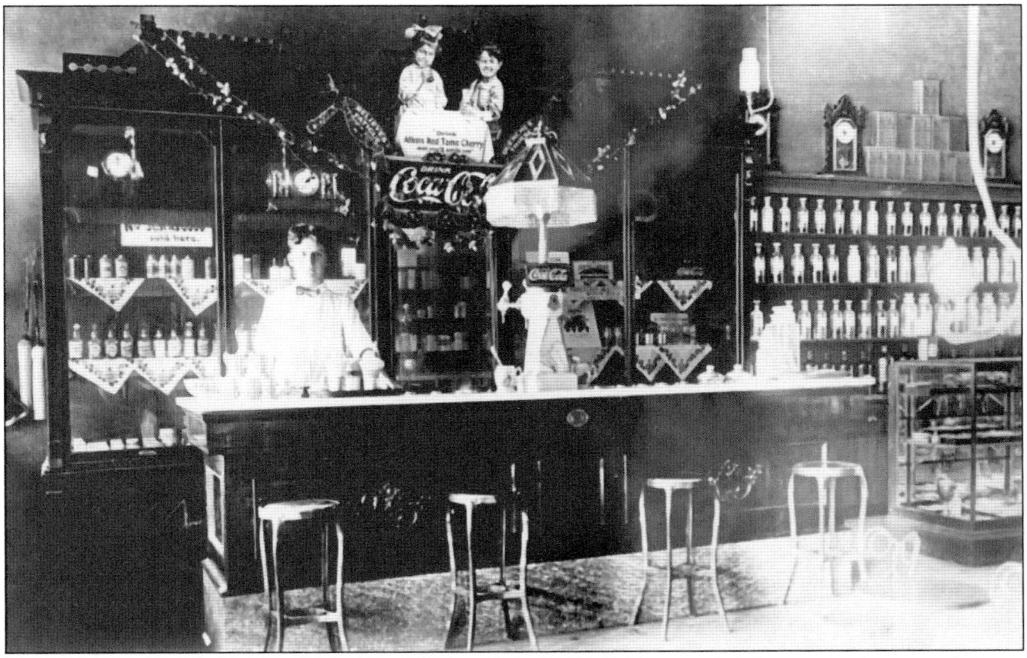

During the early 1900s, there were two drugstores on Main Street in Mulvane. A photograph from that era shows the soda fountain in the Butterfield Drug Store. Shoppers could take a break to enjoy a Coca-Cola and a snack on a warm afternoon. (Courtesy of the Mulvane Historical Museum.)

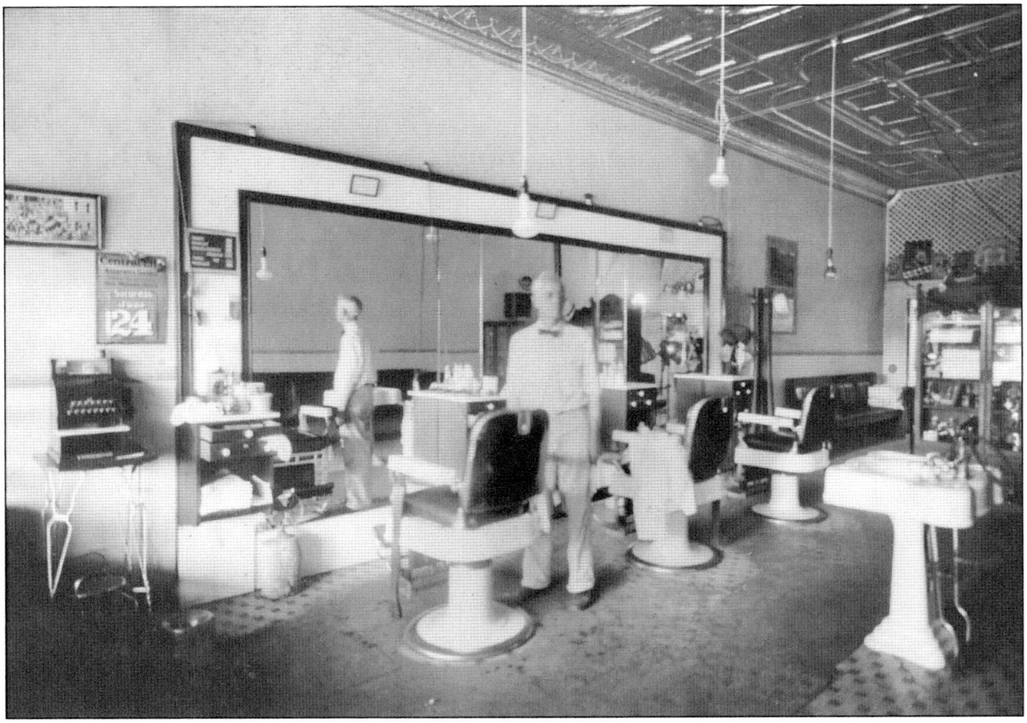

In this 1920s photograph, Jim Clark is seen in his Main Street barbershop. When Mary Lyon was 10 years old, her parents died. Clark and his wife raised Mary, and she used the Clark name, even though she was never formally adopted. (Courtesy of the Mulvane Historical Museum.)

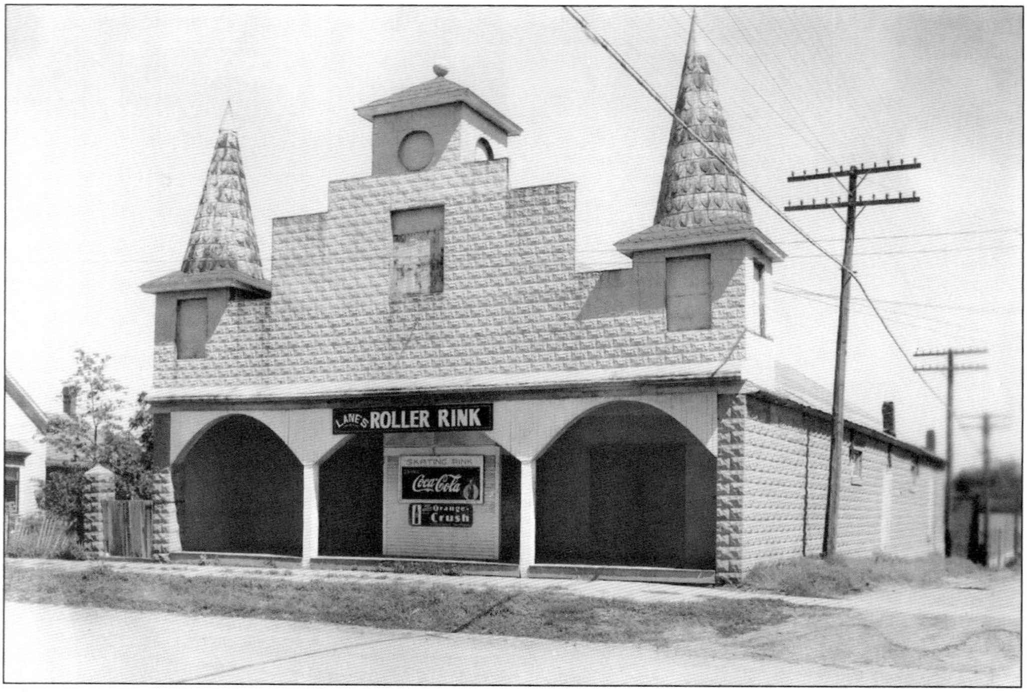

This interesting building stood on the east side of First Street, just north of Main Street. It was built as an opera house, but it also served as a grocery store. It is shown here in the mid-1940s, when it housed Lane's Roller Rink. (Courtesy of the Mulvane Historical Museum.)

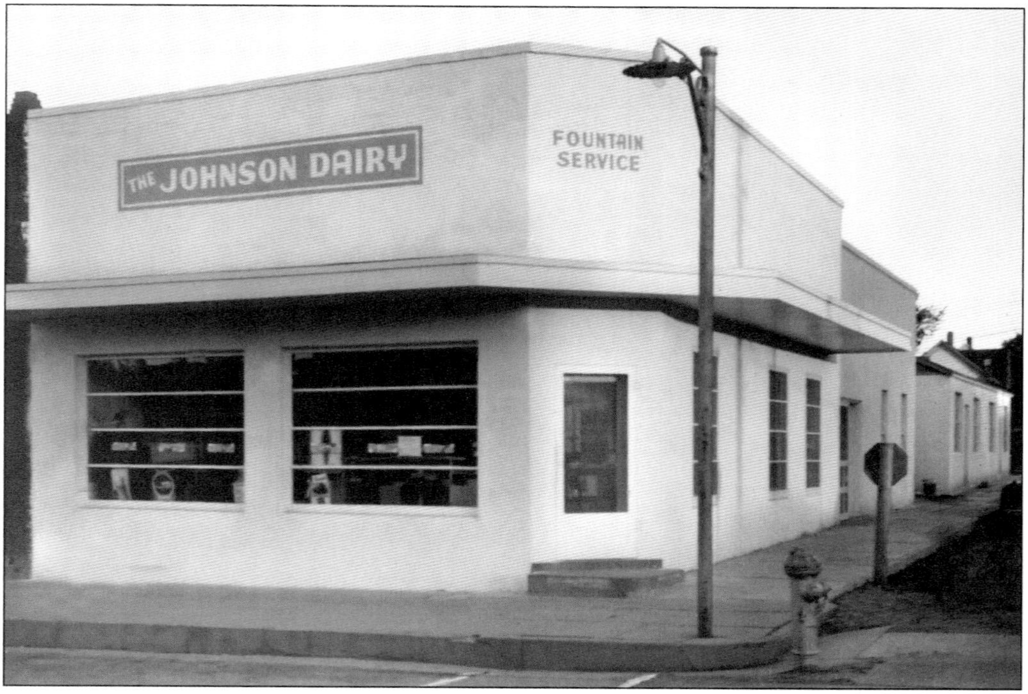

The Johnson Dairy, on the southeast corner of First and Main Streets, is seen here in 1947. In addition to selling milk and other dairy products, Johnson's had a soda fountain where people could buy ice cream and other treats. (Courtesy of the Mulvane Historical Museum.)

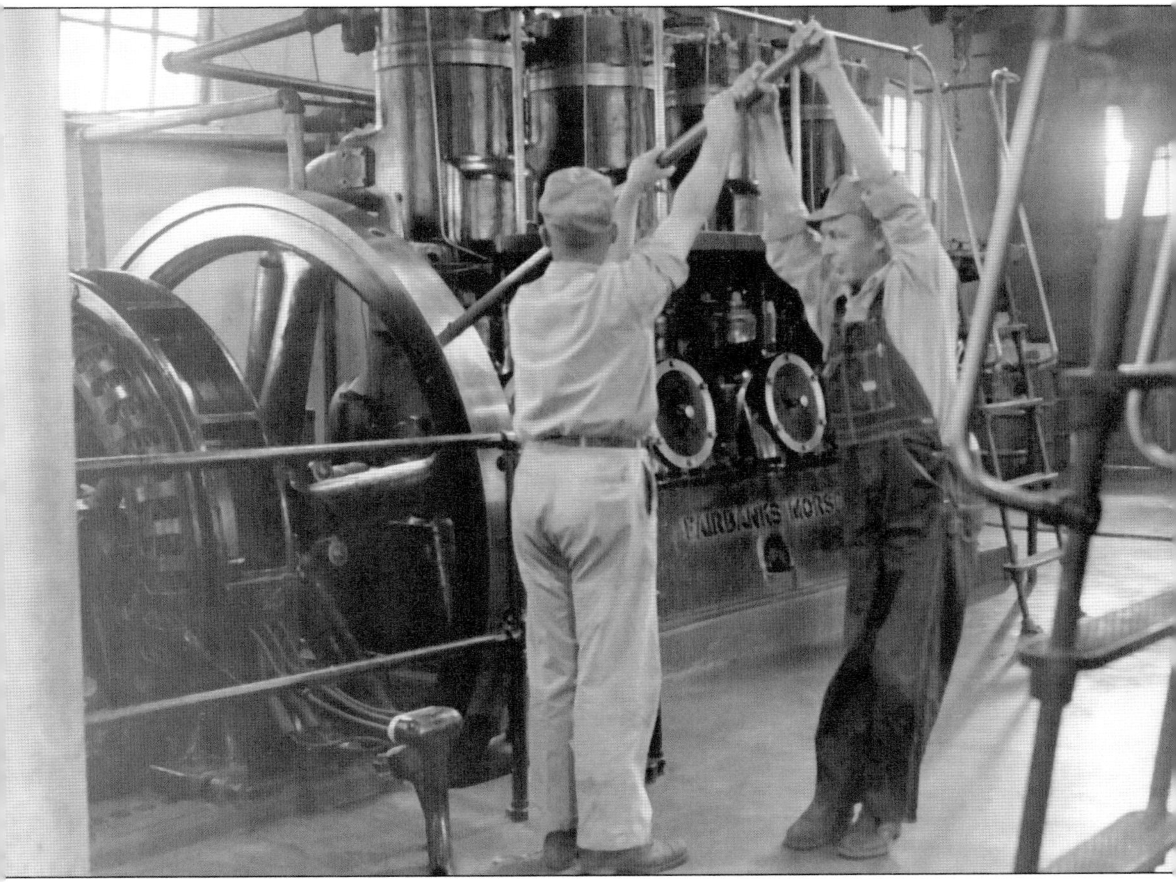

In 1947, Mulvane needed a new crankshaft for the four-cylinder engine that helped supply power to the town. This photograph, taken that year, shows employees working to install the crankshaft. Plant superintendent E.D. Fisher reported that, while the engine was being repaired, R.L. King was busy on the streets, installing cross arms and cables onto new utility poles. Another of King's duties was to trim tree limbs and branches that threatened power lines. (Courtesy of the Mulvane Historical Museum.)

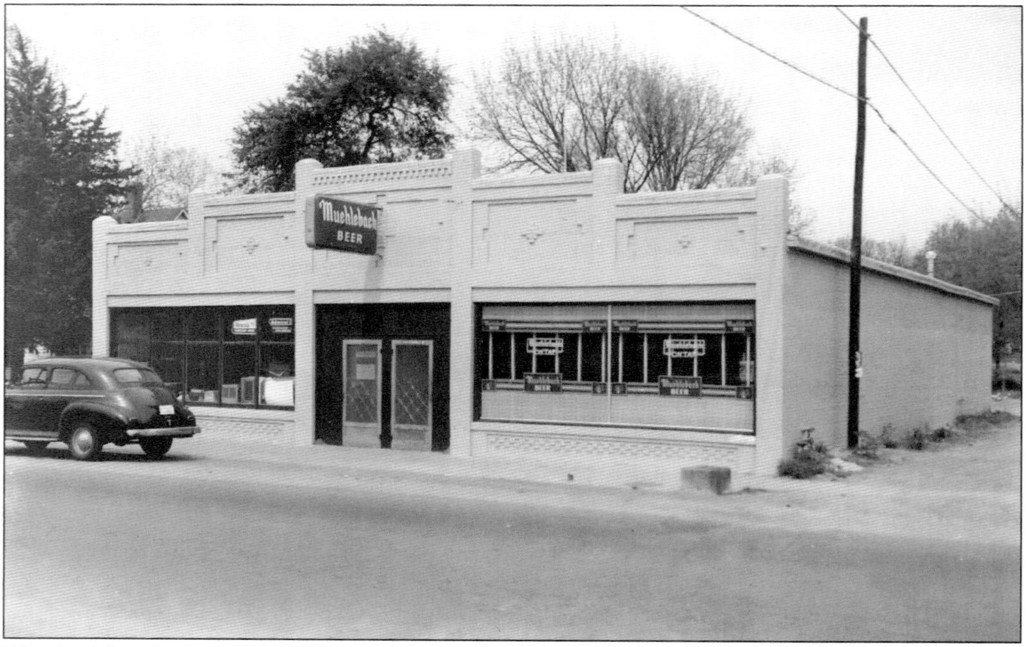

This building began as an auto parts store and was later a pool hall. In this photograph, possibly from the 1950s, Muehlebach Beer is being advertised on the sign and in the front window. The building was divided into two halves (note the two doors); the other side of the building housed an appliance shop. (Courtesy of the Mulvane Historical Museum.)

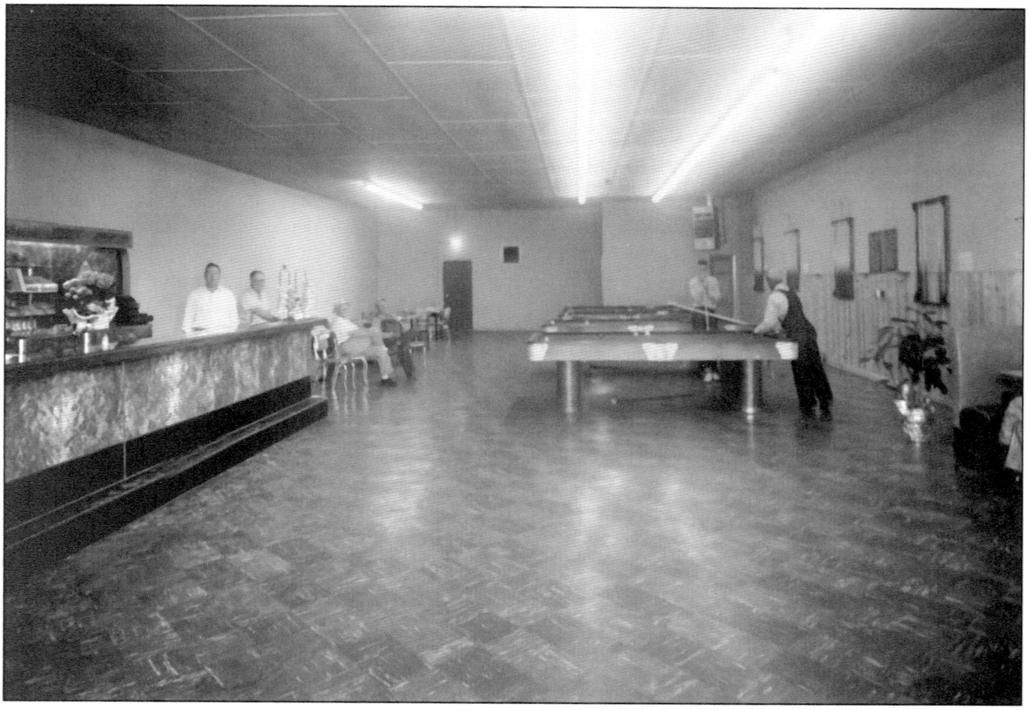

This photograph, taken during the same era, shows the inside of the pool hall. A couple of men enjoy a game of pool while a small group of men are visiting with one another. The building as it is today can be seen in chapter eight. (Courtesy of the Mulvane Historical Museum.)

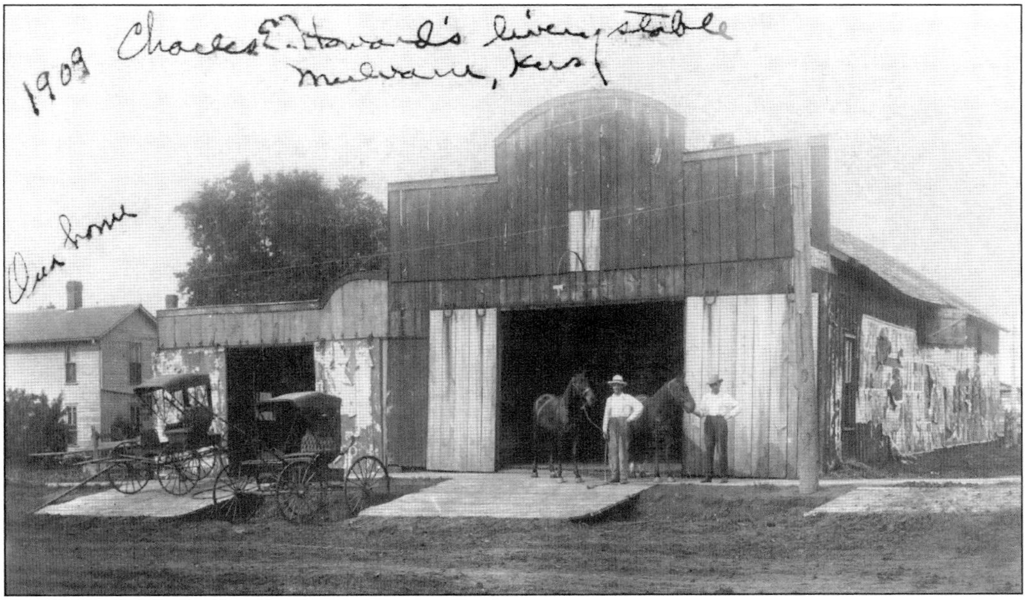

Agriculture was, and still is, a large part of Mulvane's economy. Charles Edwards's livery stable, where horses and wagons could be kept, is seen here in 1909. The two-story house on the left side of the photograph was the Edwards family home. (Courtesy of the Mulvane Historical Museum.)

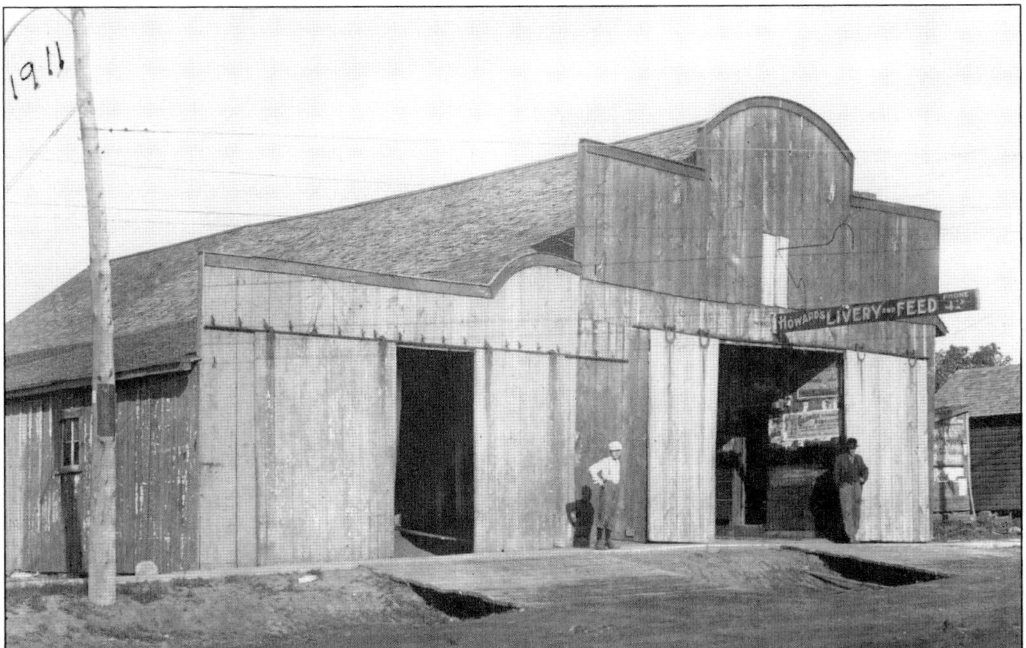

The Edwards livery stable is shown from another angle in this 1911 photograph. The gentleman in the doorway is believed to be Charles Edwards, and the boy is thought to be his son. Agriculture and agricultural support have been a key part of the Mulvane economy since the town's founding. (Courtesy of the Mulvane Historical Museum.)

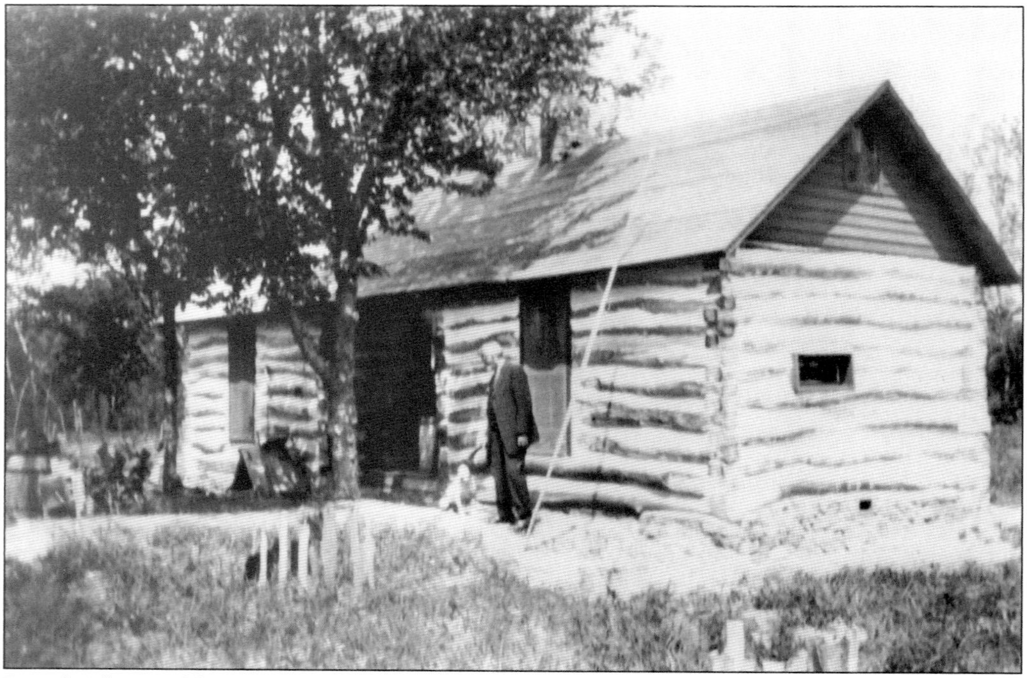

David Alley and his dog are seen standing outside of his log cabin around 1900. The cabin was located on the Arkansas River northwest of Mulvane. The cabin was typical for its day and would have provided surprisingly comfortable accommodations. (Courtesy of the Mulvane Historical Museum.)

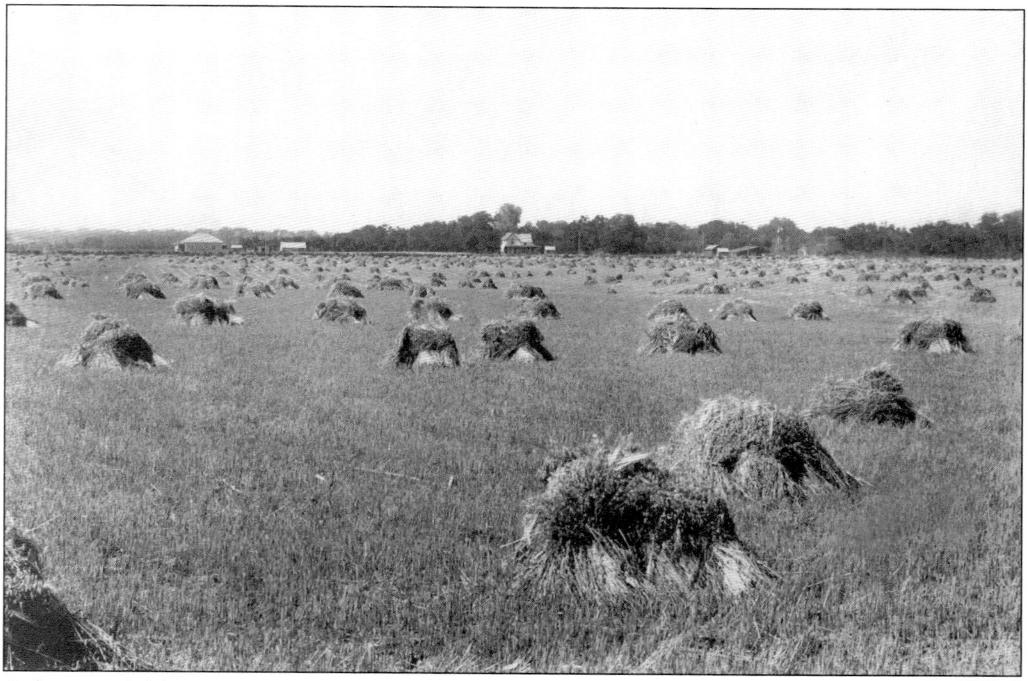

A farmer's field just outside of Mulvane is seen in this photograph, probably taken in the 1920s. The city's water tower can be seen on the left. Shocks of oats are spread throughout the field before being moved to grain bins. (Courtesy of the Mulvane Historical Museum.)

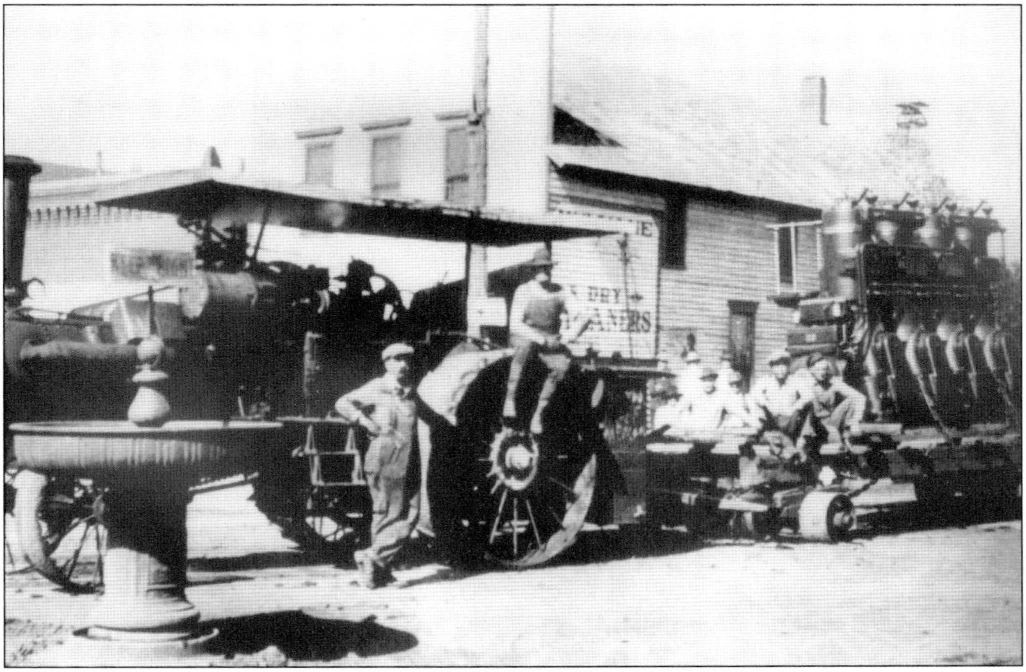

Farming has undergone dramatic changes through the years. This 1920 photograph shows Ben Bidwill (seated on the steel wheel) and his tractor. The setting is the intersection of First and Main Streets, next to the water fountain for horses. (Courtesy of the Mulvane Historical Museum.)

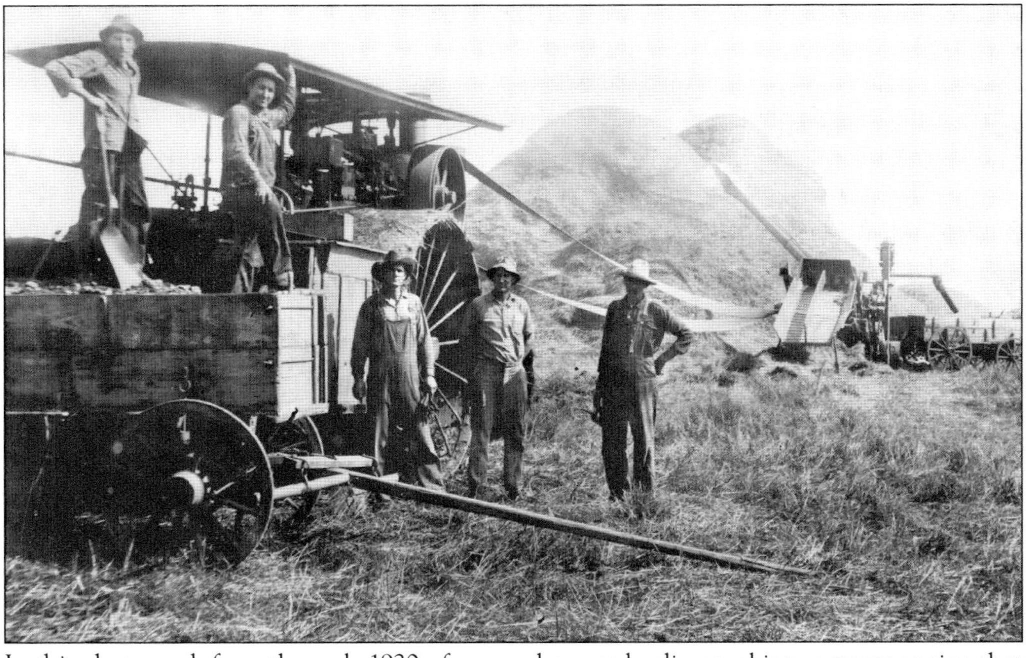

In this photograph from the early 1920s, farm workers are loading coal into a steam engine that powers a thresher. The first steam-powered thresher in Mulvane arrived in 1885, when George H. Howard moved his farming operations to rural Mulvane from Illinois. (Courtesy of the Mulvane Historical Museum.)

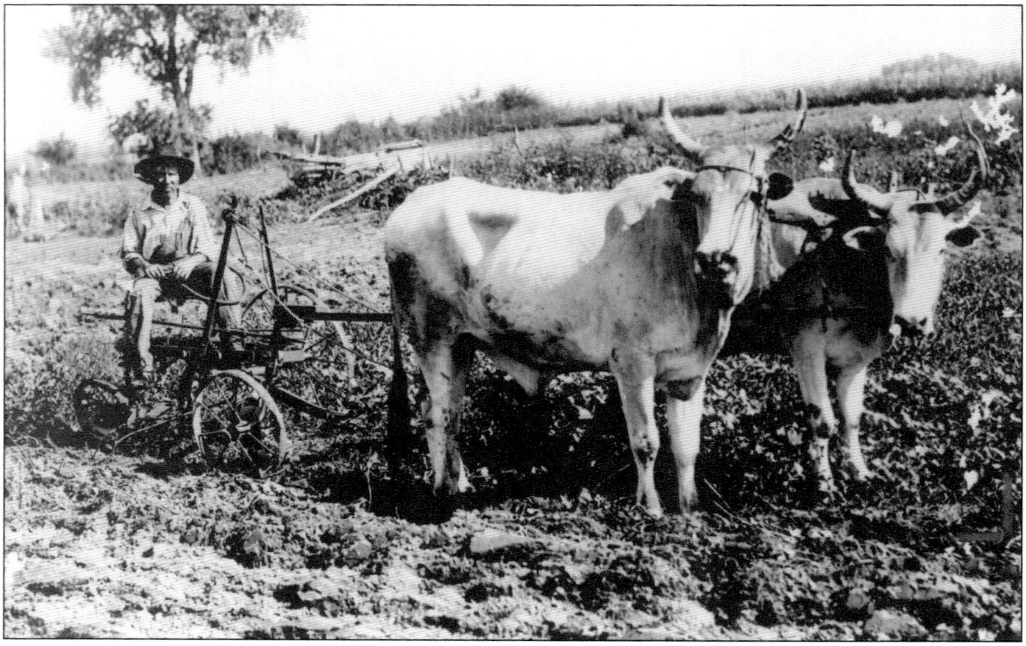

Mulvane farmer Fred Logan is shown using cattle to work his field in 1928. Cattle were used on rare occasions to power farm implements. It was far more common to use horses or mules when machinery was not available to the farmer. (Courtesy of the Mulvane Historical Museum.)

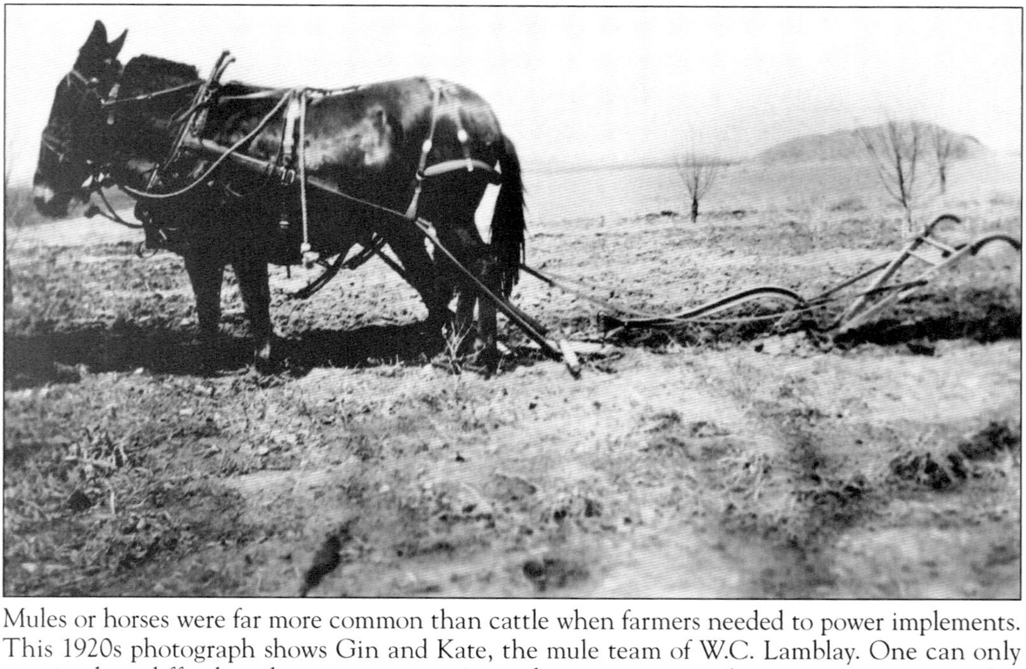

Mules or horses were far more common than cattle when farmers needed to power implements. This 1920s photograph shows Gin and Kate, the mule team of W.C. Lamblay. One can only imagine how difficult and time-consuming it was for a person to produce a crop or raise a garden using tools like this. (Courtesy of the Mulvane Historical Museum.)

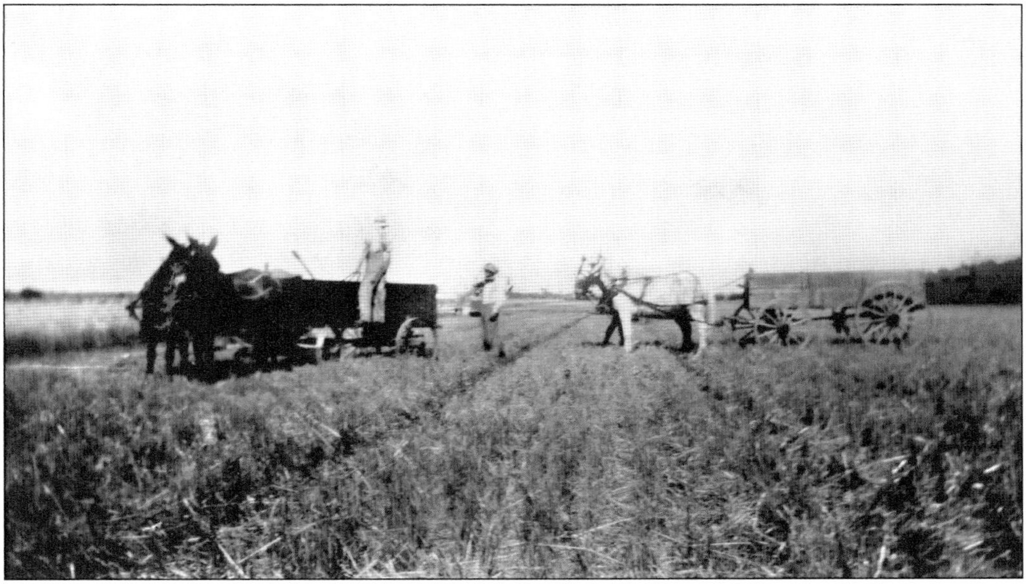

Two farmers are seen working in a field in the 1920s, a time that preceded the widespread use of trucks and tractors. The crop would be loaded into the wagons by hand and taken to town to be sold. Such a process made for long workdays. (Courtesy of the Mulvane Historical Museum.)

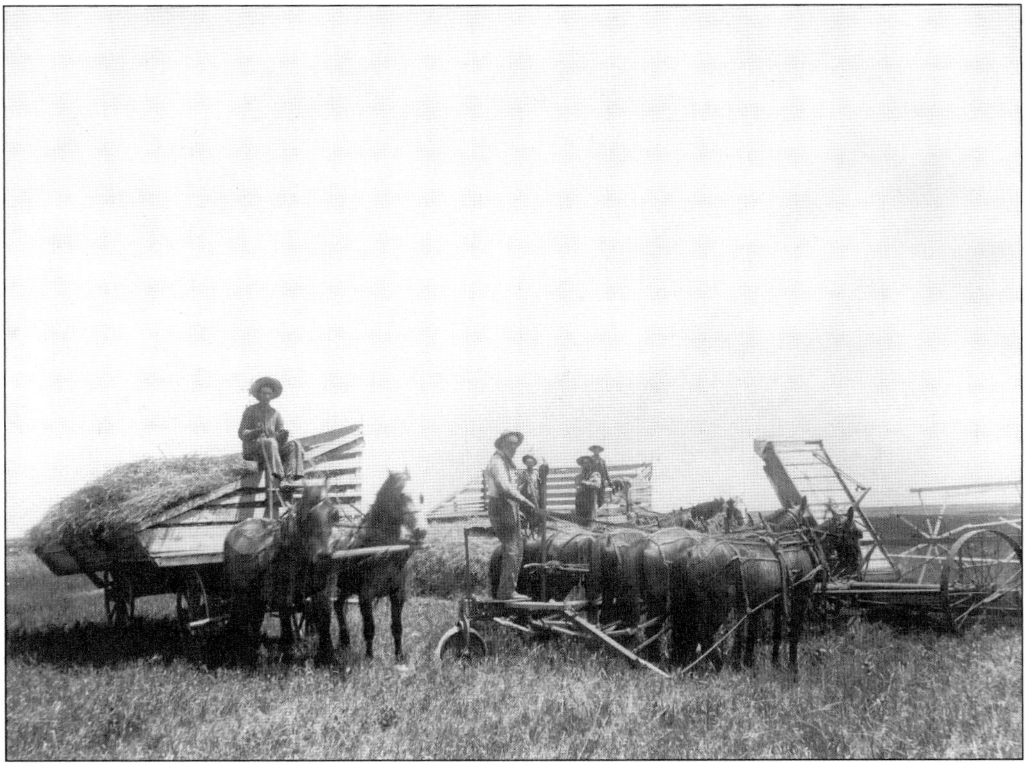

In this photograph from the early 1920s, a farmer uses a header to harvest his grain. In the days that preceded combines, a header was a way to harvest the crop and bundle it into shocks so that the heads of the grain could be threshed at a later time. (Courtesy of the Mulvane Historical Museum.)

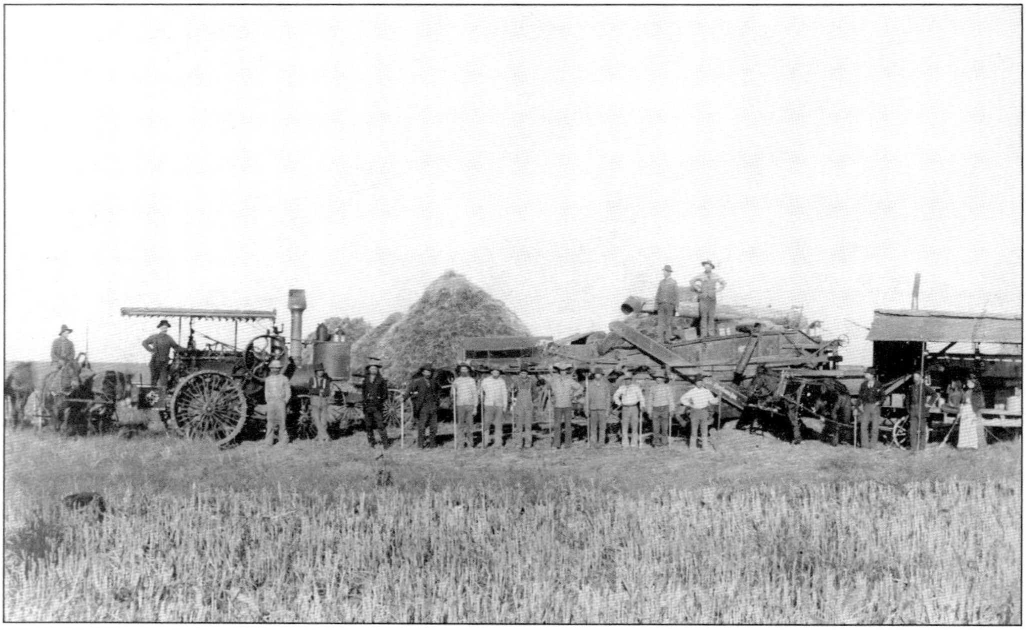

This photograph from the 1920s shows a full crew working to bring in a harvest. In this era, many farm implements were introduced into farming operations. A farmer's wife can be seen on the far right. It was not uncommon to see women working in the fields next to men. (Courtesy of the Mulvane Historical Museum.)

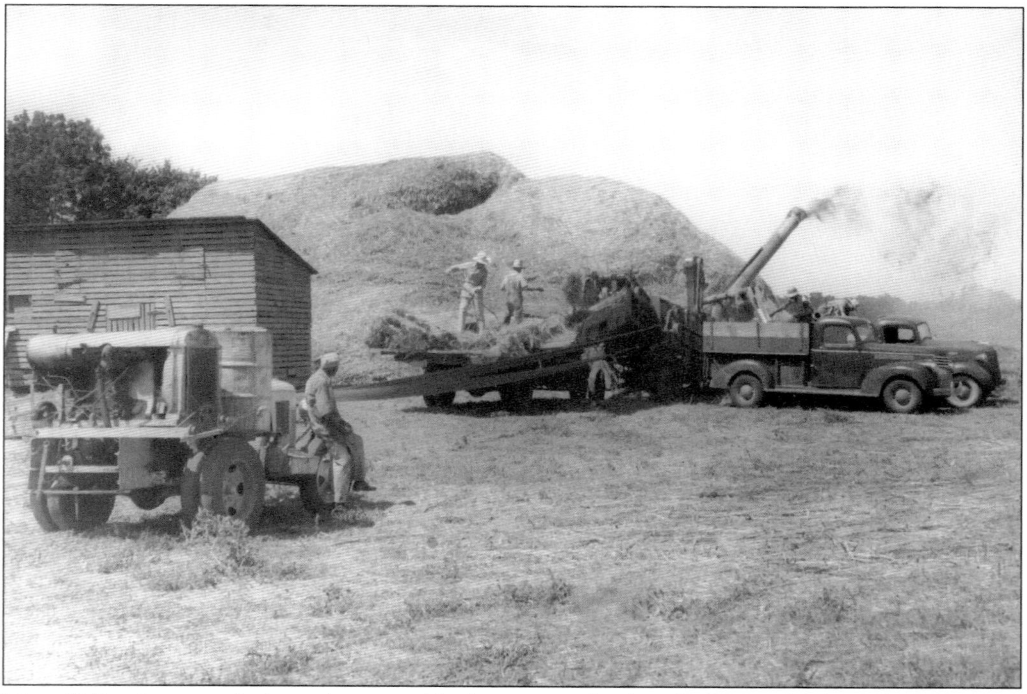

This 1940s photograph shows how quickly farming evolved with the availability of mechanized equipment. Notice the difference from the previous photographs in the sizes of the harvests and crews. The evolution of modern farming helped make Kansas the "breadbasket of the nation." (Courtesy of the Mulvane Historical Museum.)

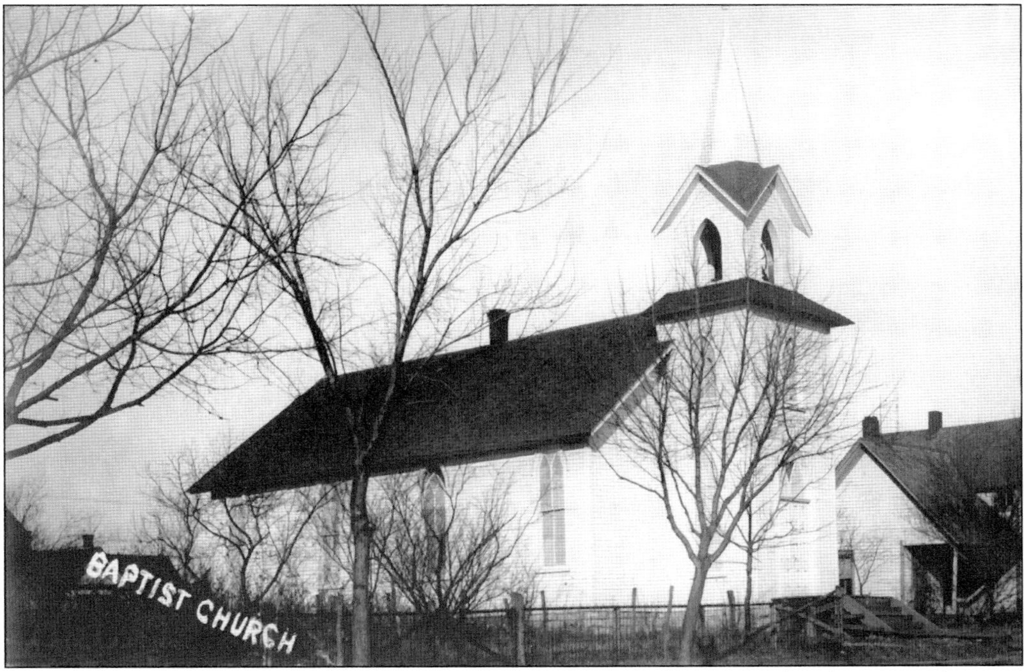

As is the case with most small towns across the country, Mulvane's early churches were a big part of the community. This building was an early home of the Baptist Church of Mulvane, which was founded in 1947 and is thriving today. (Courtesy of the Mulvane Historical Museum.)

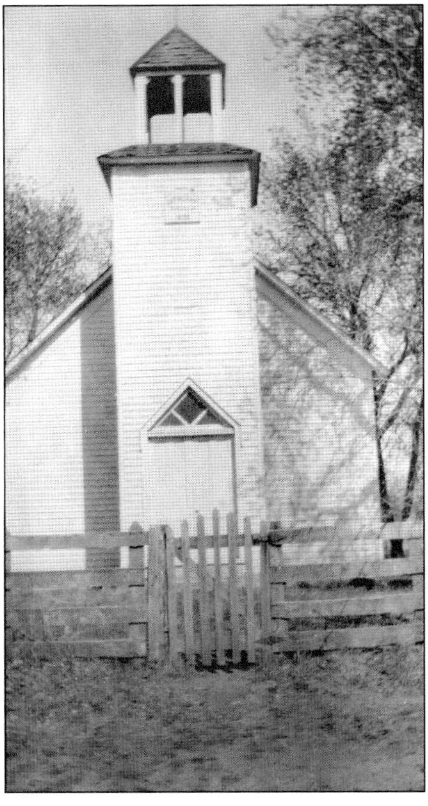

This is a photograph of the Evangelical Lutheran Church of Mulvane, which existed from 1881 to 1927. Because of difficulty finding ministers, the church disbanded on May 27, 1927, and its members began attending Lutheran services at the Immanuel Lutheran Church in Wichita. The land on which this church stood is now a family home. (Courtesy of the Mulvane Historical Museum.)

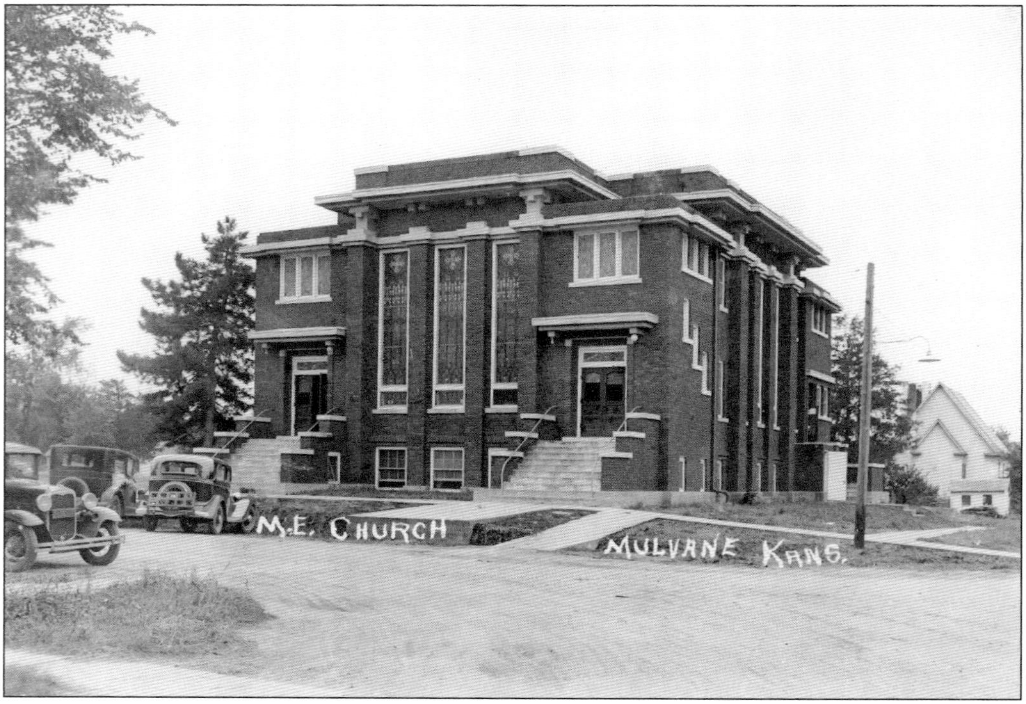

The Mulvane Methodist Church was founded soon after the town was formed in 1879. This church building was erected in 1918 at a cost of $27,600 and is still in use today. (Courtesy of the Mulvane Historical Museum.)

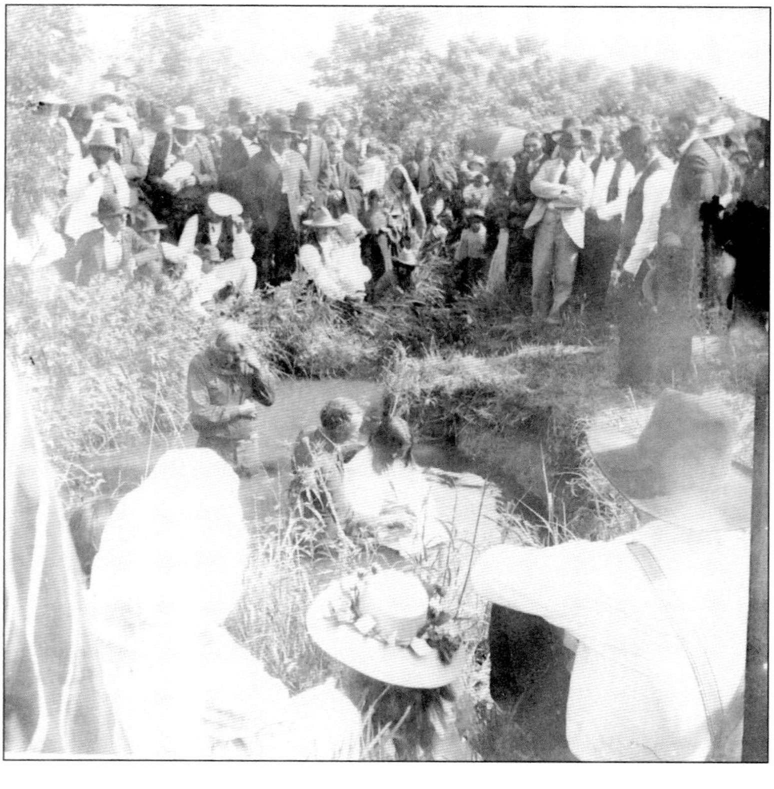

Shown here is an outdoor baptism. Not much is known of this particular event, but it offers an interesting glimpse into church services in Mulvane in the early 20th century. The date of the service and the name of the church are not known. (Courtesy of the Mulvane Historical Museum.)

Four

EARLY SCHOOLS

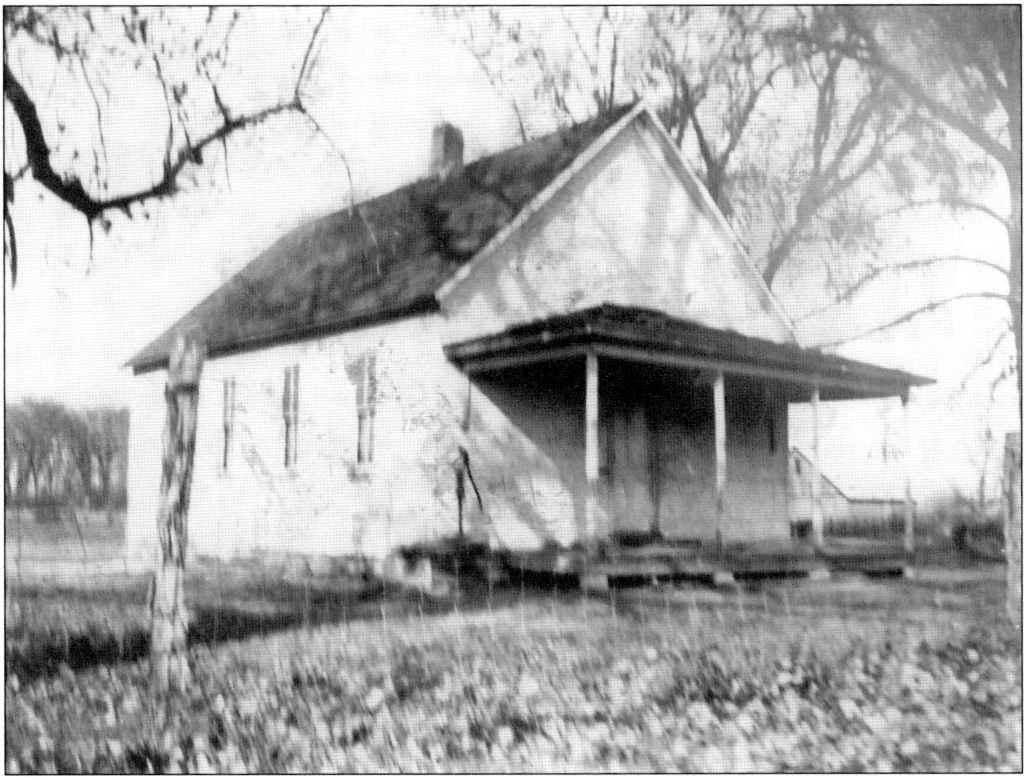

Shown here is the Salem School in rural Sumner County at the turn of the 20th century. Typical of rural schools of the day, this was a one-room school in which all grade levels were taught. The chimney in the middle of the roof reveals the location of the building's only source of heat. (Courtesy of the Mulvane Historical Museum.)

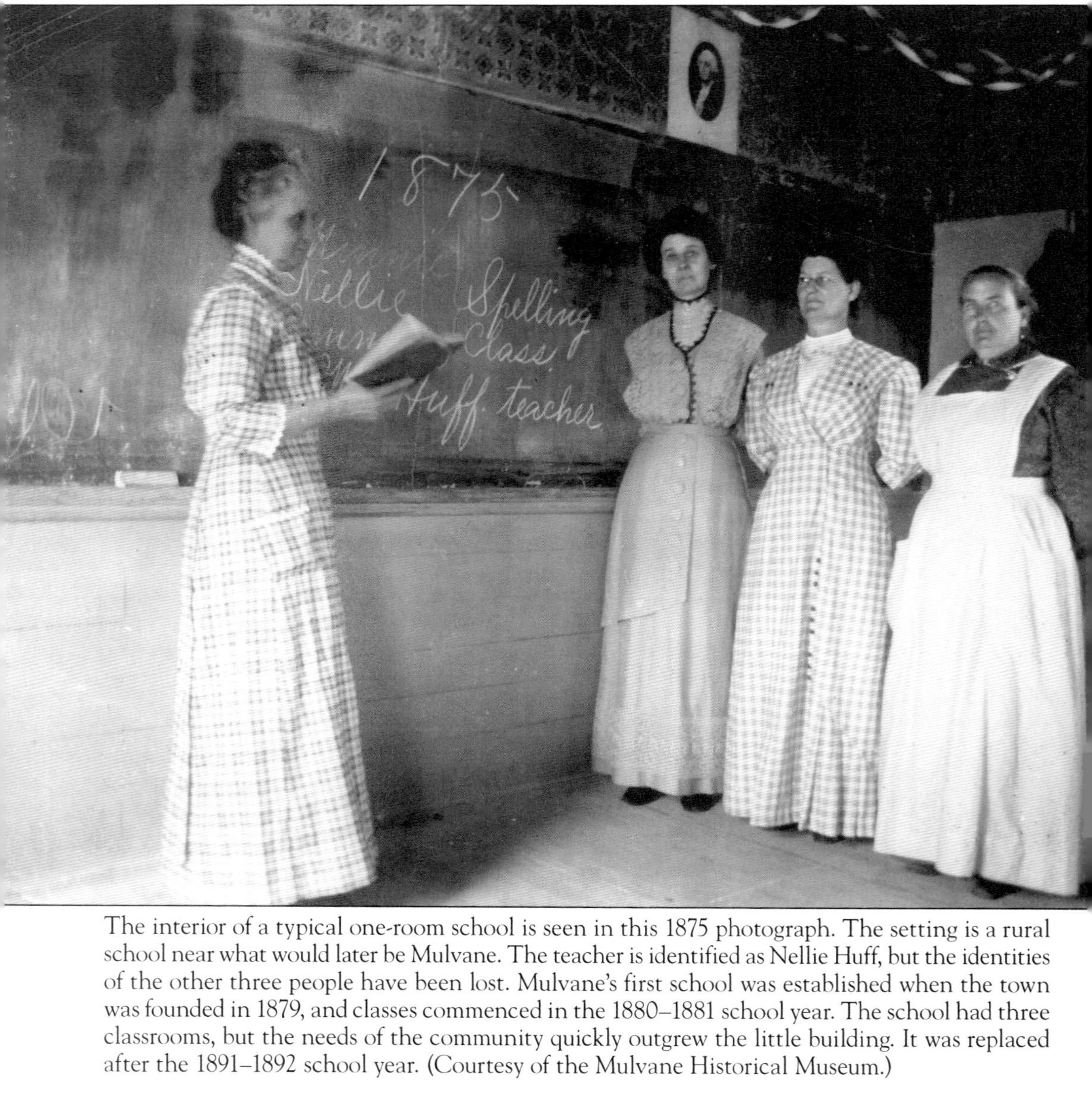

The interior of a typical one-room school is seen in this 1875 photograph. The setting is a rural school near what would later be Mulvane. The teacher is identified as Nellie Huff, but the identities of the other three people have been lost. Mulvane's first school was established when the town was founded in 1879, and classes commenced in the 1880–1881 school year. The school had three classrooms, but the needs of the community quickly outgrew the little building. It was replaced after the 1891–1892 school year. (Courtesy of the Mulvane Historical Museum.)

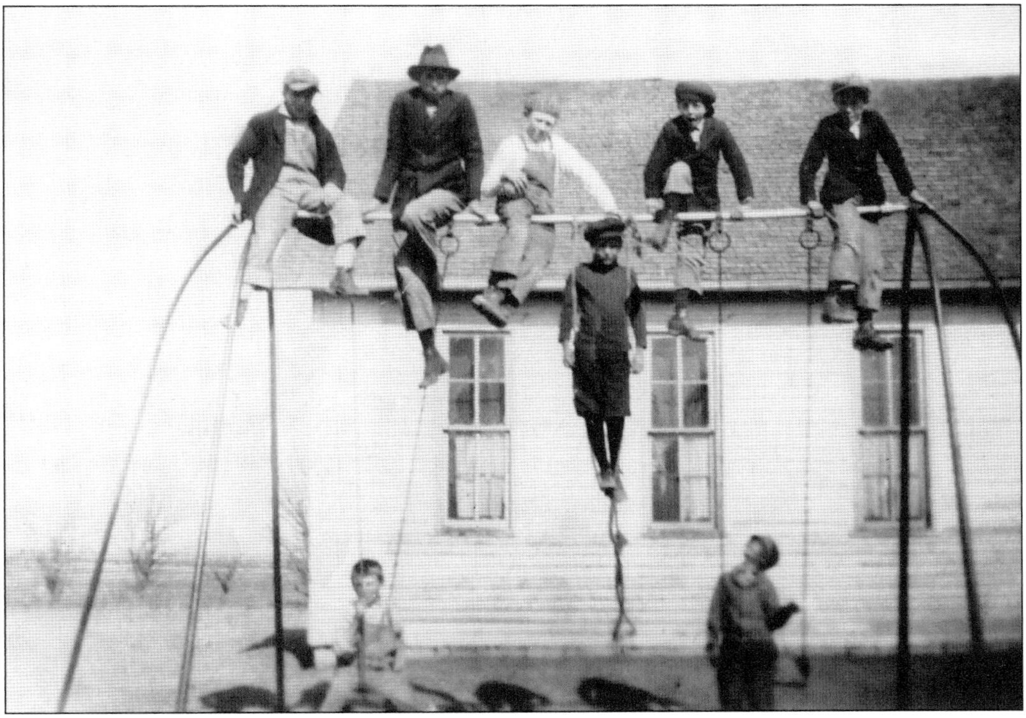

This fun photograph was taken at the turn of the century at the Grand Prairie School near Mulvane. Several boys demonstrate their bravado on a playground swing, while one nervous onlooker evaluates the situation. Another student is in a swing, apparently indifferent to it all. (Courtesy of the Mulvane Historical Museum.)

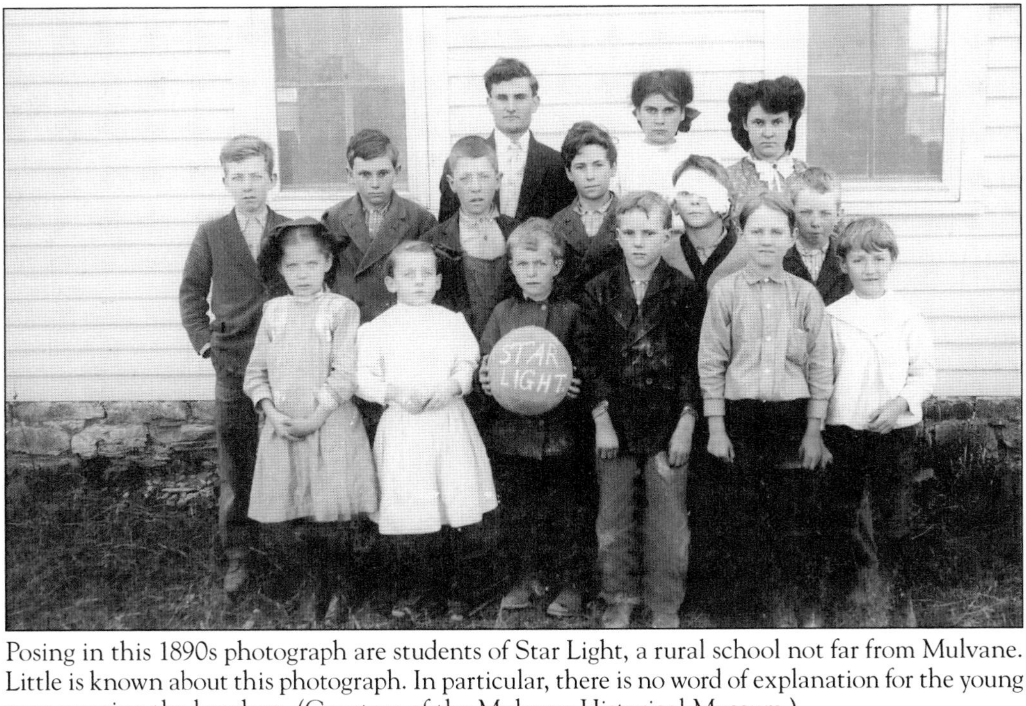

Posing in this 1890s photograph are students of Star Light, a rural school not far from Mulvane. Little is known about this photograph. In particular, there is no word of explanation for the young man wearing the bandage. (Courtesy of the Mulvane Historical Museum.)

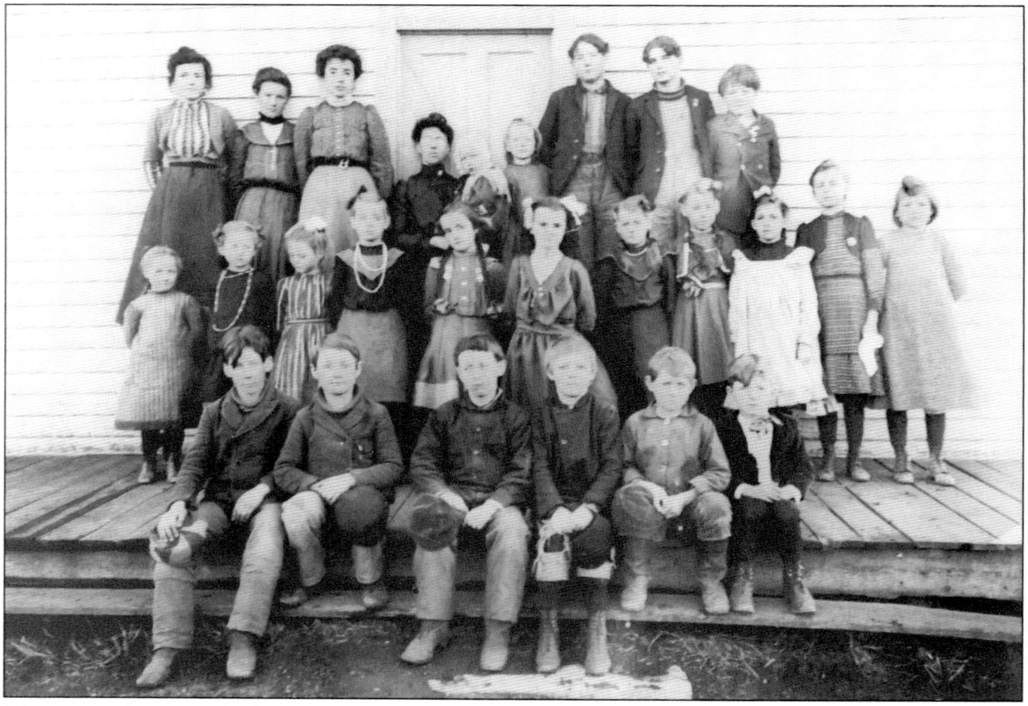

This 1910 photograph shows the elementary school students of the Central School District. The teacher was Ethel Huffington (back row, holding baby). She was responsible for 24 students, covering the gamut in age and education. It would have been a big challenge for a teacher of the day. (Courtesy of the Mulvane Historical Museum.)

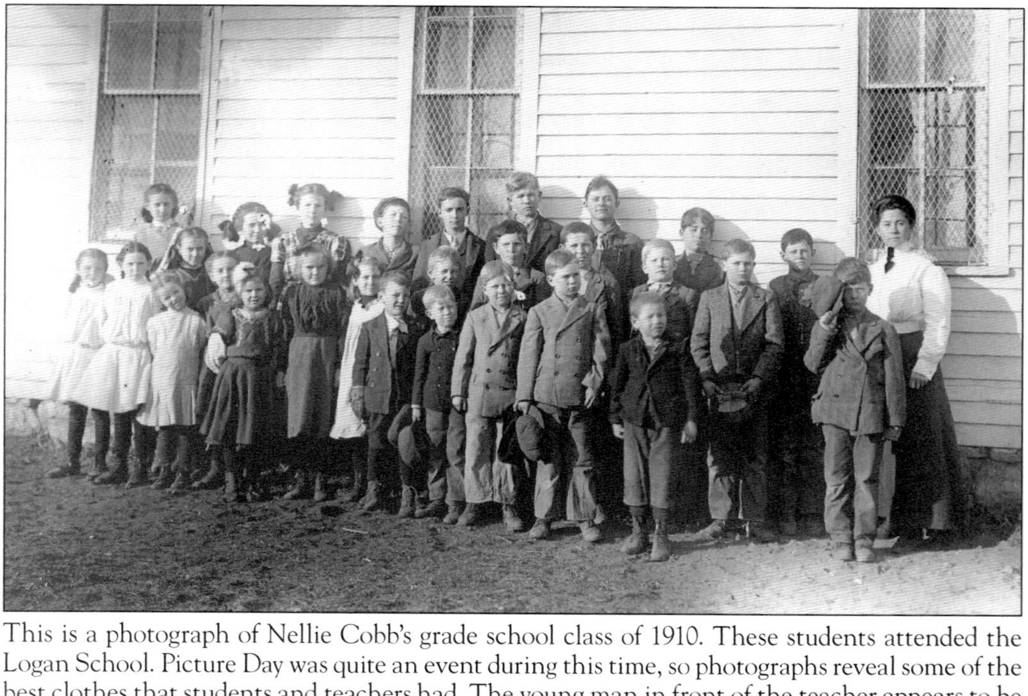

This is a photograph of Nellie Cobb's grade school class of 1910. These students attended the Logan School. Picture Day was quite an event during this time, so photographs reveal some of the best clothes that students and teachers had. The young man in front of the teacher appears to be shielding his eyes from the sun with his cap. (Courtesy of the Mulvane Historical Museum.)

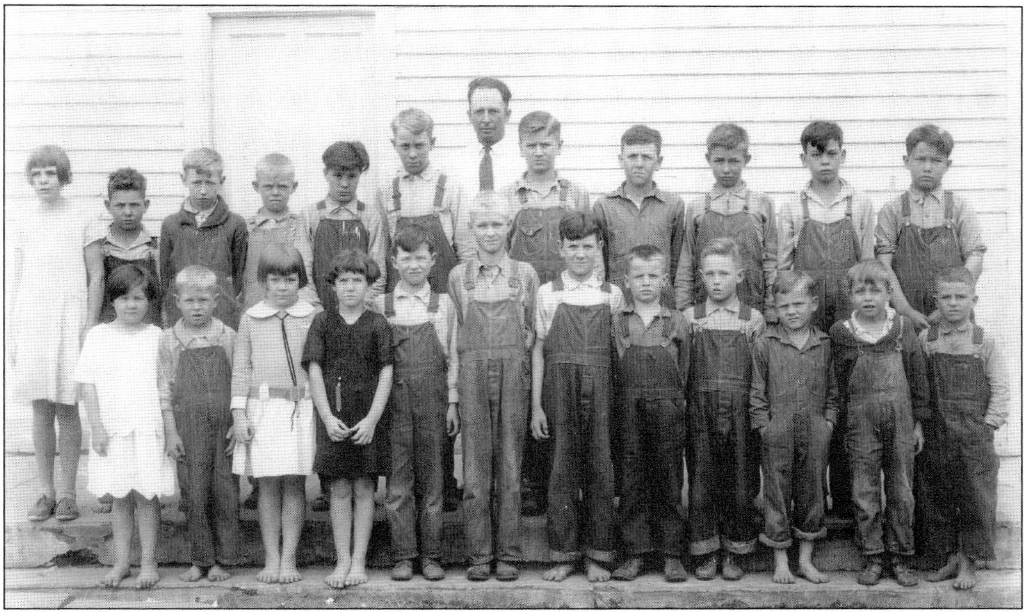

Robert Duvall's class at the Valley School near Mulvane is seen in this photograph from 1926 or 1927. The Valley School was located in Sumner County between Mulvane and Belle Plaine. It is interesting to note how many of the children are barefoot in this photograph. (Courtesy of the Mulvane Historical Museum.)

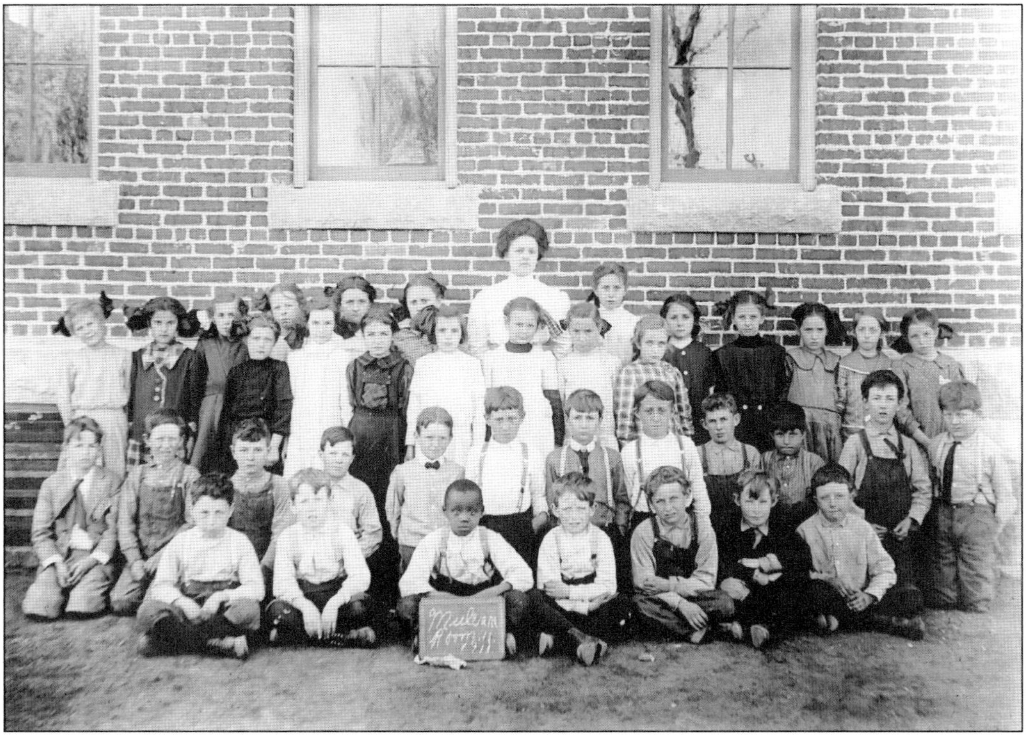

This is one of the earliest photographs of Mulvane students. It is from 1911 and shows the grade-school class of Room Four. The teacher is not identified, but there were 37 pupils in her class. It was an early sign of the growth of Mulvane. (Courtesy of the Mulvane Historical Museum.)

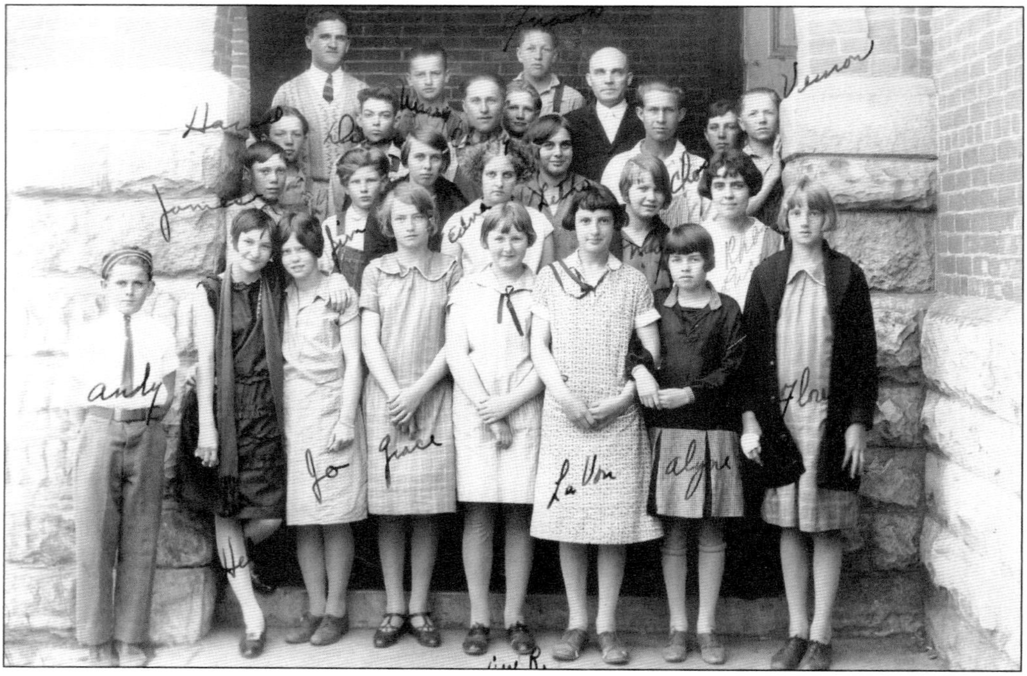

Mulvane Grade School's seventh-grade class poses for a photograph in 1926. The teacher and the administrator shown here are not identified, but two pairs of girls in the first row appear to have formed friendships that could last a lifetime. (Courtesy of the Mulvane Historical Museum.)

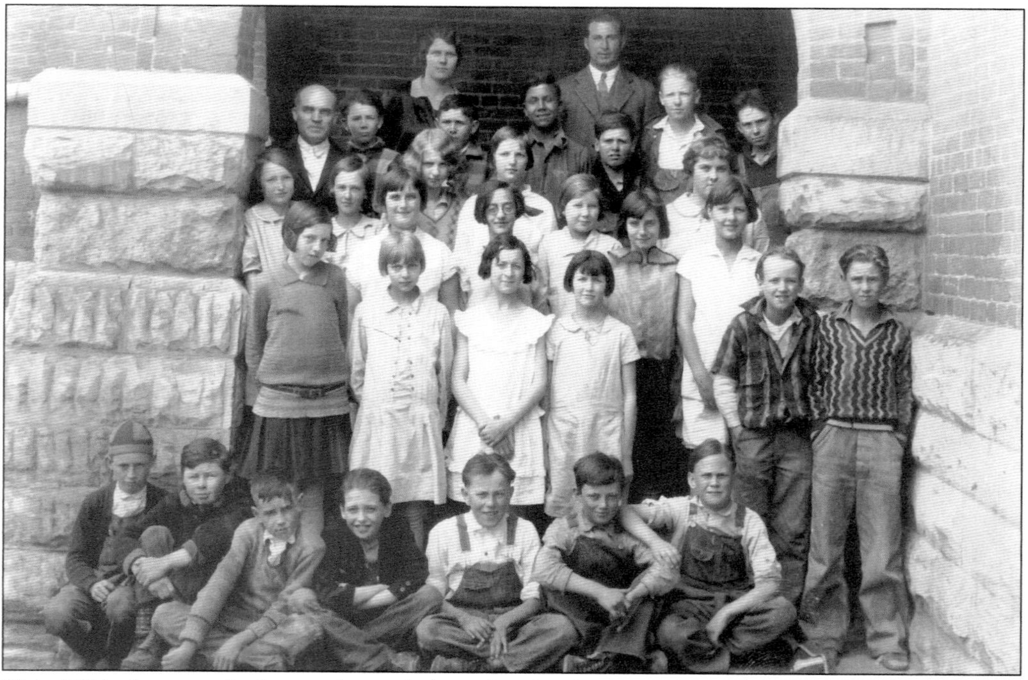

This 1934 photograph shows what is believed to be the seventh-grade class at Mulvane Grade School. The country had gone from the Roaring Twenties to the Great Depression. These young people seem unaffected by the trials of the day, but 1934 was not an easy year on the Great Plains. (Courtesy of the Mulvane Historical Museum.)

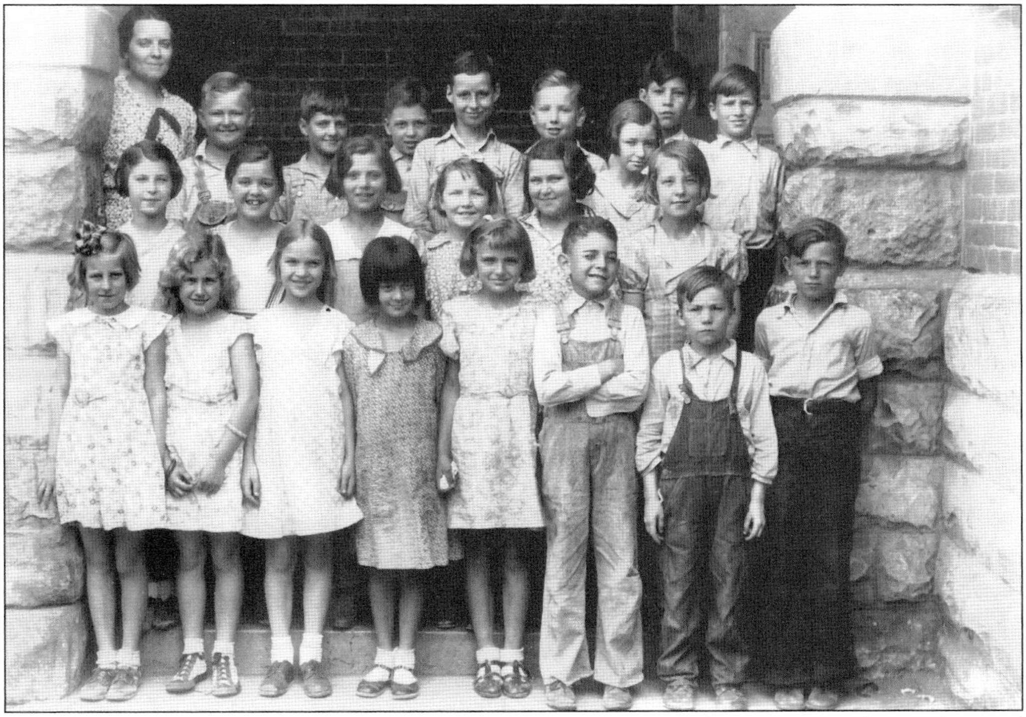

World War II was coming to a close when this photograph was taken in 1944. The teacher and her class are not identified, but this group of young people will soon begin helping to rebuild the country and the world after the devastating effects of the war. (Courtesy of the Mulvane Historical Museum.)

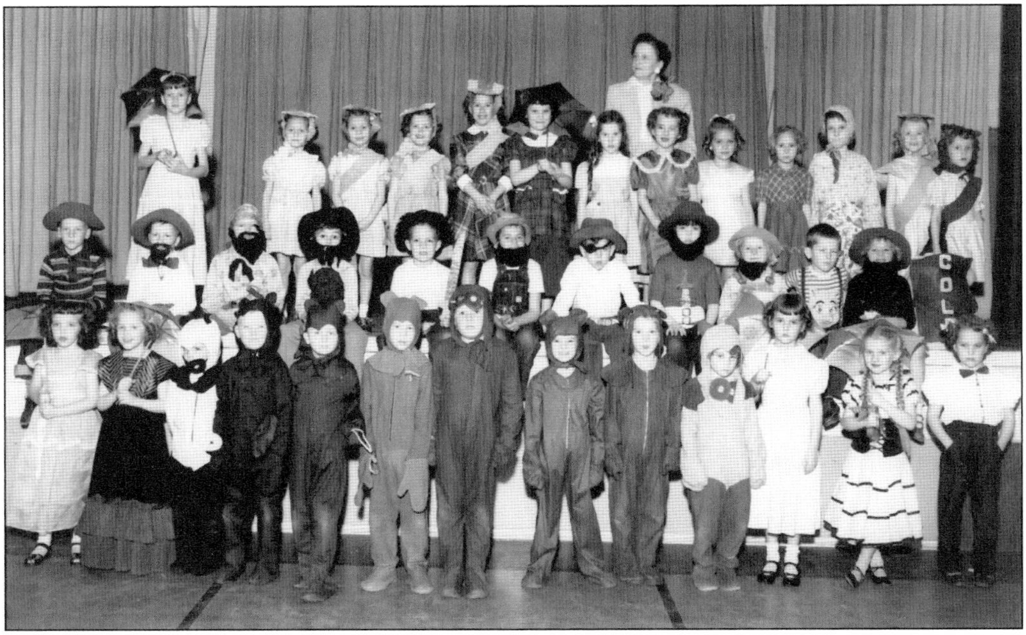

Esther Thompson poses with her Mulvane Elementary School students, who are in full costume for a school play in the 1950s. Plays were very common, and this one is unique in the elaborateness of the costumes, most of which were made by hand. (Courtesy of the Mulvane Historical Museum.)

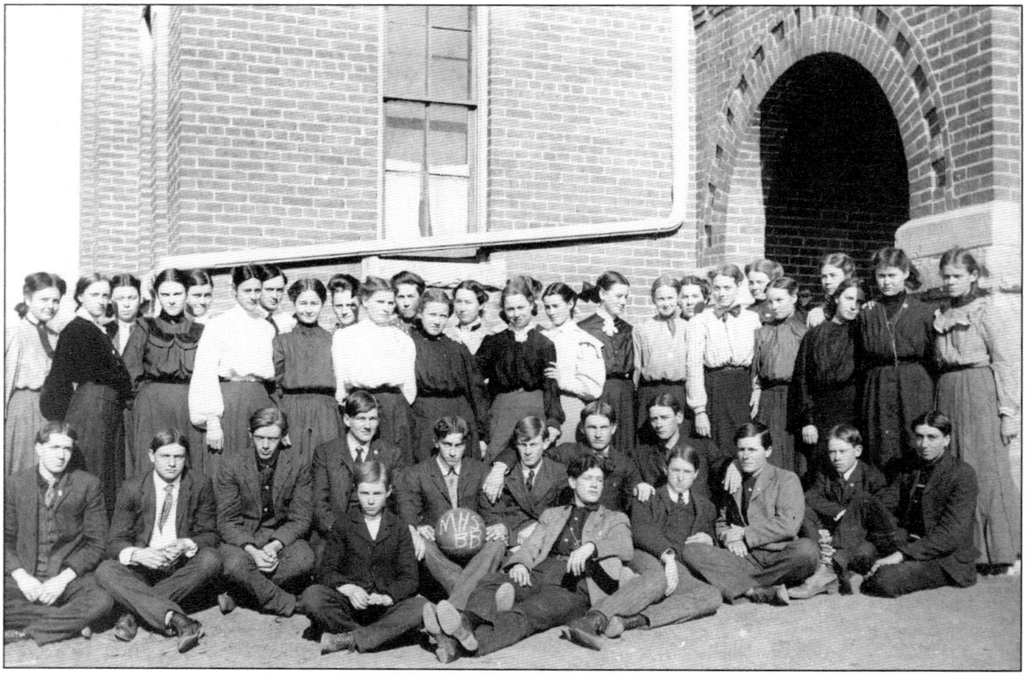

This 1920s photograph shows one of the first groups of students to attend the high school that opened in 1919. Members of the Mulvane varsity basketball team are seated on the ground. Suits and ties were the order of the day for the boys. (Courtesy of the Mulvane Historical Museum.)

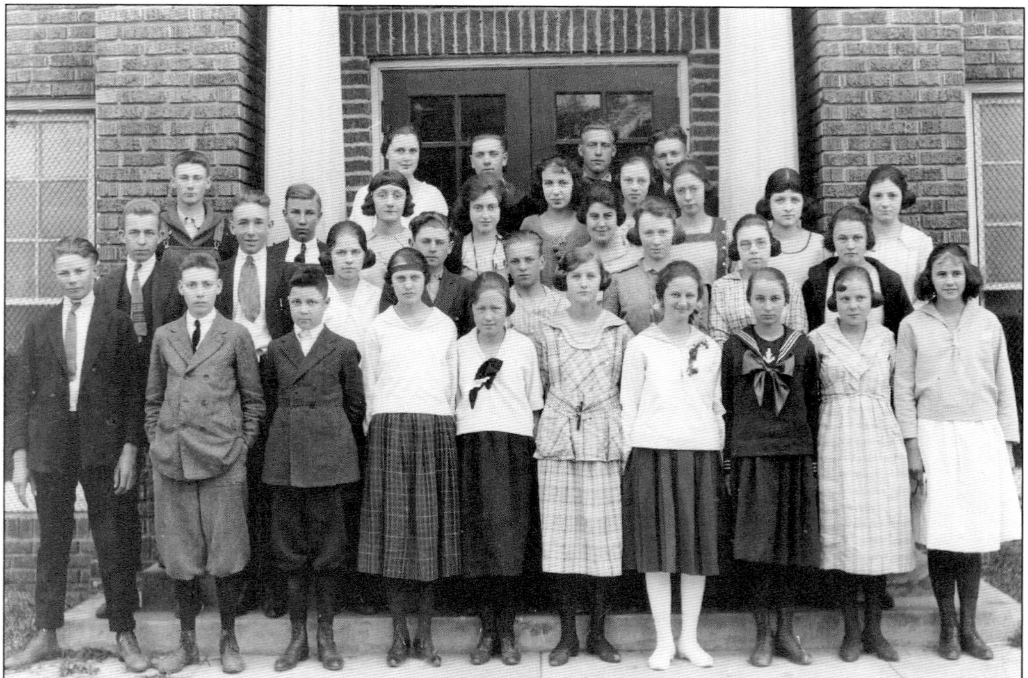

Shown here is Mulvane High School's graduating class of 1924. This was the first group of students to complete all four years in the new high school building. This was also among the first classes to be known as the Mulvane Wildcats. (Courtesy of the Mulvane Historical Museum.)

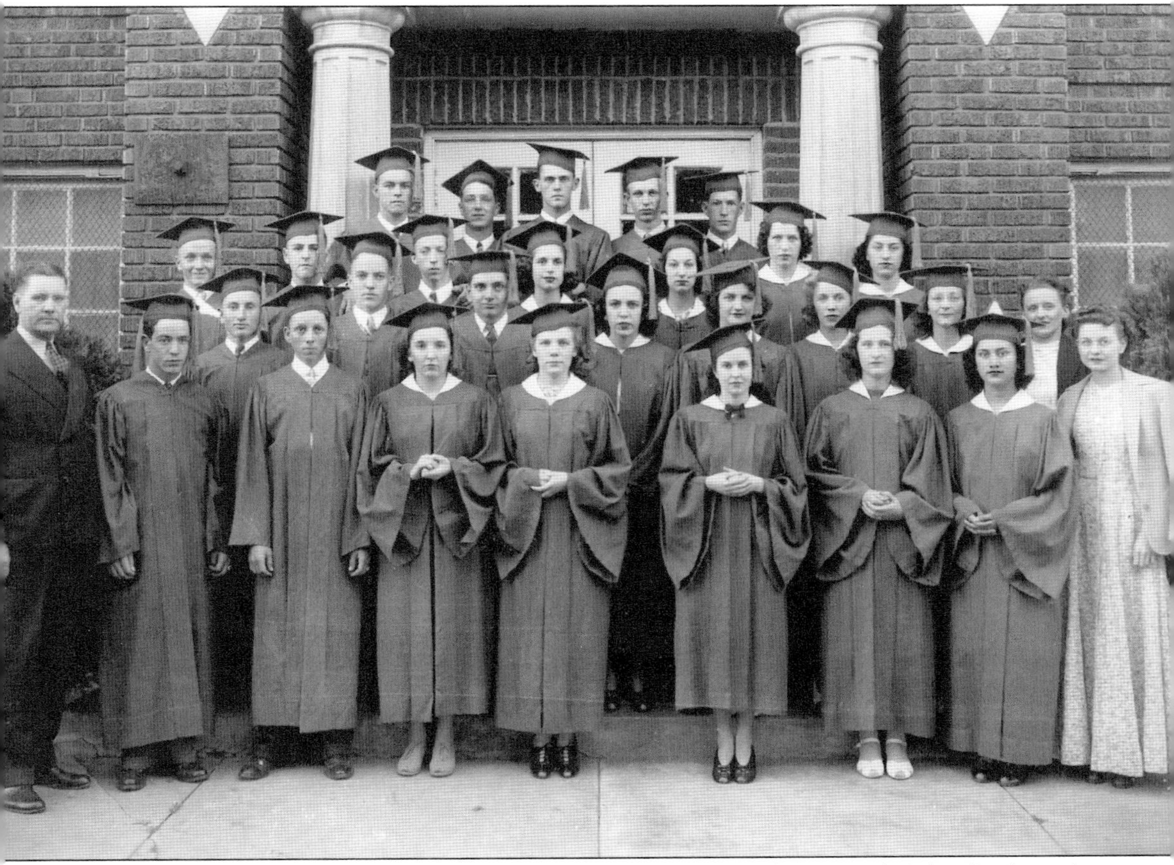

Caps and gowns are the order of the day in this photograph of Mulvane High School's class of 1942. There were 27 students in the class, 10 of whom were young men. Most of them would serve in the military during World War II. (Courtesy of the Mulvane Historical Museum.)

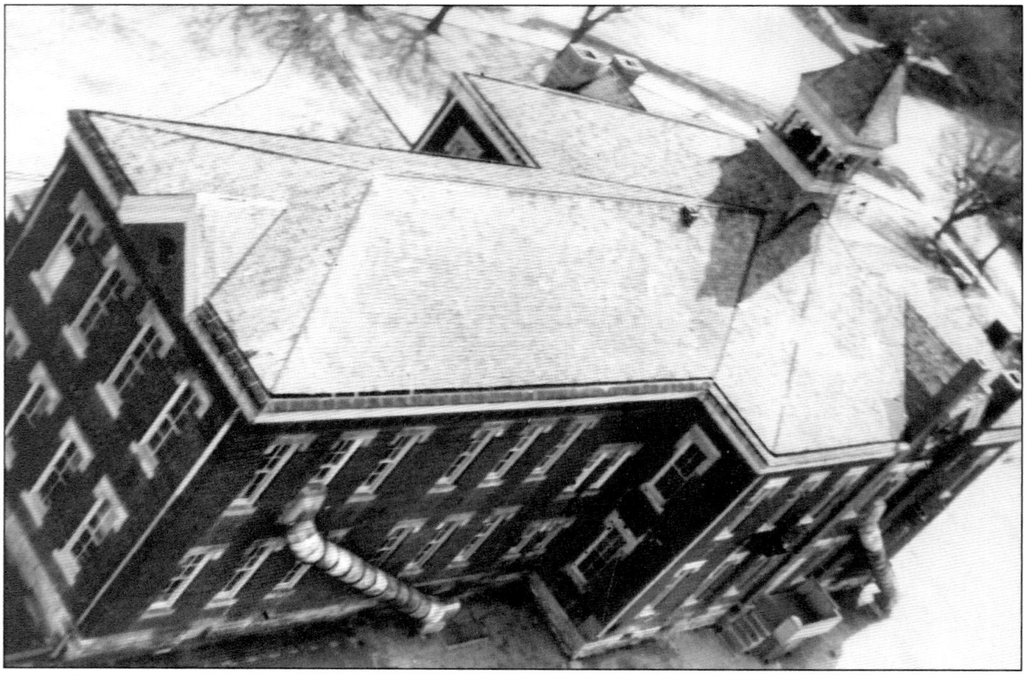

This photograph of the grade school was taken in 1927 by a brave photographer who climbed to the top of the Mulvane water tower. The school building was first used in 1892 and was modified and expanded until it was razed in 1949. On the near side of the building is the tube-slide fire escape. In the event of fire, students were instructed to climb out the window and slide to the ground below. (Courtesy of the Mulvane Historical Museum.)

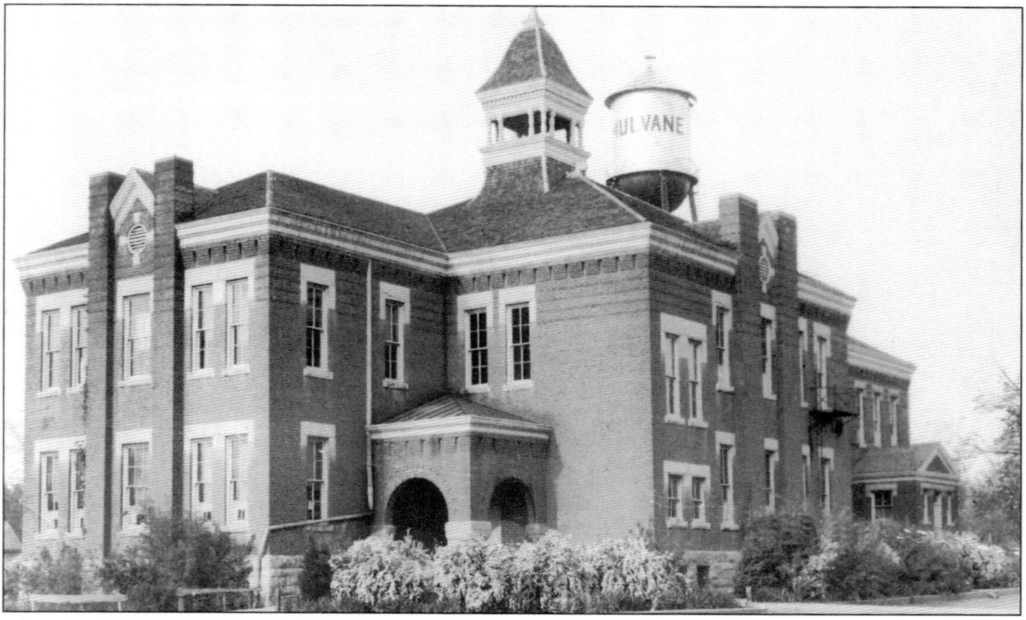

This photograph was taken in the mid-1940s as the grade school was in the final years of use. It served the community for almost 60 years before it had to be replaced in 1949. The water tower referenced in the previous caption can be seen just behind the building. (Courtesy of the Mulvane Historical Museum.)

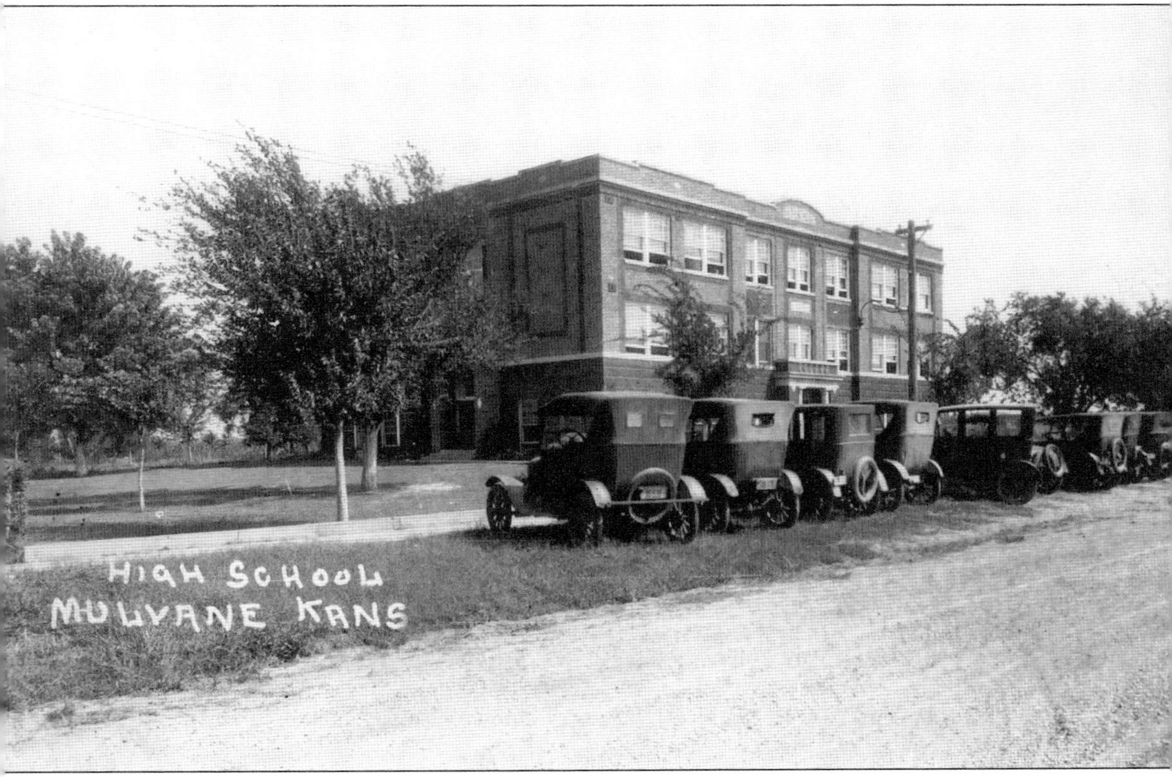

Mulvane High School is seen here shortly after it opened in 1919. It was the first time that high school students attended classes in a separate building. The needs of the day had evolved to a point where a separate high school was needed. In 1921, green and white were formally adopted as the school's colors, and the Wildcat mascot was officially adopted. The school included a small auditorium and a small gymnasium that were used until 1937, when a school addition was completed. This large brick structure was used until 1955. (Courtesy of the Mulvane Historical Museum.)

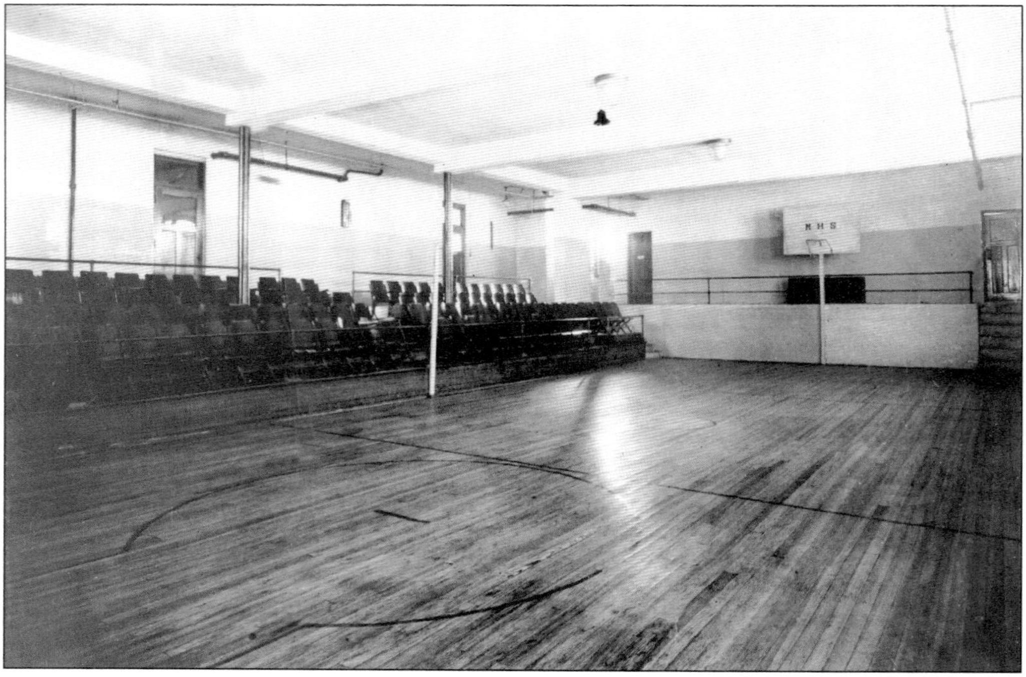

The high school's gymnasium (above) and auditorium (below) were quite small, and the gymnasium was not practical for interscholastic competition. A new gymnasium and auditorium were built in 1937, the cost covered by WPA funds. In 1949, the high school was torn down, and a new junior high school was built in its place. The gym and the auditorium were expanded, remodeled, and included in the new junior high school. Mulvane school enrollment continued to increase, requiring continual expansion and remodeling throughout the 1960s. (Both, courtesy of the Mulvane Historical Museum.)

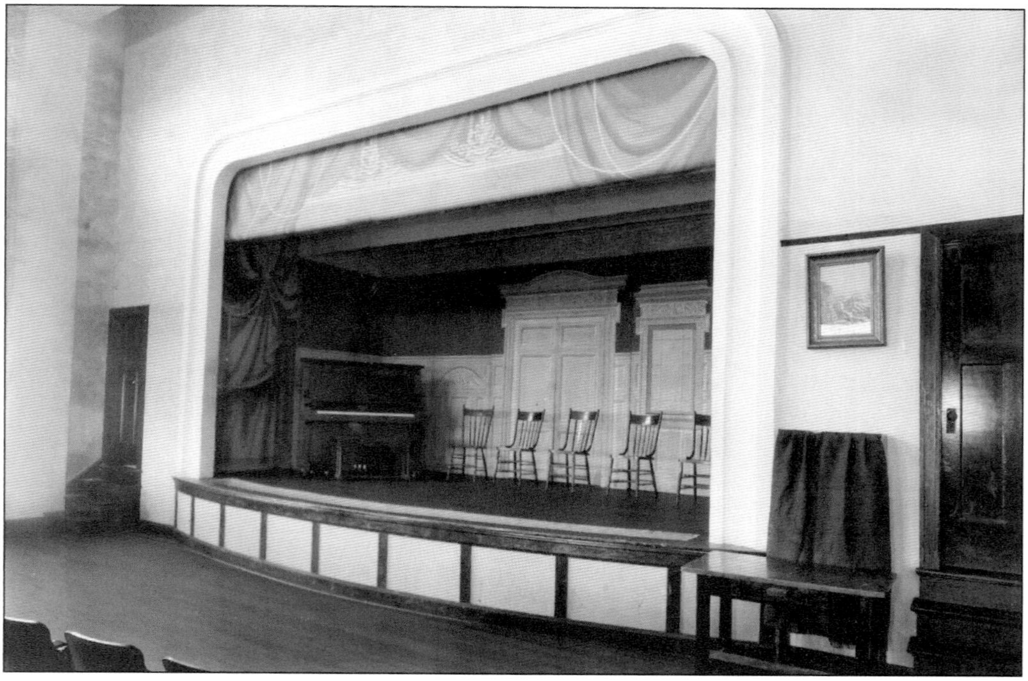

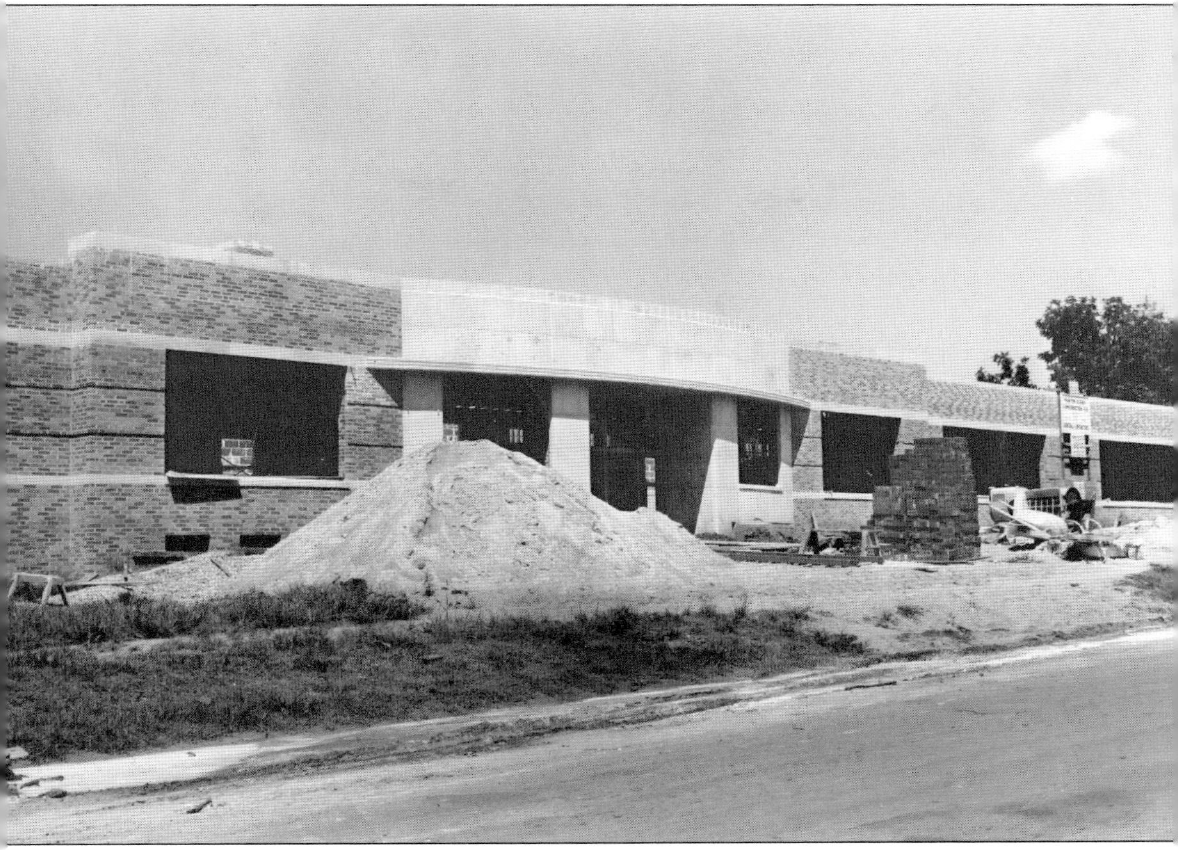

Construction of Mulvane Primary School is under way in 1960–1961. In January 1964, the school was renamed Munson Primary School in honor of W.D. Munson, who served as the superintendent of schools from 1950 until his retirement in 1964. It was during his tenure that Mulvane saw the construction of a new high school, a new middle school, and the new primary school that bore his name. Munson also oversaw numerous remodeling projects and upgrades to school buildings, school grounds, and athletic facilities. (Courtesy of the Mulvane Historical Museum.)

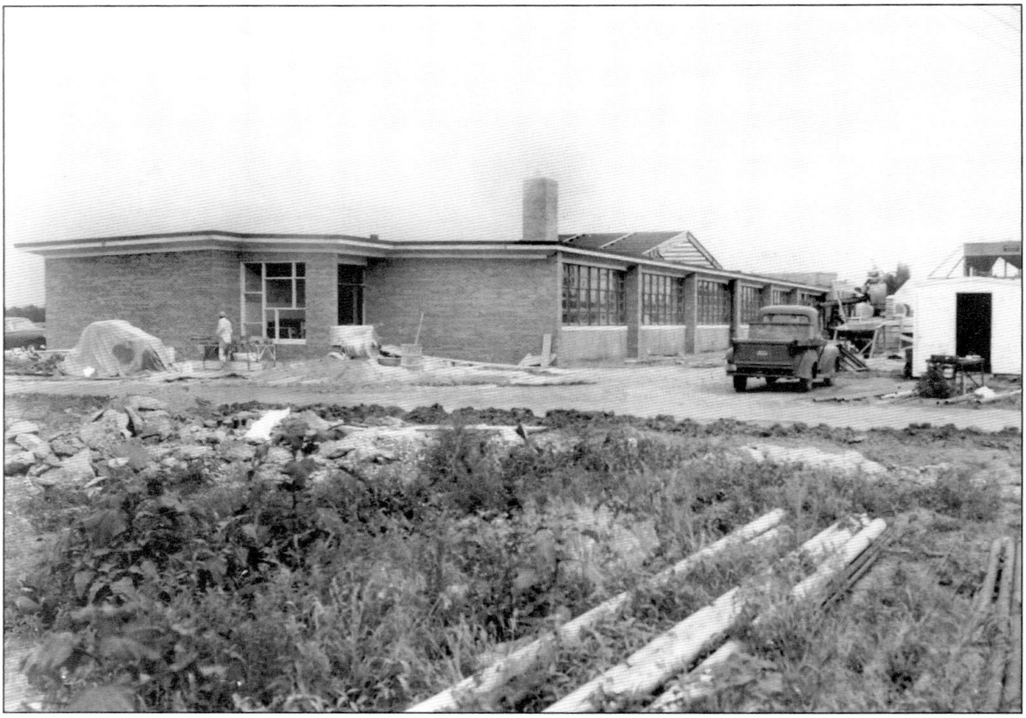

These two photographs were taken during the construction of Mulvane High School in 1954. The 1919 high school was ready to be replaced, so this new school was built. Superintendent Munson and the school board secured federal funds to help pay for the construction project, and the school was ready for students on the first day of classes in 1954. This building, still in use today, currently houses Mulvane Middle School. (Both, courtesy of the Mulvane Historical Museum.)

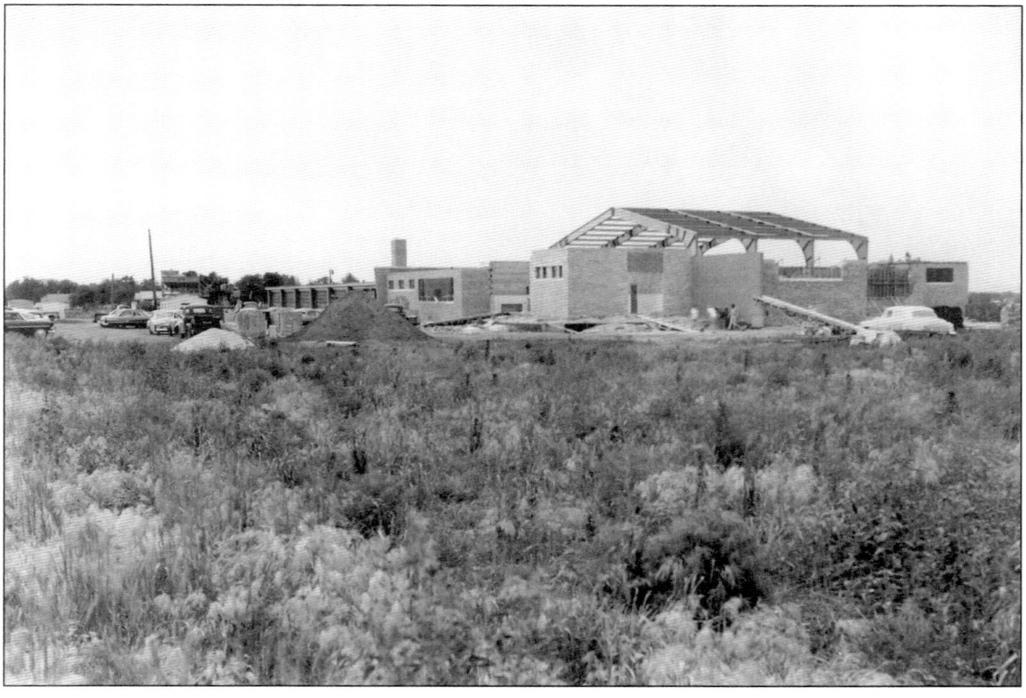

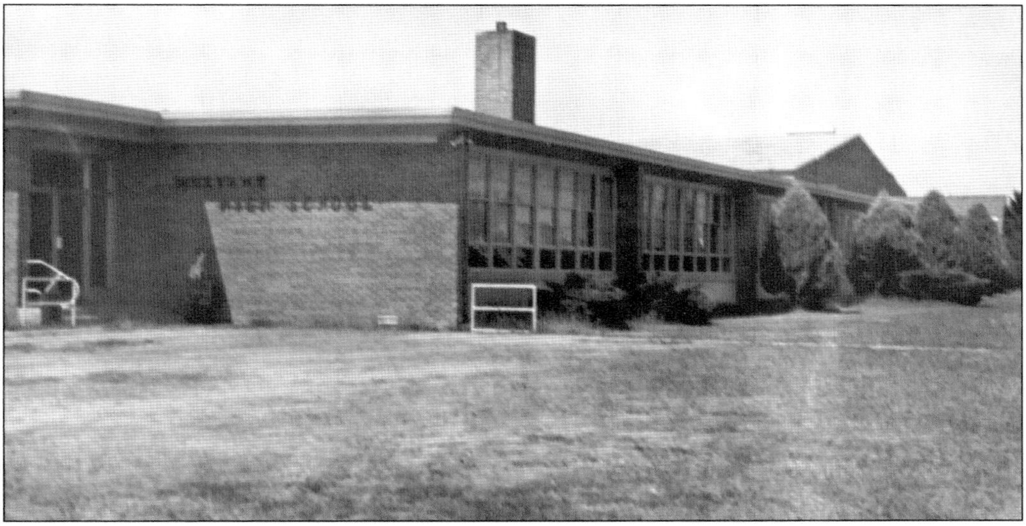

These two photographs show the high school after construction was completed. In the aerial view (below) can be seen the areas behind the school that would eventually be converted to athletic fields. The school building wasn't the only thing that was new in 1955. The school also approved a new alma mater that year. Mulvane High School student G.C. Daniels wrote it, and it is still being used today. (Both, courtesy of the Mulvane Historical Museum.)

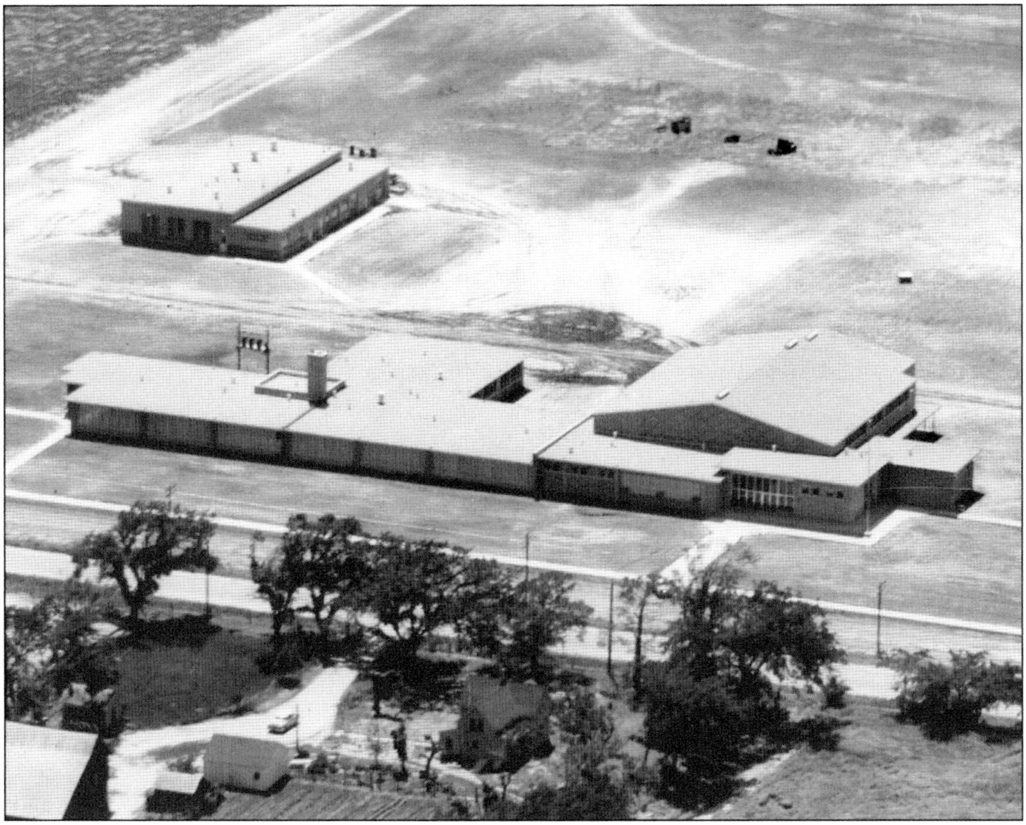

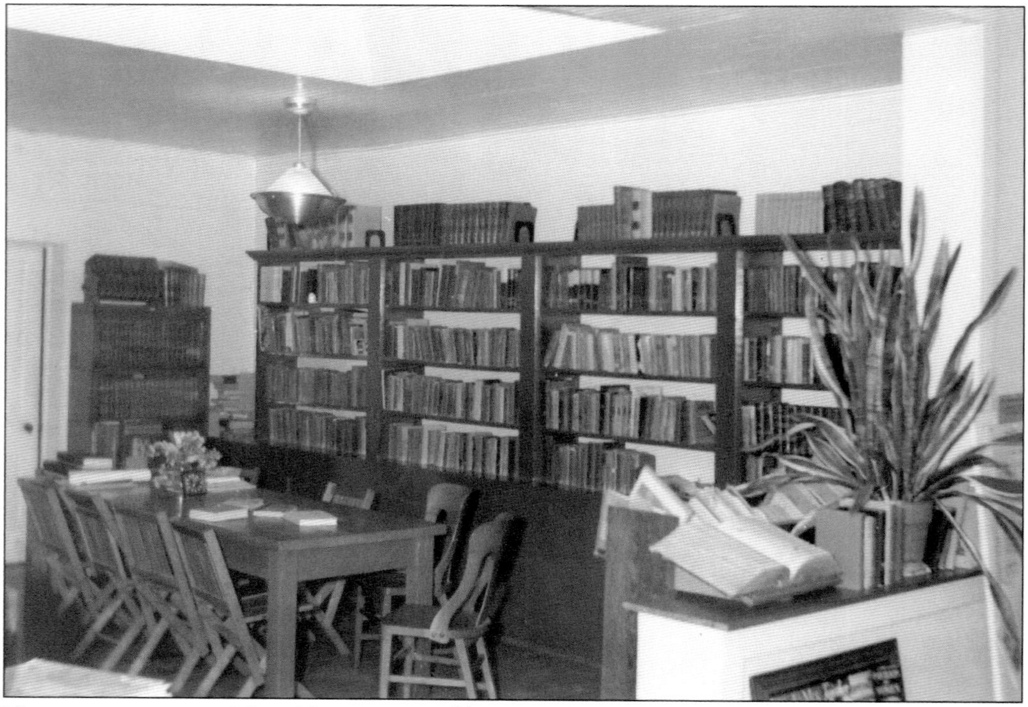

Here are two views of the old community library in downtown Mulvane. It was formerly on the north side of Main Street between First and Second Streets. The library was small and limited, and the community's needs quickly exceed the library's resources. Today, the library is in the theater building, which was modified for the purpose. Both children and adults utilize its services. (Both, courtesy of the Mulvane Historical Museum.)

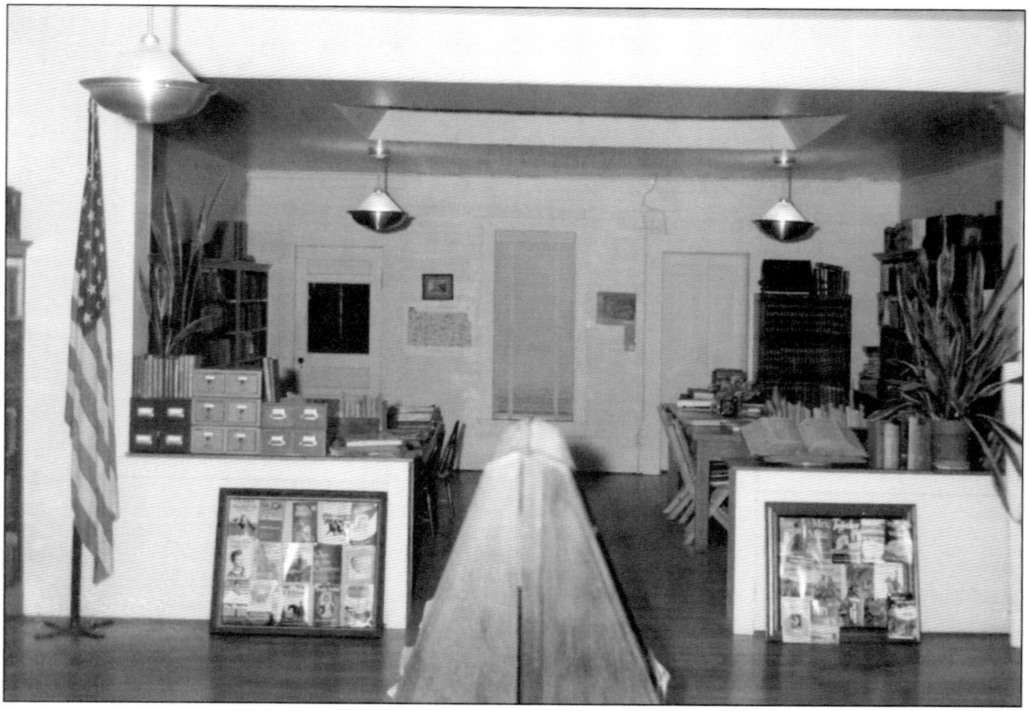

Five

EARLY SPORTS

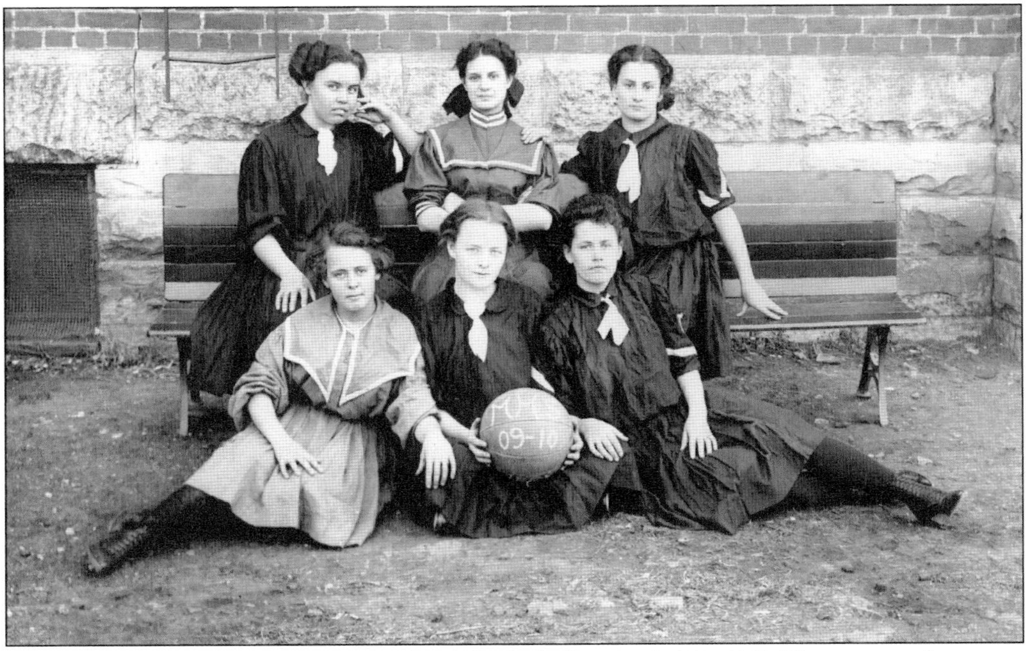

Shown here is the Mulvane High School girls' basketball team of 1909–1910. There is no information about how many games they won that season, but it shows that girls' basketball has been popular in Mulvane for a long time. It is interesting to note that the team had only six players. (Courtesy of the Mulvane Historical Museum.)

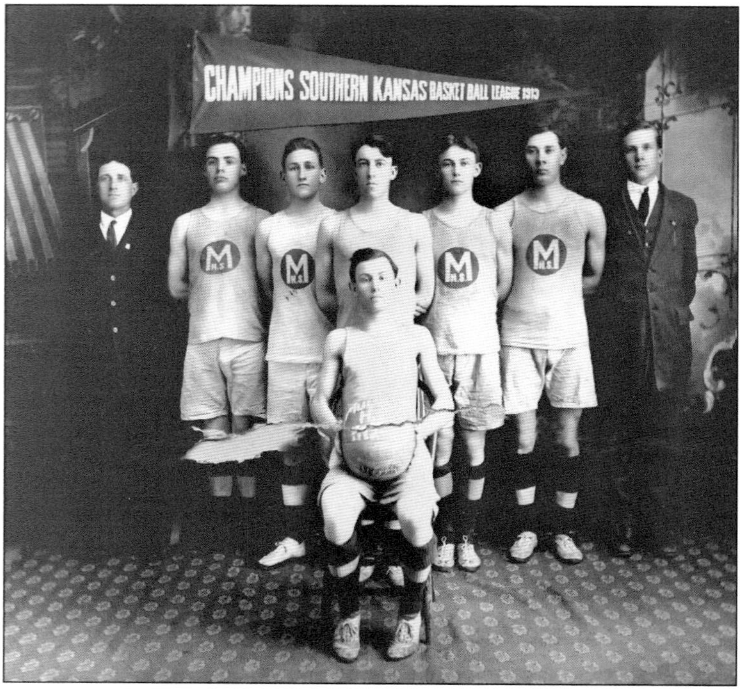

This is a photograph of Mulvane High School's first basketball champions. The team won the 1912–1913 Southern Kansas Basketball League title. At that time, students at all grade levels attended classes in the same building. With only six players on the team, foul trouble and injuries had to be avoided. (Courtesy of the Mulvane Historical Museum.)

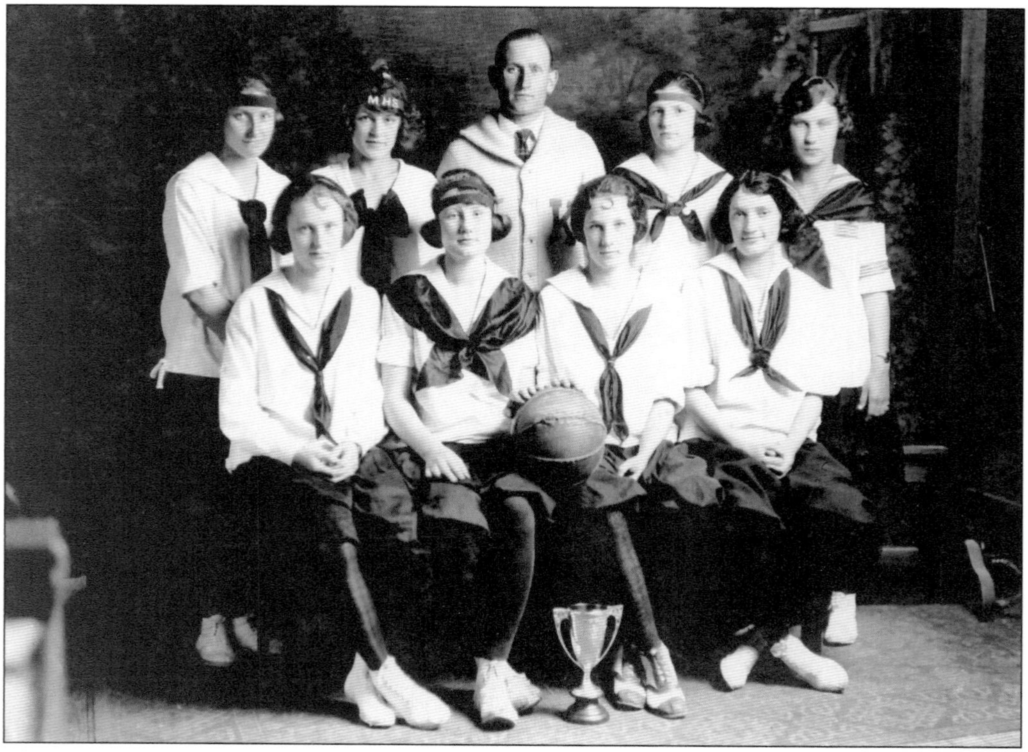

The 1920–1921 girls' basketball team of Mulvane High School poses for a photograph. The uniforms look very nautical, and it is apparent that the use of headbands is nothing new. (One player even has MHS on her headband.) The trophy indicates that it was a successful year. (Courtesy of the Mulvane Historical Museum.)

This is a photograph of the Mulvane High School basketball team of 1921–1922. Shown here are, from left to right, (first row) David Sherman (coach), Mason Sealock, and Herbert Butterfield; (second row) Frank Harris, Richard Hamler, and Orville Woolery. (Courtesy of the Mulvane Historical Museum.)

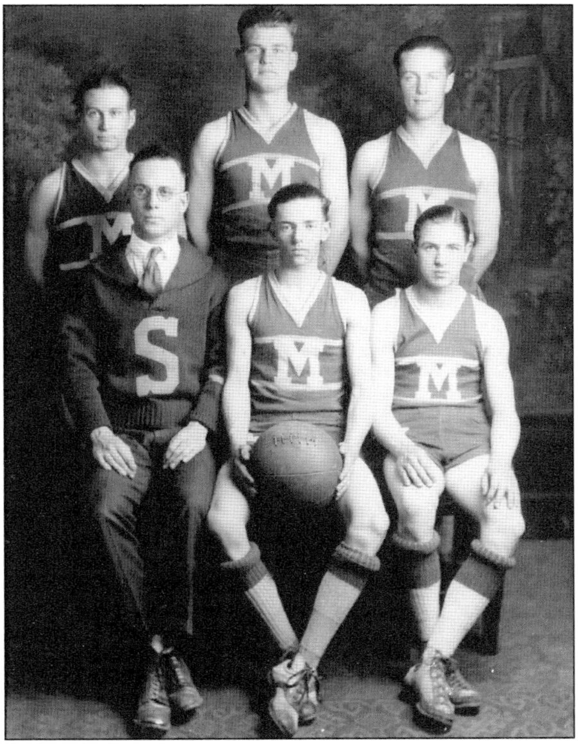

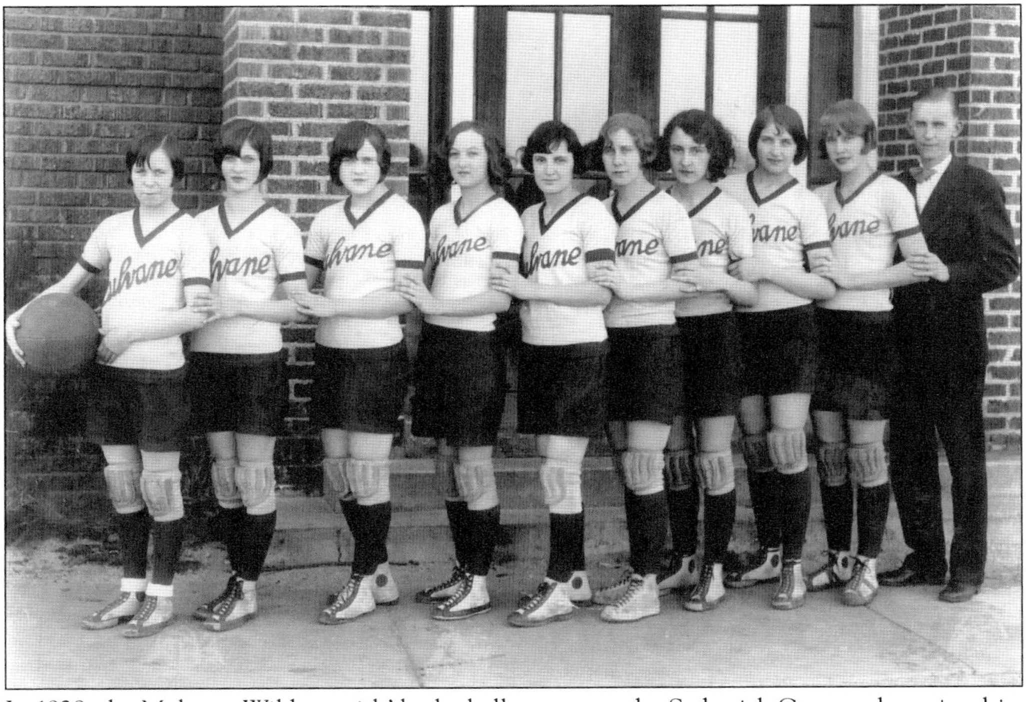

In 1928, the Mulvane Wildcats girls' basketball team won the Sedgwick County championship. Players on that team were, from left to right, Margaret Putman, Nellie Stewart, Cleo Burgess, Norma White, La Von Howard, Rose Callagy, Beth Higginson, Joan Grimstead, and Lillie Callagy. The coach was Paul Rider. (Courtesy of the Mulvane Historical Museum.)

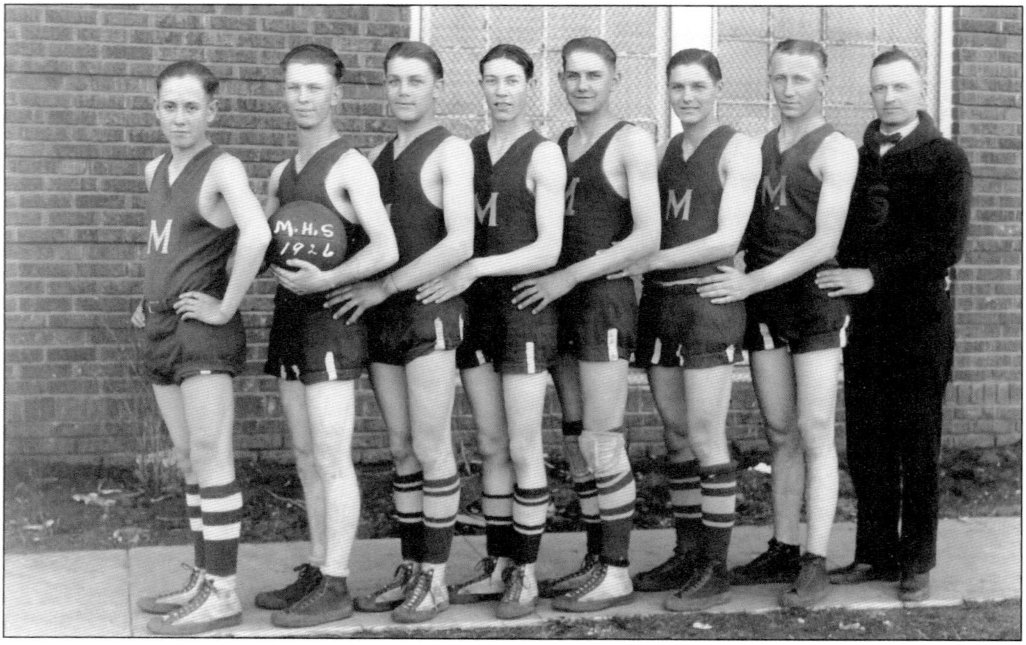

This is a photograph of the 1925–1926 basketball team at Mulvane High School. By this time, the team was known as the Mulvane Wildcats, and the school colors were green and white. That season's roster was increased to seven players, which would have provided a little team depth. (Courtesy of the Mulvane Historical Museum.)

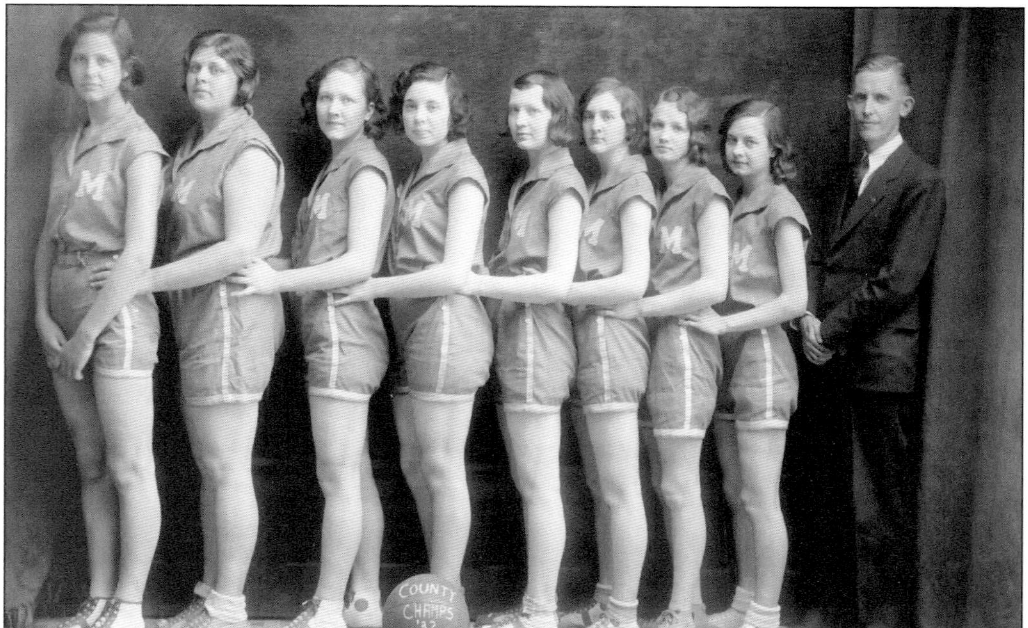

In 1932, the Mulvane Wildcats girls' basketball team won another Sedgwick County championship under the guidance of coach Paul Rider (far right). Players on that team were, from left to right, Maryan Bowens, Katherine Heersche, Dorothy Ripper, Marceille Butts, Ina Loper, Irene Howard, Mary Sumpter, and Doris Putman. (Courtesy of the Mulvane Historical Museum.)

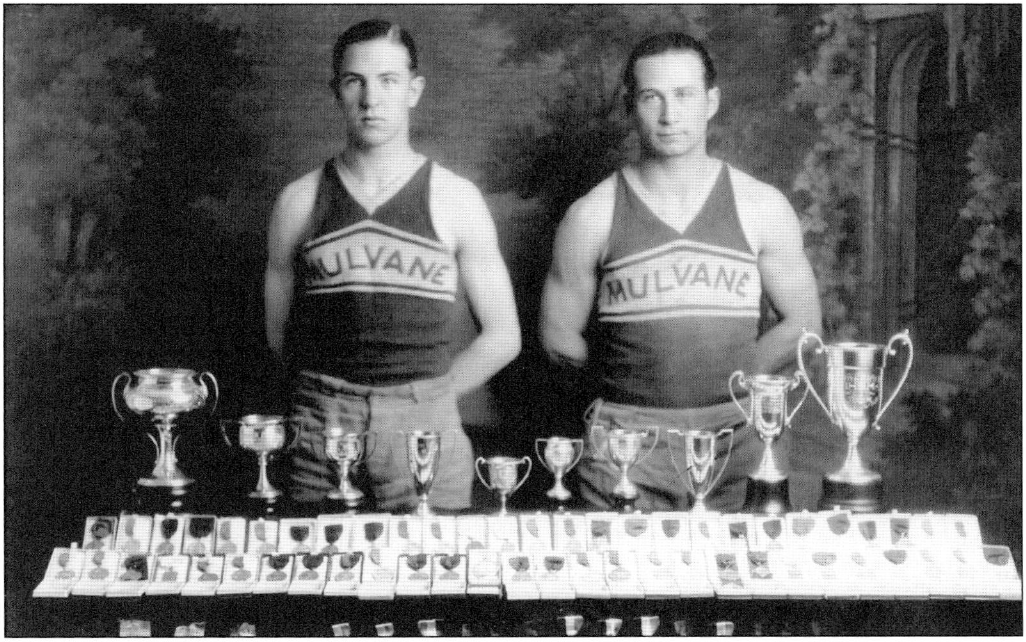

In 1923, Herbert Butterfield (left) and Frank Harris led Mulvane to a third-place finish at the state track meet in Emporia. Harris finished the meet with high-point honors for individual competitors. Butterfield and Harris pose with the trophies and medals they earned that year. (Courtesy of the Mulvane Historical Museum.)

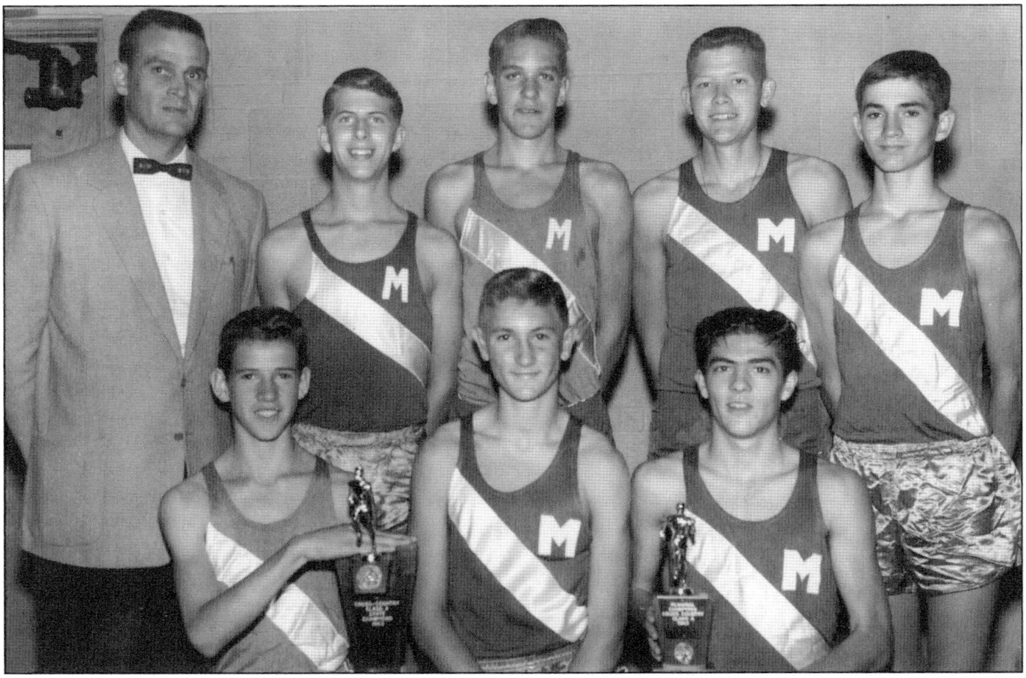

In 1963, the Mulvane Wildcats cross-country team won the state championship. Shown here are, from left to right, (first row) Bill Grieve, Mike Tarry, and Terry Cook; (second row) Clint Hill (coach), Doug Irvin, Kent Stotts, Dave Farber, and Curt Crow. (Courtesy of the Mulvane Historical Museum.)

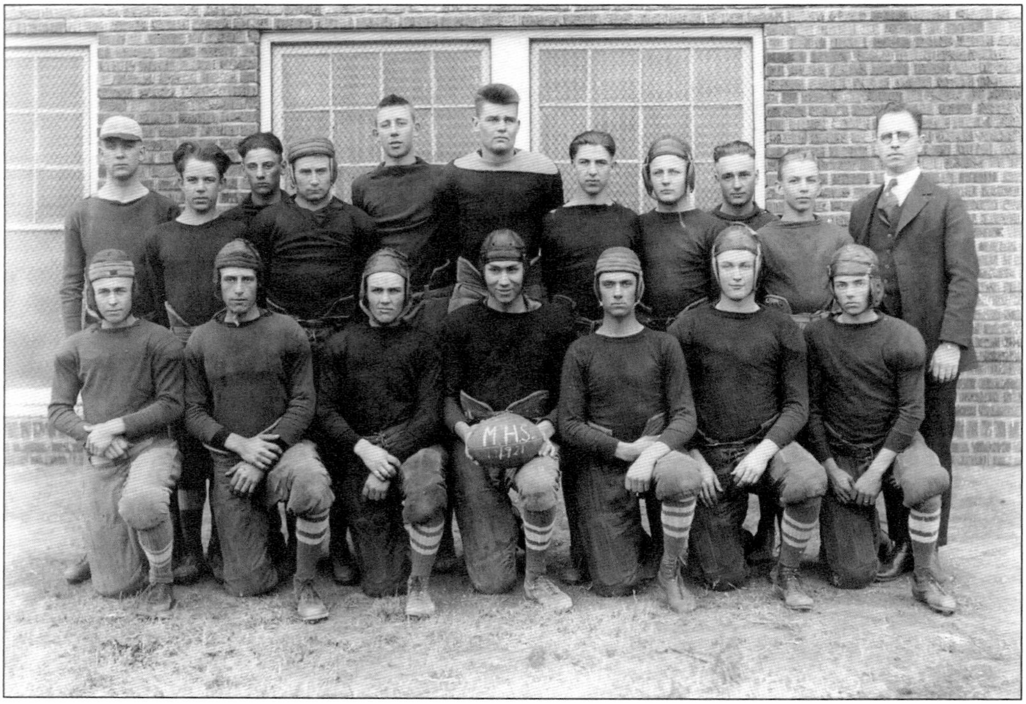

In 1921, the Mulvane High School football team had a remarkable year. It finished the campaign with a record of 10-0, winning 10 shutouts and outscoring its opponents 383-0. The closest game the team played was a 10-0 victory over Winfield. (Courtesy of the Mulvane Historical Museum.)

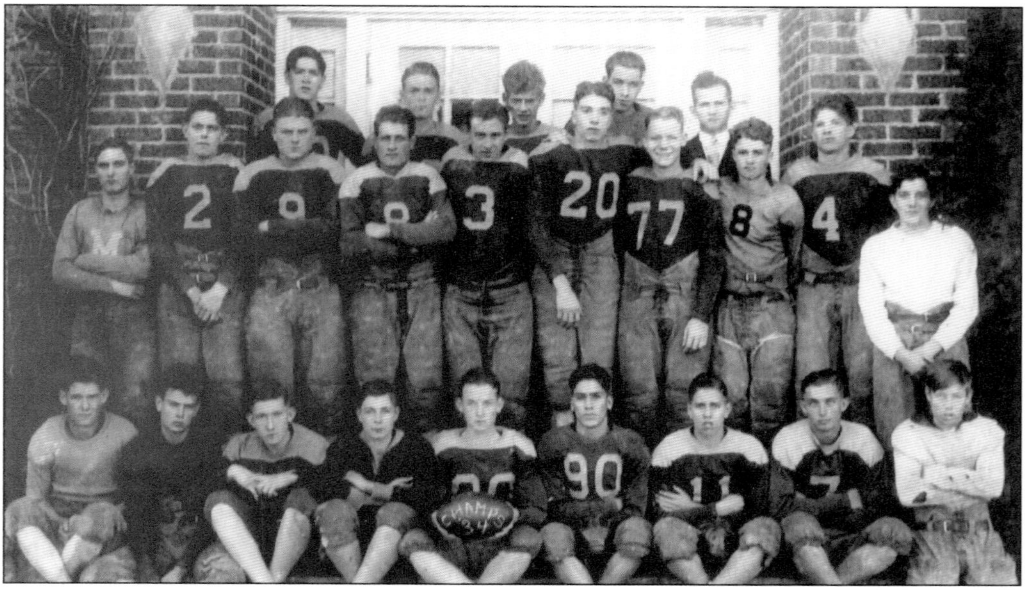

In 1934, the Mulvane Wildcats won another football championship. George Norton, who is on the far right in the back row, coached the team. By this time, Mulvane was making a name for itself as one of the strongest football programs in Kansas. (Courtesy of the Mulvane Historical Museum.)

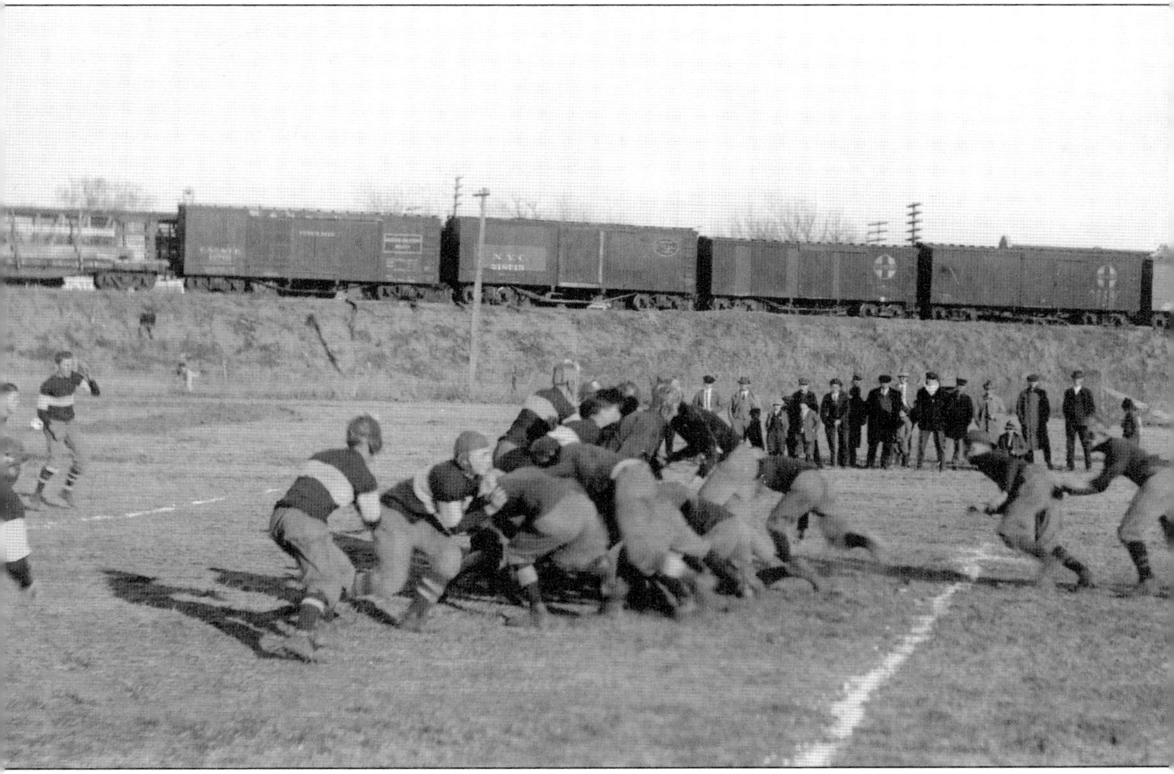

This is a rare in-game photograph of a Mulvane Wildcat football contest played in the 1920s. Specifics of the game are unknown, but the Wildcats are moving the football. Perhaps the most interesting thing about this image is the equipment. The shoulder pads seem to leave a little to be desired, and the helmets are leather. At least three players on the visiting team have chosen to play without headgear, including one in the middle of the line—he is visible in the center of the photograph if one looks closely. (Courtesy of the Mulvane Historical Museum.)

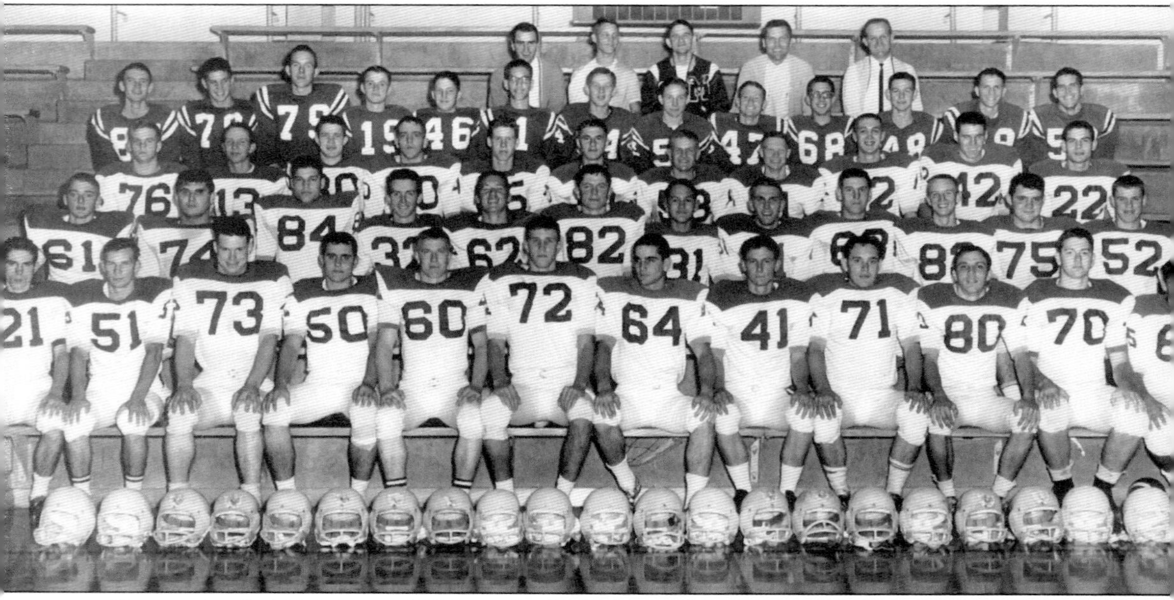

This is the 1964 Mulvane Wildcats football team, which finished the season undefeated and ranked second in Class A in Kansas. The Wildcats were a dominant team at the time, putting together consecutive undefeated seasons between 1963 and 1965. At that time, it was the longest winning streak in Kansas. (Courtesy of the Mulvane Historical Museum.)

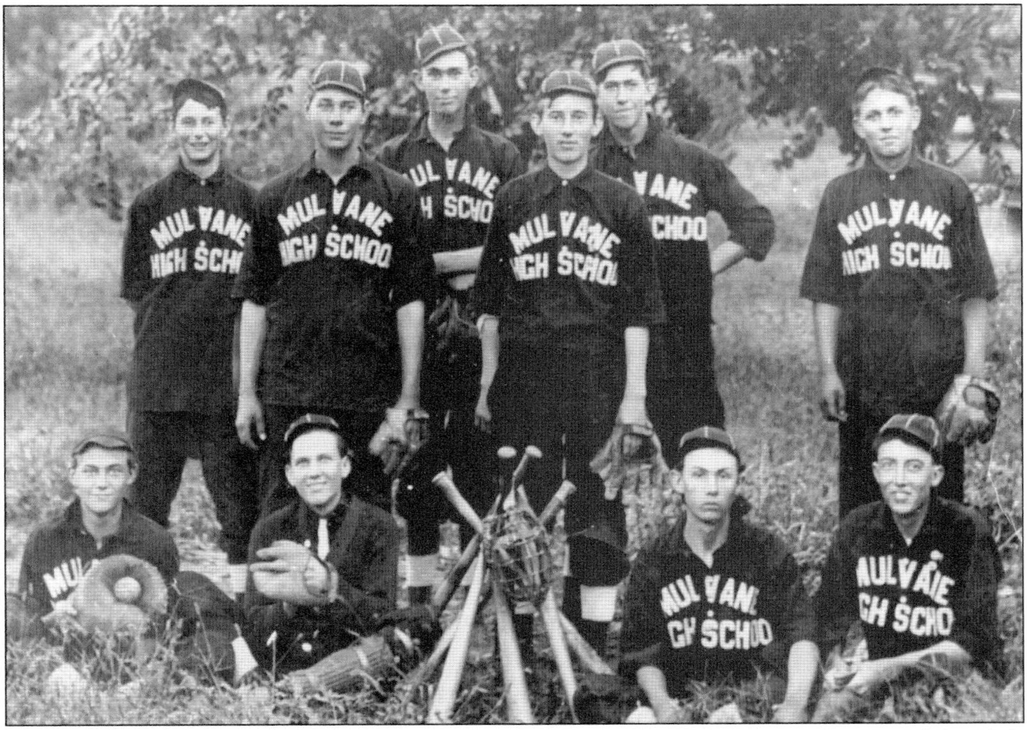

This c. 1920 photograph shows a Mulvane High School baseball team. Since the turn of the 20th century, baseball has been a very popular sport in Mulvane. Nonprofessional and semi-pro teams have been a big part of Mulvane's summer activities. (Courtesy of the Mulvane Historical Museum.)

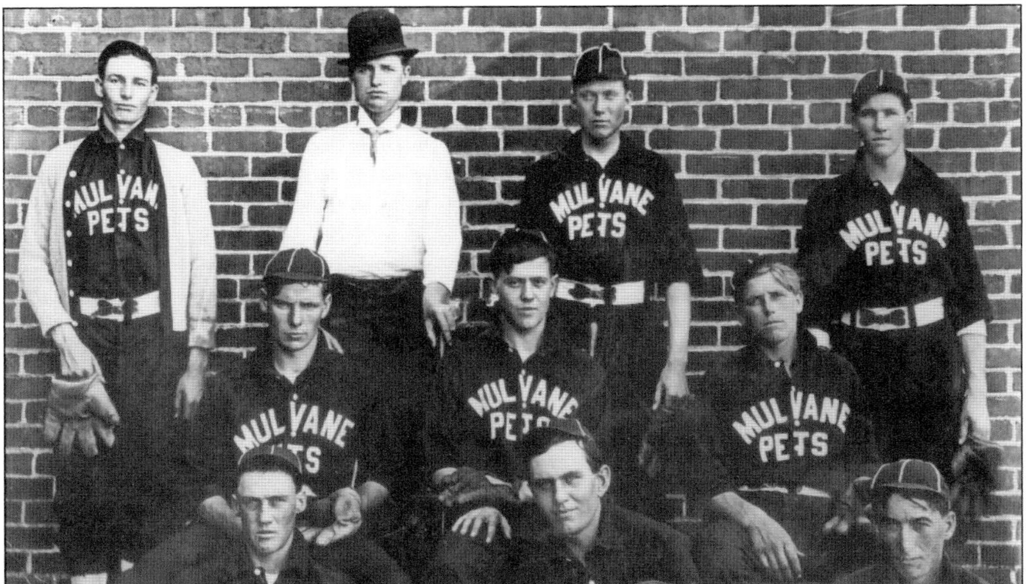

The Mulvane Pets played baseball from 1908 to 1910. Members of the team included, from left to right, (first row) Wiley Penny, Lawrence Johnson, and Charley Glaser; (second row) Ray Gillet, Andrew Miller, and Herb Gilles; (third row) Perley Fisher, Ernest Fisher, Henry Storey, and Earl Gill. (Courtesy of the Mulvane Historical Museum.)

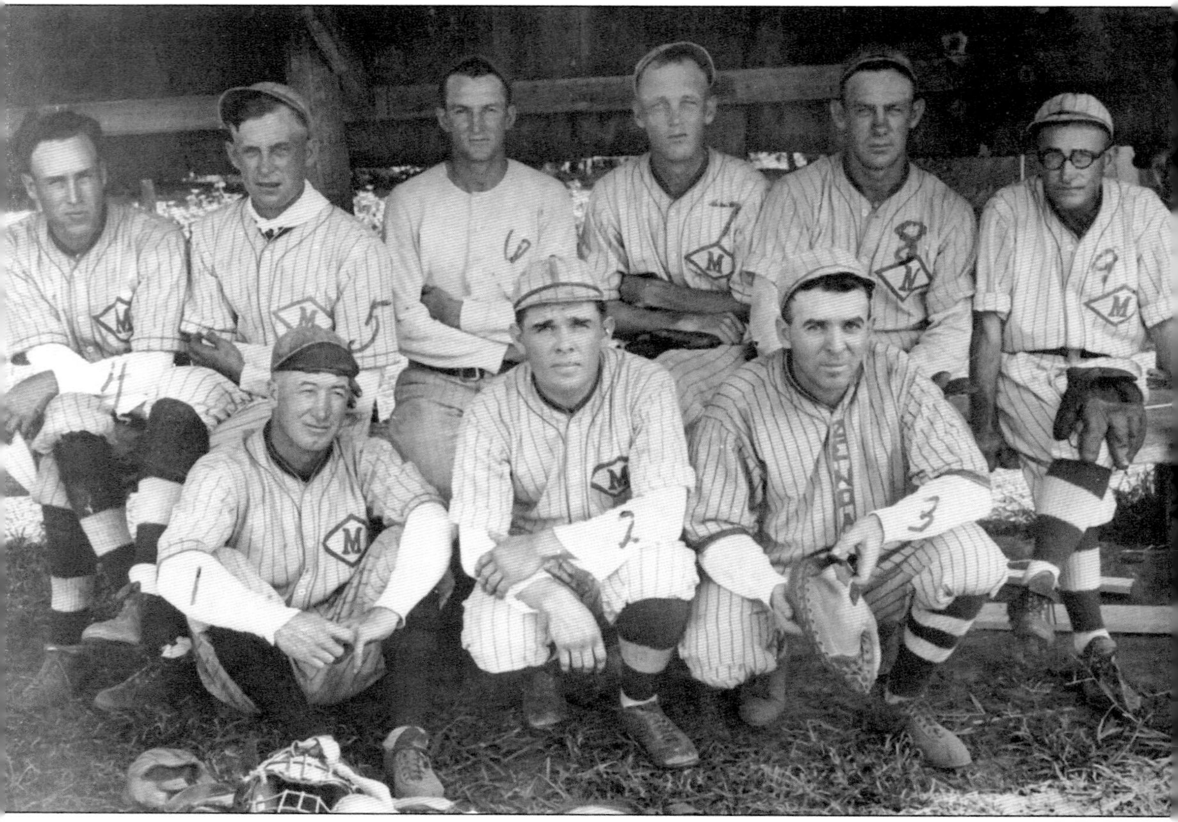

This is a Mulvane baseball club that played games around 1915. Members of this team are, from left to right, (first row) Leo Turley, Mike Rhodes, and Raleigh Wentworth; (second row) Ral Davis, Clyde Travis, Earl Wentworth, Doc Bruncher, Squid Travis, and Short Martin. It was common for "town teams" from small Kansas communities to play against one another on the weekend. Rivalries could get pretty intense, and bragging rights were routinely exercised. (Courtesy of the Mulvane Historical Museum.)

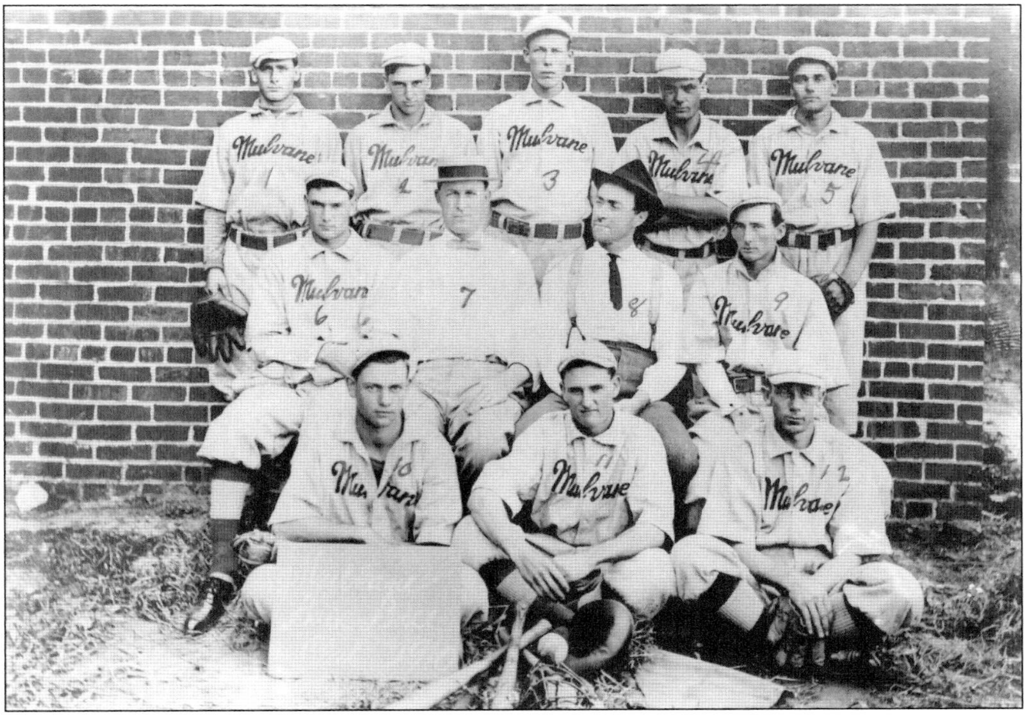

Members of the Mulvane baseball club of 1910 pose for a photograph. Shown here are, from left to right, (first row) Ted Citizen, Earnest Thompson, and Clarence Reynolds; (second row) Lawrence Thompson, Ike Thompson, Bob Seyfer, and Merle Smith; (third row) Clyde Smith, Ray Thompson, Cliff Rucker, Edgar Thompson, and Frank Reynolds. (Courtesy of the Mulvane Historical Museum.)

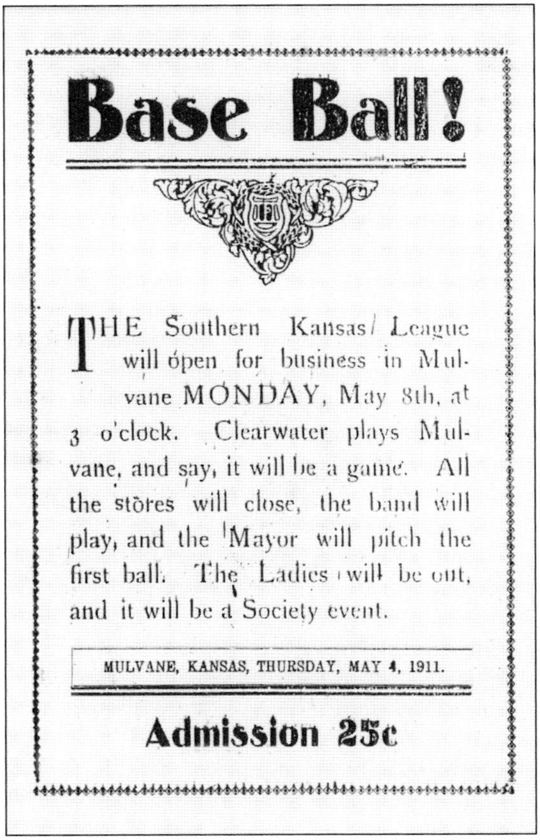

This poster from 1911 announces the opening of another baseball season. In the days that preceded radio and television, a baseball game was a community event that would draw large crowds. This poster describes a festive environment with bands and lots of excitement. Admission was only 25¢. (Courtesy of the Mulvane Historical Museum.)

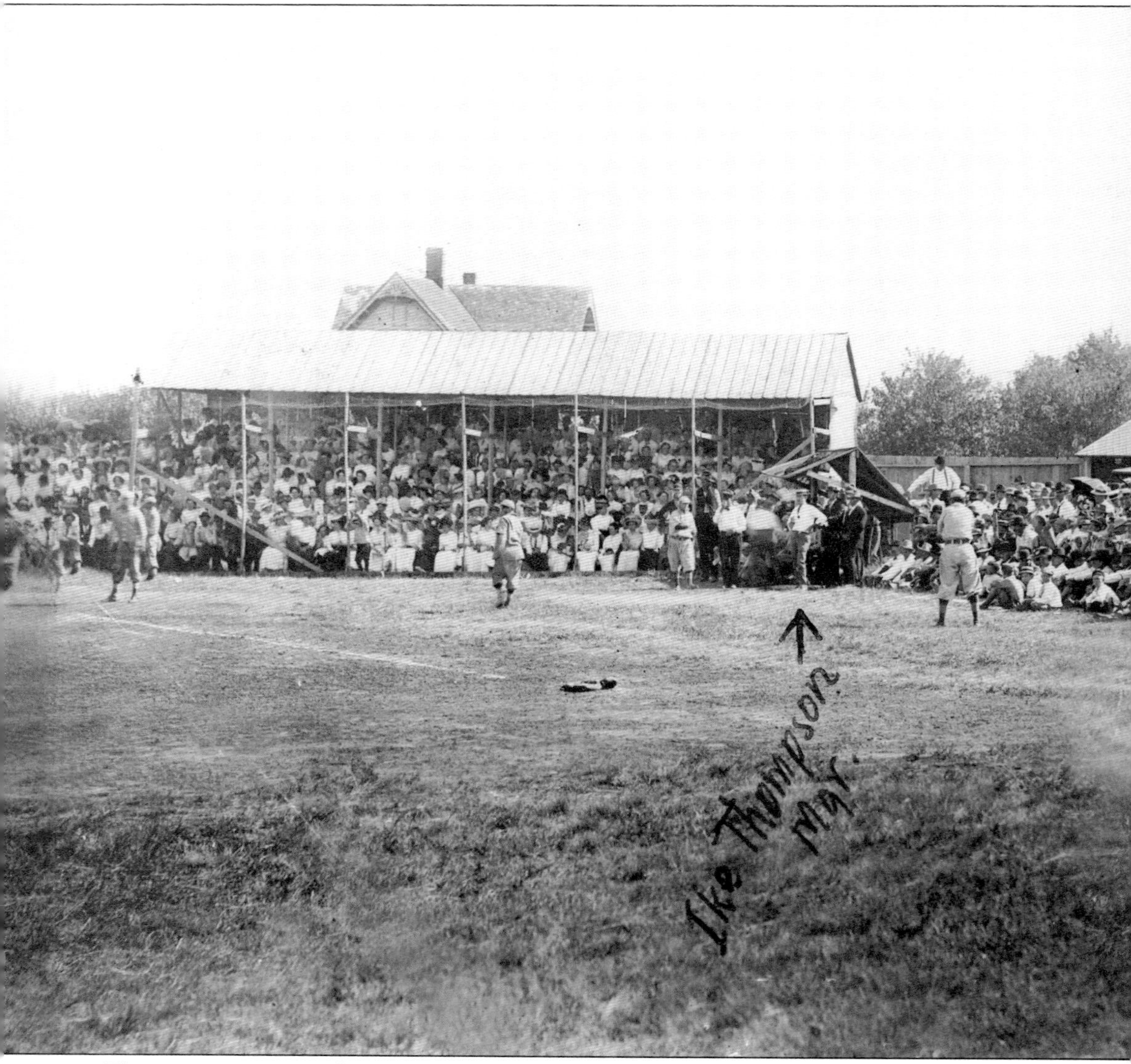

This is a rare in-game photograph of early-20th-century baseball. Shown here is the 1911 Southern Kansas League Championship Game, which saw Mulvane playing at nearby Clearwater. Mulvane manager Ike Thompson can be seen in a white shirt with his hands on his hips. He is standing at the Mulvane bench. The crowd has exceeded the capacity of the grandstand, and spectators

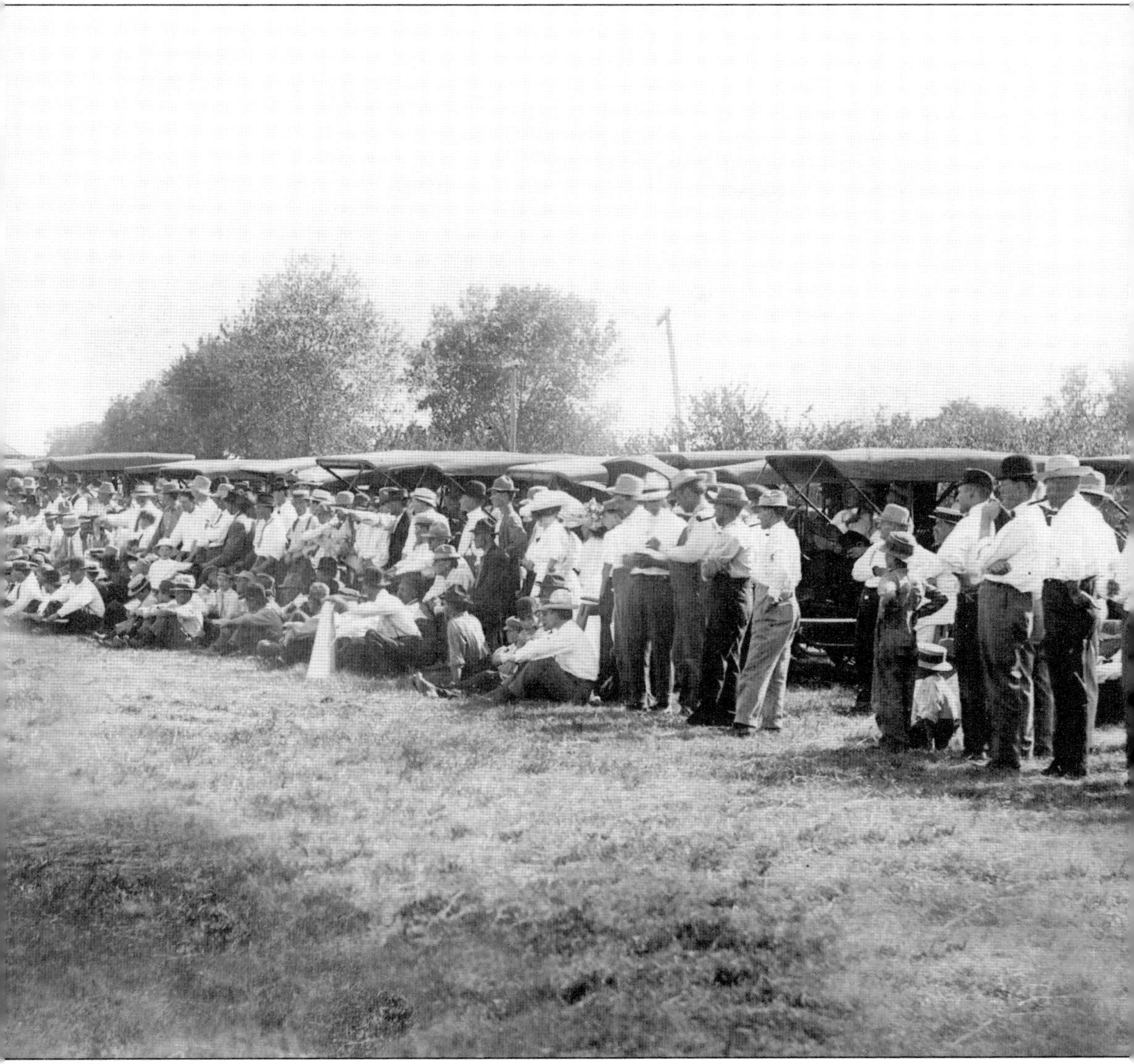

line the playing field along both foul lines. A baseball game of this sort was a festive event, so spectators would wear their best clothes. There is no information regarding who won the game. (Courtesy of the Mulvane Historical Museum.)

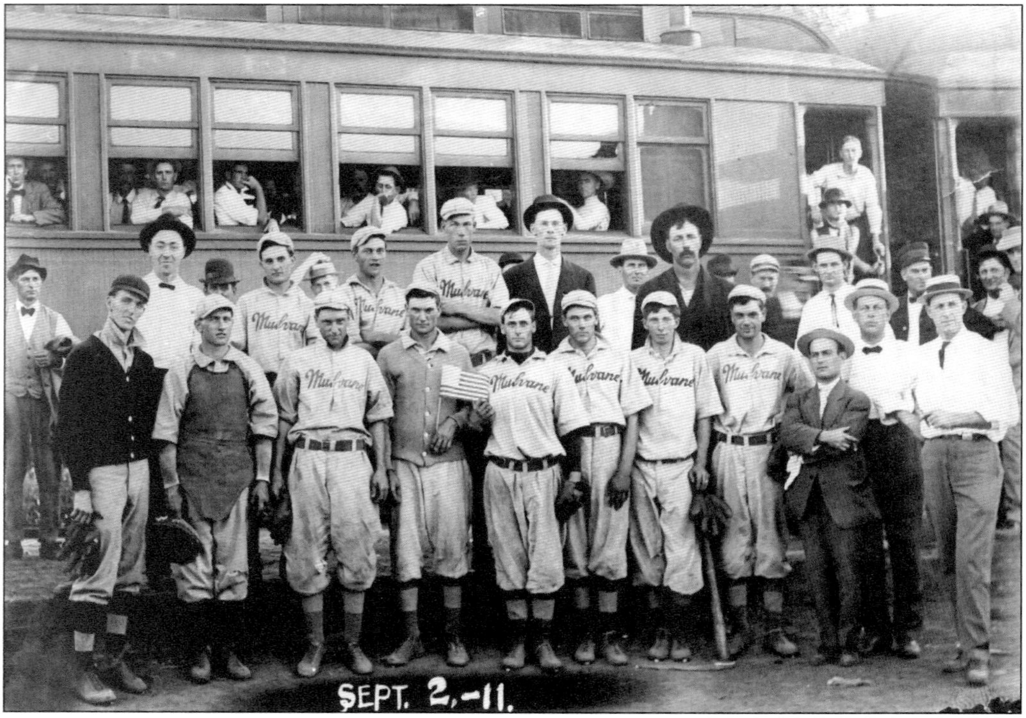

On September 2, 1911, Mulvane prepares to make the journey to Clearwater for the championship game. One notable player in the game was Carl Mays, who is wearing a warm-up jacket on the left side of the photograph. (Courtesy of the Mulvane Historical Museum.)

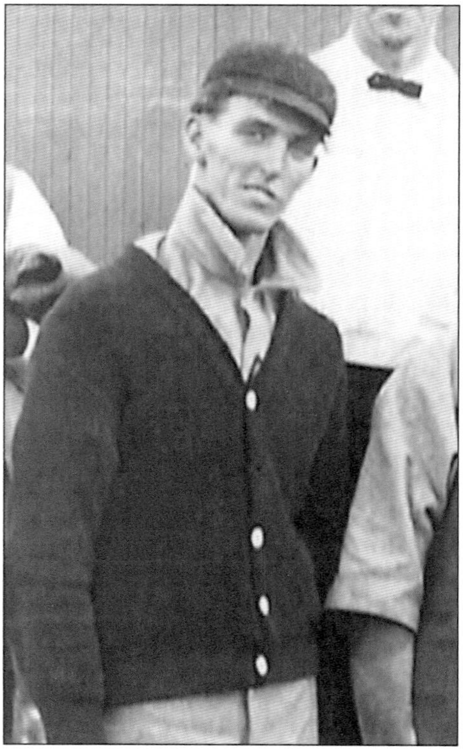

Carl Mays prepares for the trip to Clearwater. Mays pitched in the big leagues for 15 seasons and four different teams. He won over 200 games during his career. His 1921 season with the New York Yankees was his best, with a 27-9 record and an ERA of 3.05. (Courtesy of the Mulvane Historical Museum.)

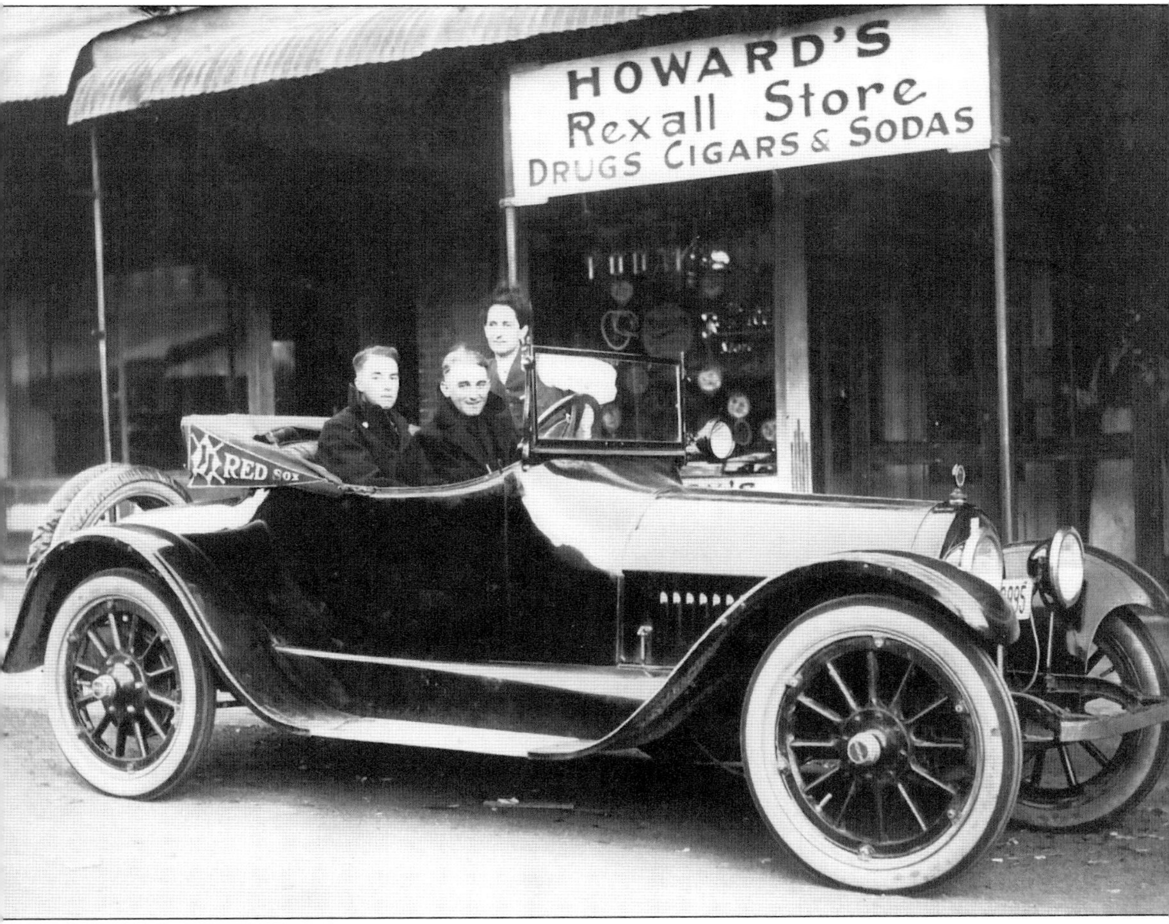

Carl Mays visits with his friend Roy Howard, who owned a drugstore in Mulvane. Mays was pitching with the Boston Red Sox when this photograph was taken. During an outstanding big-league career, Mays's career record was 207-126 with an ERA of 2.92. He pitched in the World Series in 1915, 1916, 1918, and from 1921 through 1923. He twice led the American League in complete games and twice led the league in shutouts. He won 20 or more games in five different seasons. He had a great career in baseball that some think could have put him in the Hall of Fame. Today, he is remembered for a very tragic event, if he is remembered at all. (Courtesy of the Mulvane Historical Museum.)

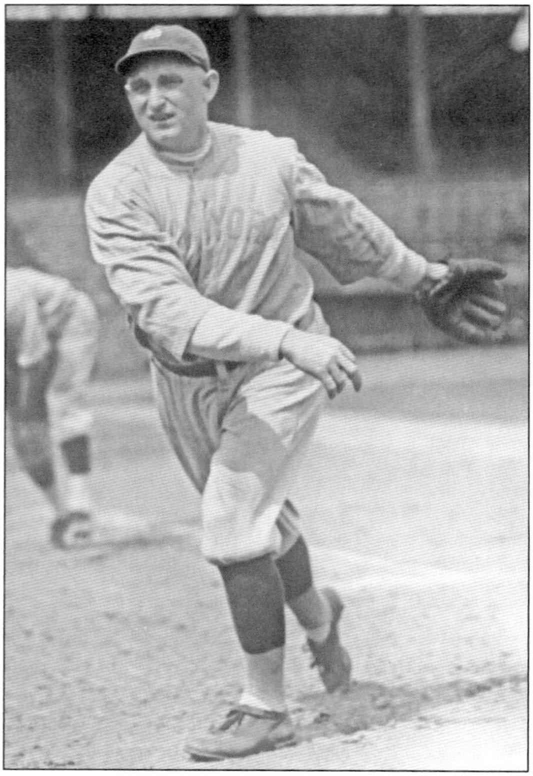

The photograph to the left shows Mays pitching with the New York Yankees. In a game between the Yankees and the Cleveland Indians on August 16, 1920, Mays hit Ray Chapman (below) in the head with a pitch. Chapman fell to the ground. He was taken to a hospital, where he died the next day without having regained consciousness. Chapman remains the only player killed in a major-league baseball game. As a result of the tragedy, Mays became one of the most unpopular players of his time. (Both, courtesy of the Library of Congress.)

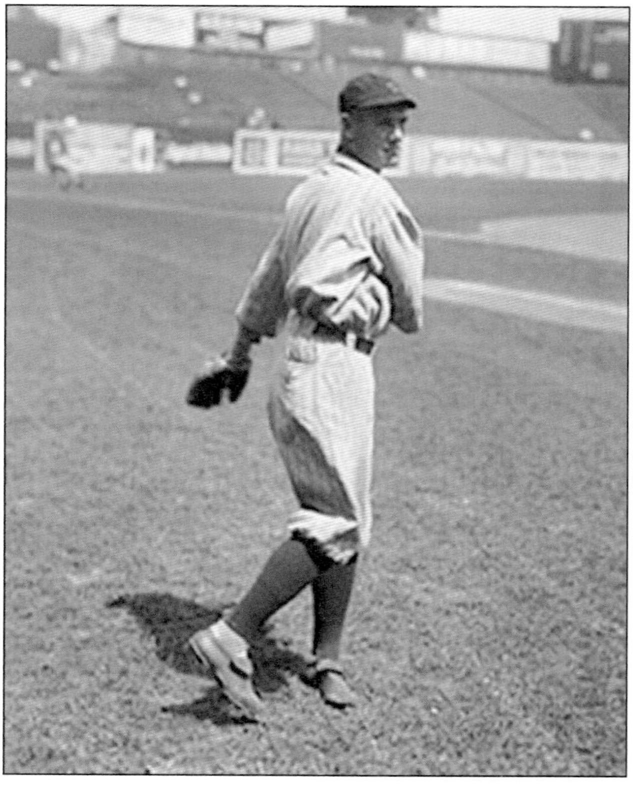

Six

Bad Days

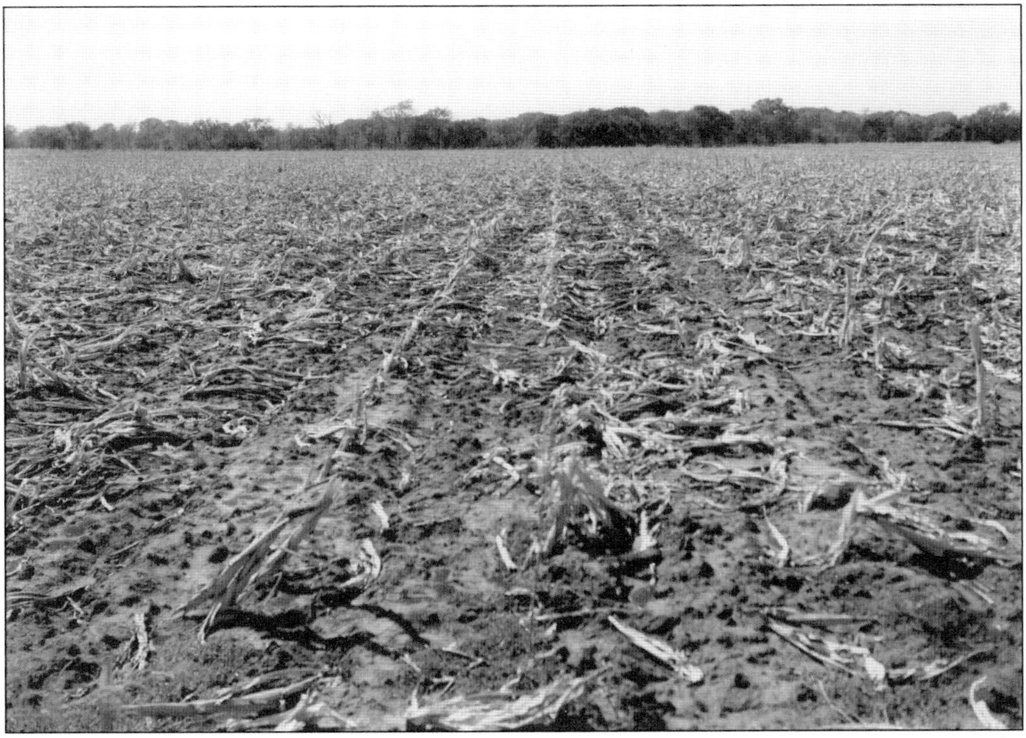

Perhaps the most destructive natural disaster to plague Mulvane has been drought. During the Dust Bowl years, many farmers faced significant financial and agricultural challenges. This 1930s cornfield in rural Mulvane testifies to the destruction that can result from strong winds and a lack of water. (Courtesy of the Mulvane Historical Museum.)

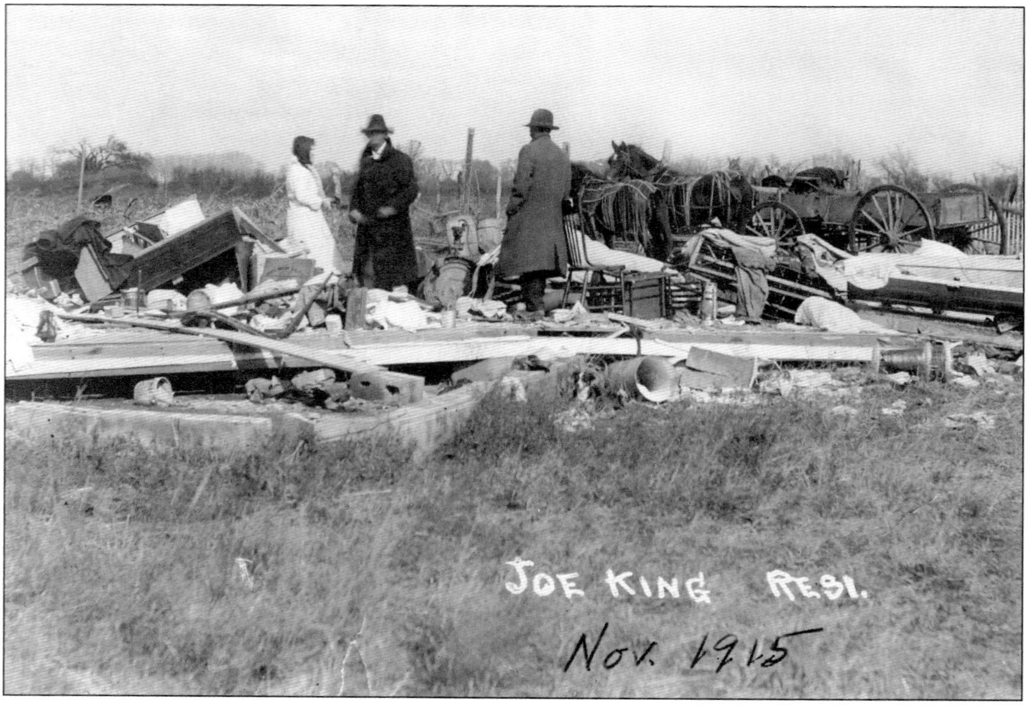

Tornadoes are a huge problem in Kansas. They usually occur in the spring but can strike in any month. In 1915, a rare November twister hit the Mulvane area, causing significant damage. In the above photograph, residents sort through the damage at the Joe King residence. The nearby farm of Abe Dye (below) was heavily damaged by the storm. (Both, courtesy of the Mulvane Historical Museum.)

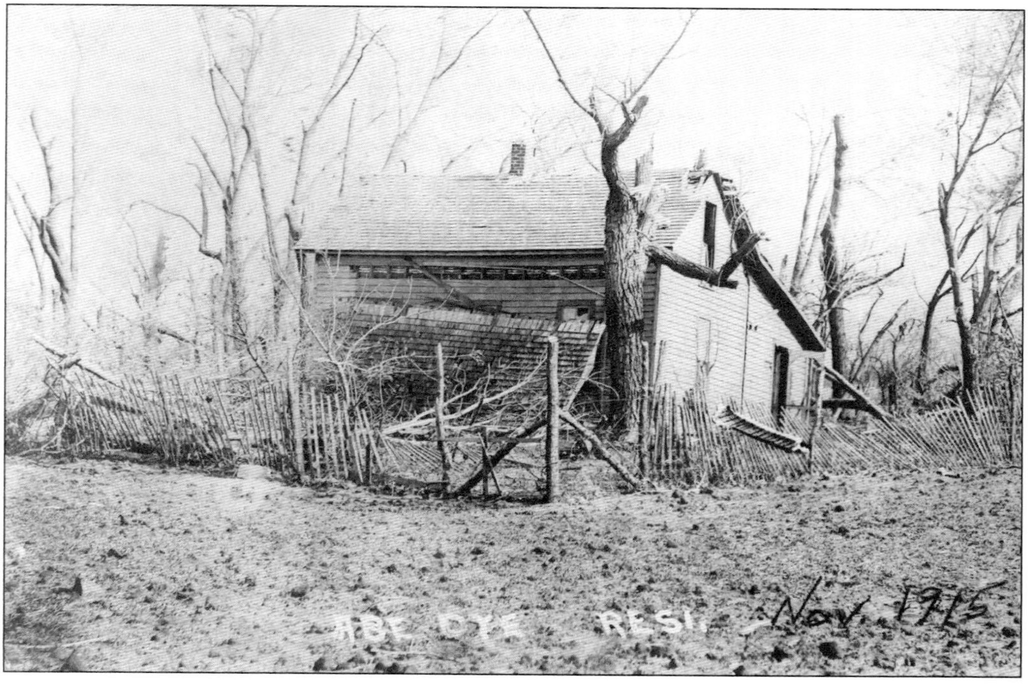

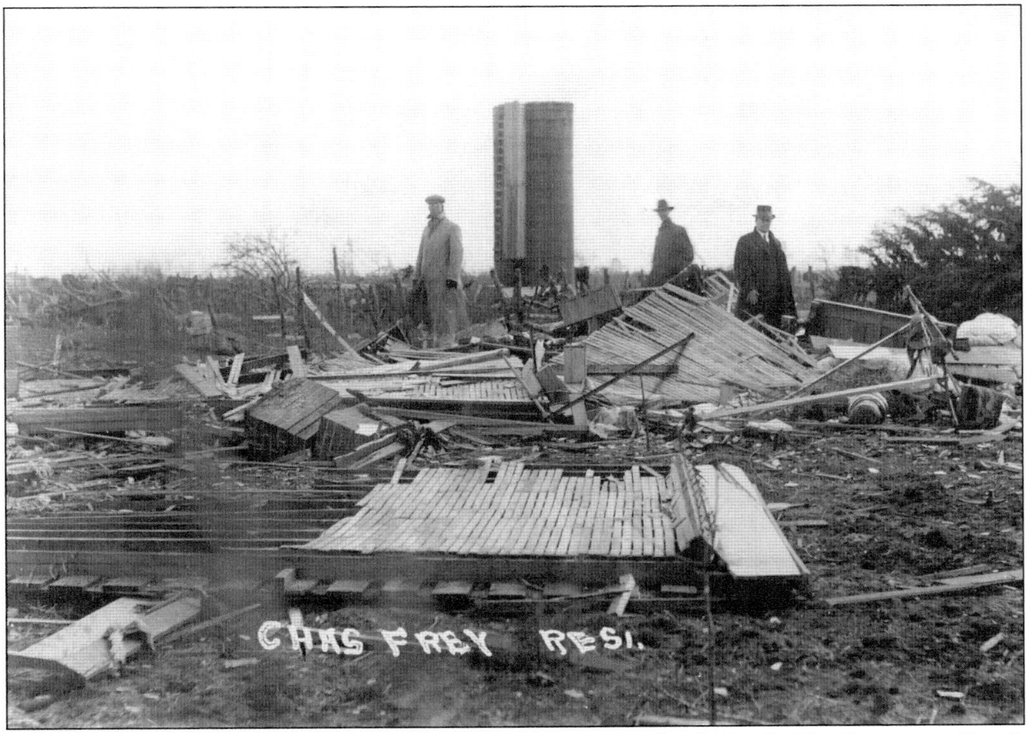

Not far away, the residence of Chris Frey (above) was completely leveled by the storm. Frank Watson's two-story farmhouse suffered significant damage (below), but the destruction of trees was overwhelming. During this time, civil defense and weather radar were non-existent. People and property were very vulnerable to storms of this sort. (Both, courtesy of the Mulvane Historical Museum.)

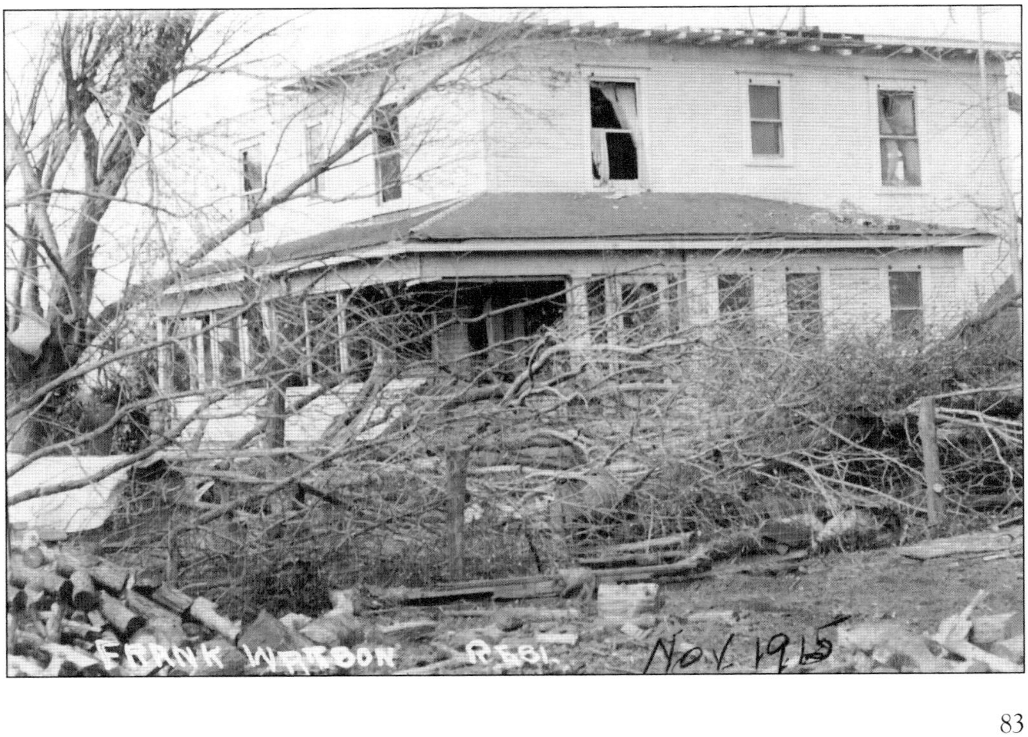

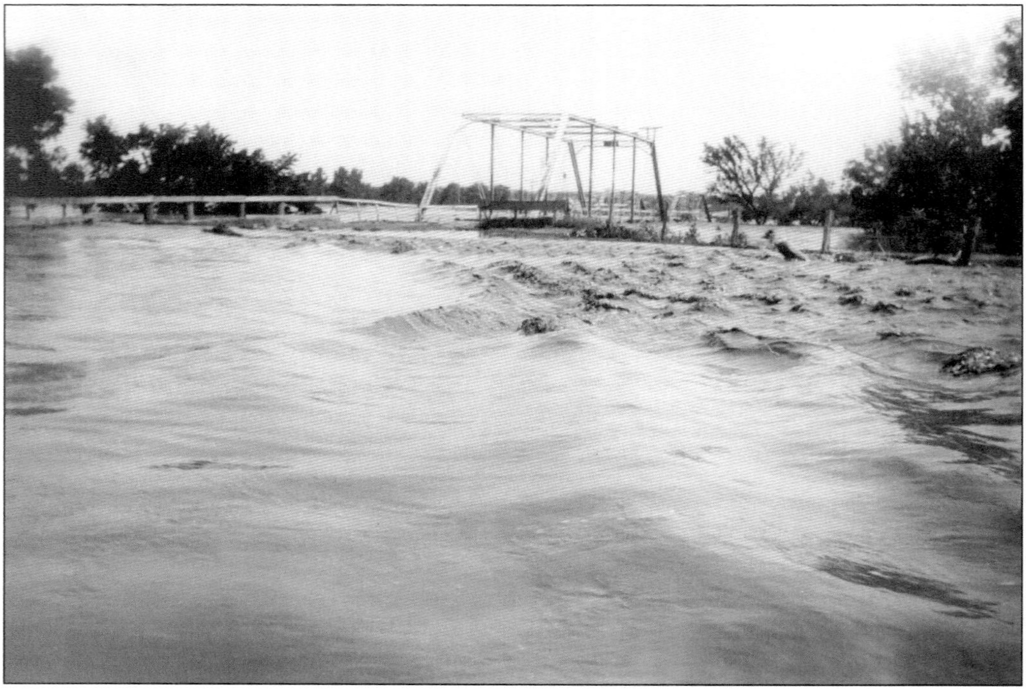

It doesn't happen often, but once in a while, rain will force the Arkansas River beyond its banks. When that happens, the results can be disastrous. Such was the case in 1923, when floodwaters rolled through the area just west of Mulvane. The above photograph shows a bridge that is at risk, while the water in the foreground has formed dangerous rapids. In the below photograph, rising floodwaters have put a Mulvane farm in jeopardy. (Both, courtesy of the Mulvane Historical Museum.)

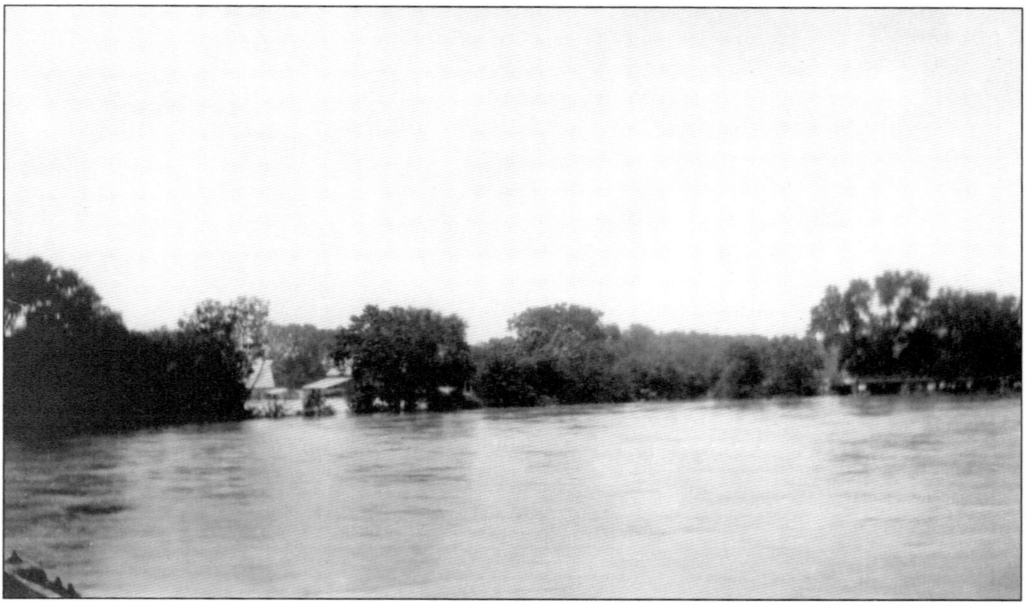

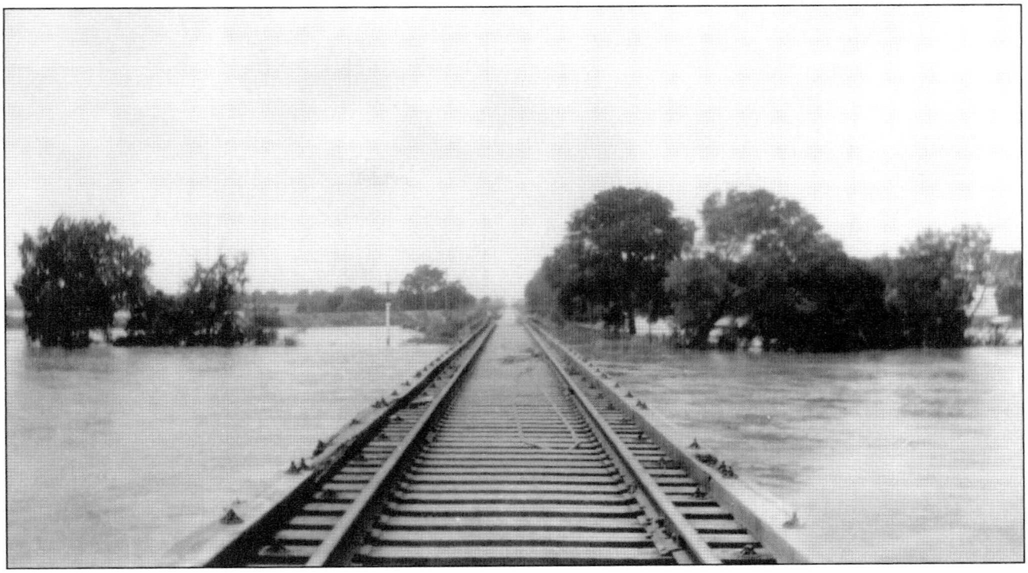

As the above photograph shows, the flood of 1923 nearly washed over the railroad tracks west of town, which would have been disastrous. As it was, the farms on either side of the tracks became isolated. The Hinkle farm (below) suffered major damage during the flood. (Both, courtesy of the Mulvane Historical Museum.)

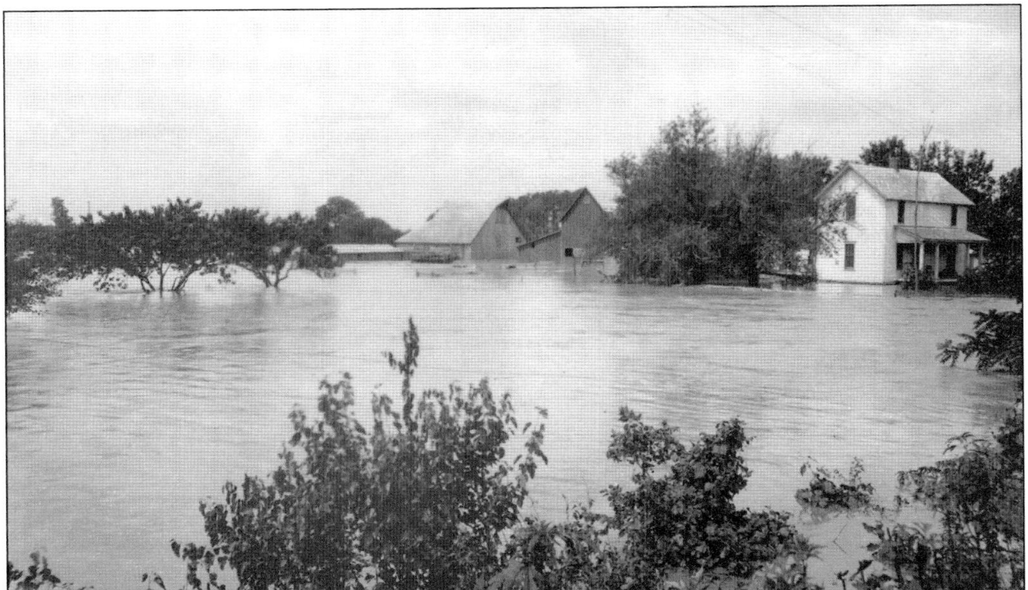

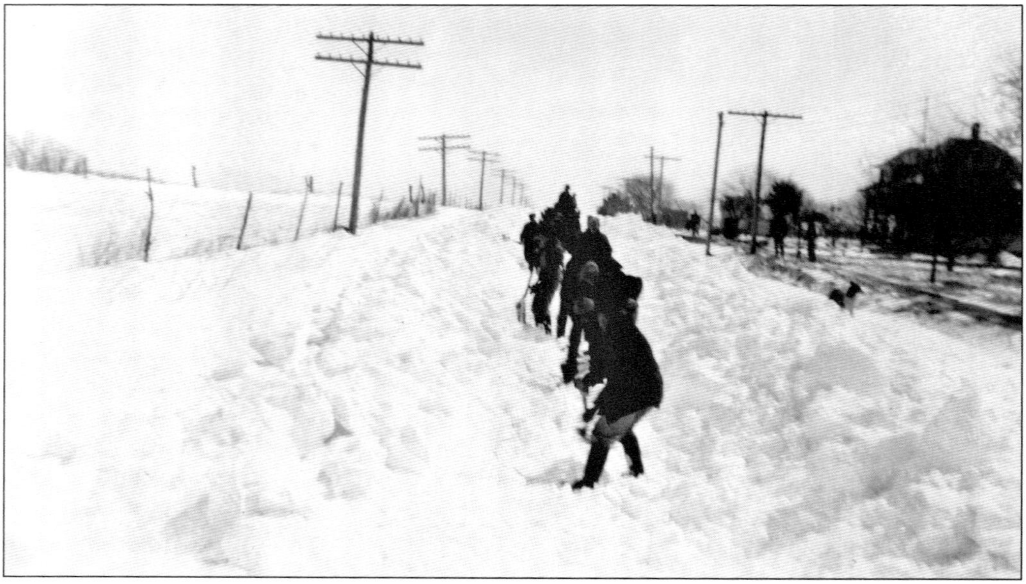

Southern Kansas isn't known for its harsh winters, but it is possible for conditions to threaten people and livestock. A blizzard hit the area in 1926, dumping snow throughout the region. Above, in the absence of snowplows, people manually cleared a snow path. In the below photograph, the heads of the mules are barely visible as they pull a wagon through the snow. (Both, courtesy of the Mulvane Historical Museum.)

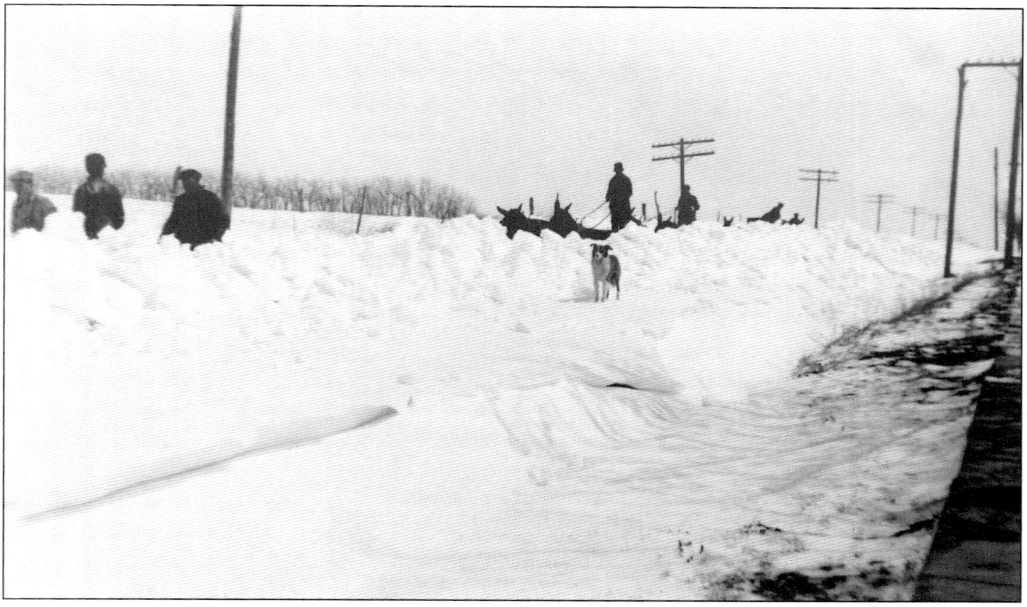

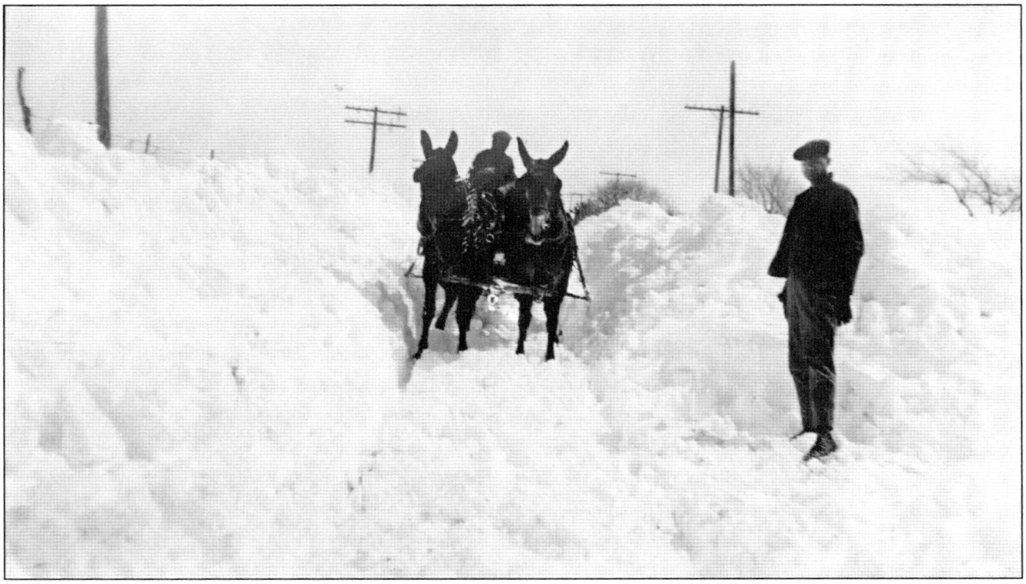

Monster snowdrifts (above) were the result of creating a path for this wagon. In the below photograph, the wagon is seen traveling west to Mulvane from east of town. Note that the path allows access to only one wagon at a time. (Both, courtesy of the Mulvane Historical Museum.)

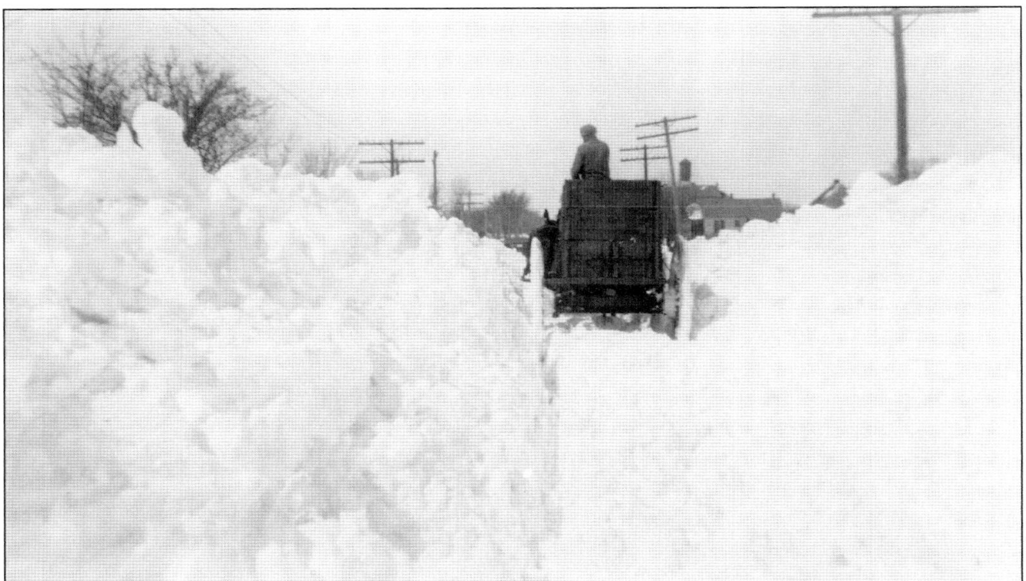

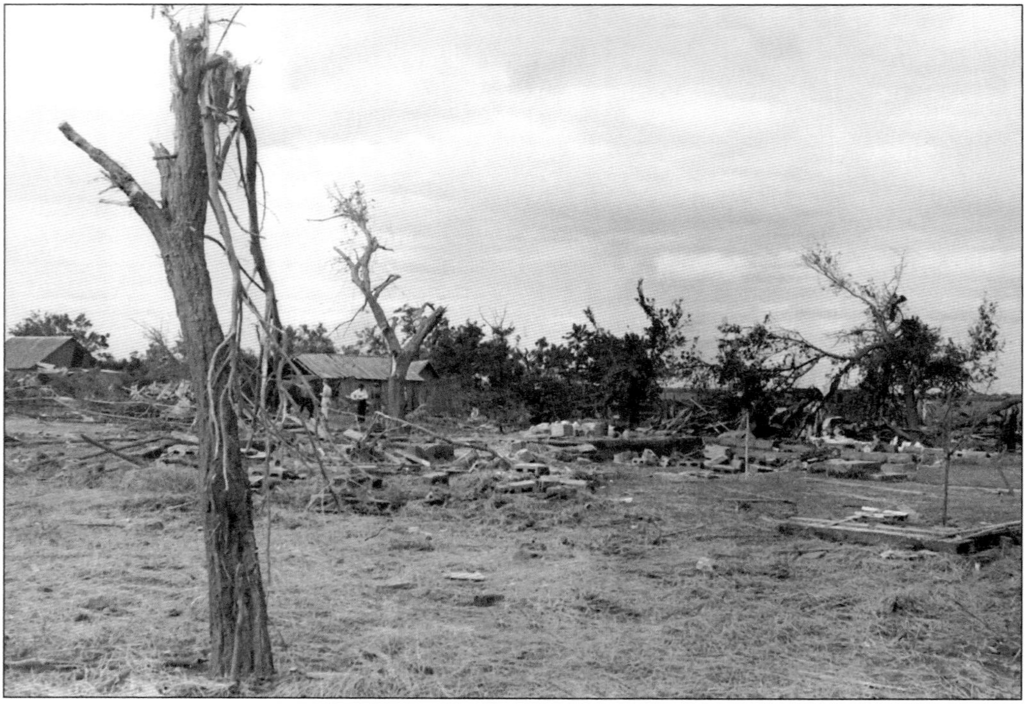

Another tornado ripped through the Mulvane area in 1942. These storms can do tremendous damage in a very short period of time. These two photographs show a farm that was almost destroyed by the 1942 twister. The cleanup after a tornado can take weeks, sometimes months, and it can be years before trees regain their shape and health. (Both, courtesy of the Mulvane Historical Museum.)

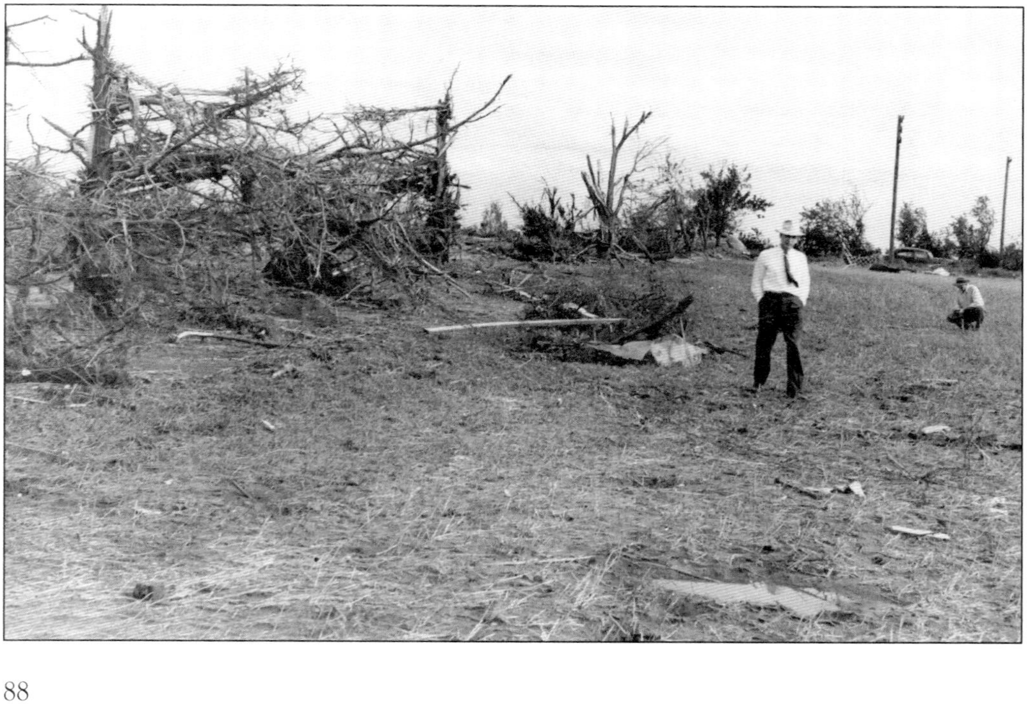

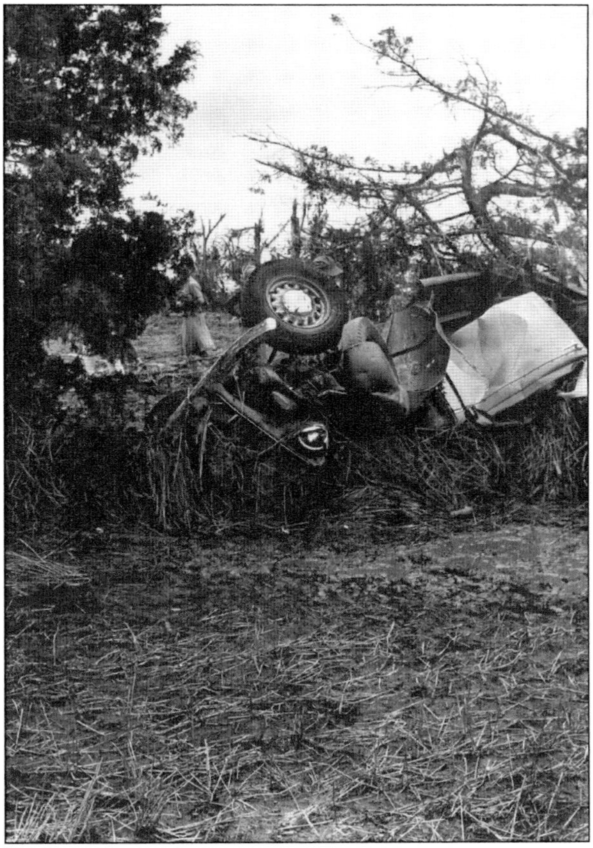

In the photograph to the right, a truck has been twisted almost beyond recognition in the 1942 storm. Below, on the property of Mulvane photographer Ralph Wright, all of the buildings have been virtually destroyed and replaced by mountains of debris. (Both, courtesy of the Mulvane Historical Museum.)

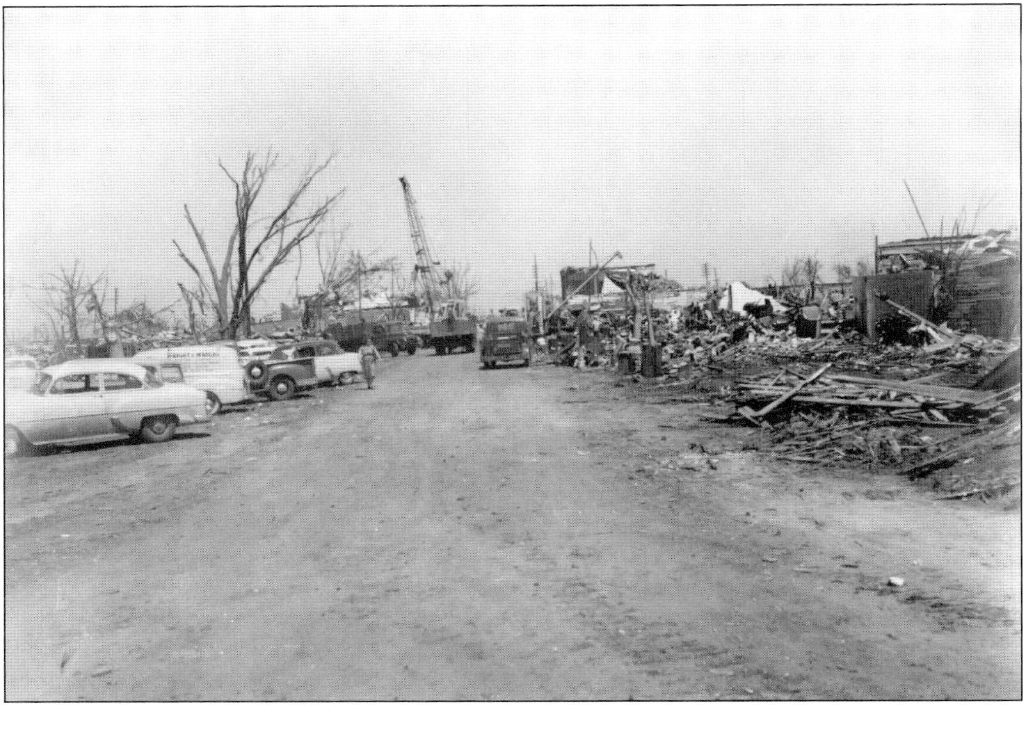

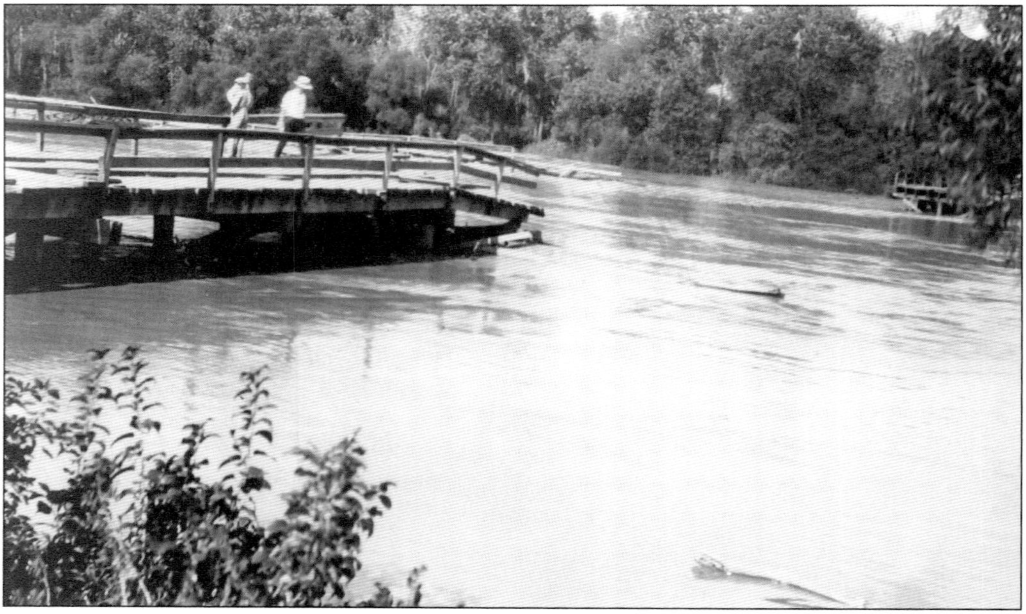

The Arkansas River jumped its banks again in 1957. Unlike the flood of 1923, this time, the water reached into the city limits. A pedestrian bridge (above) was washed away in a residential area. The below photograph shows how close the water came to some of the houses in town. (Both, courtesy of the Mulvane Historical Museum.)

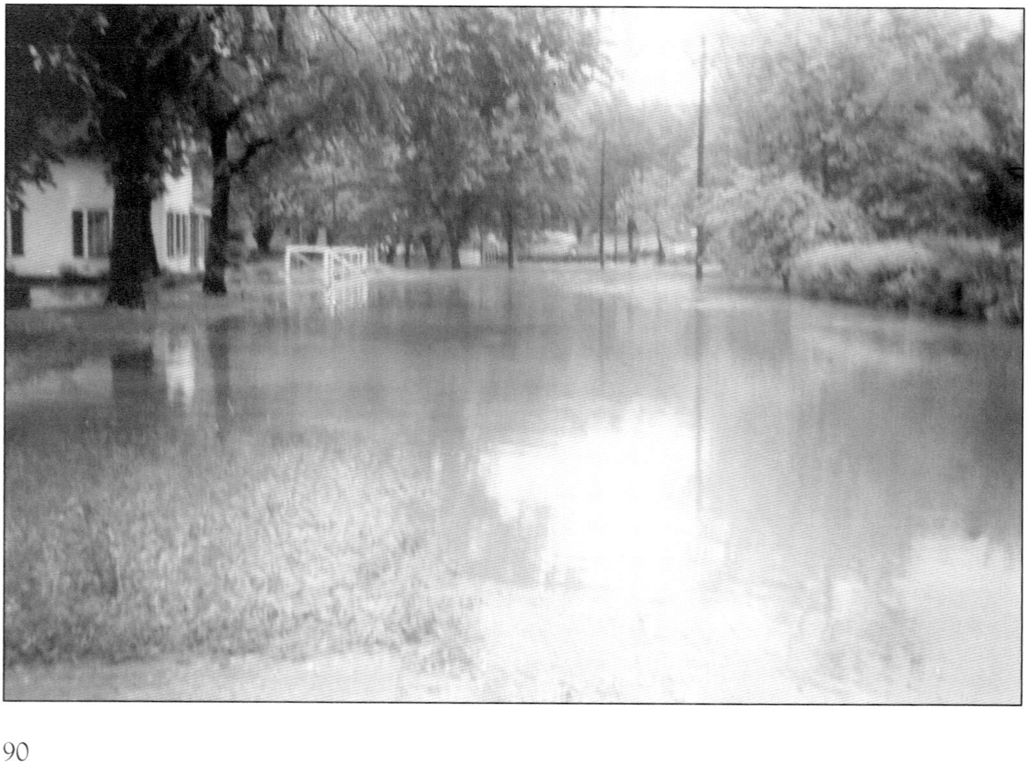

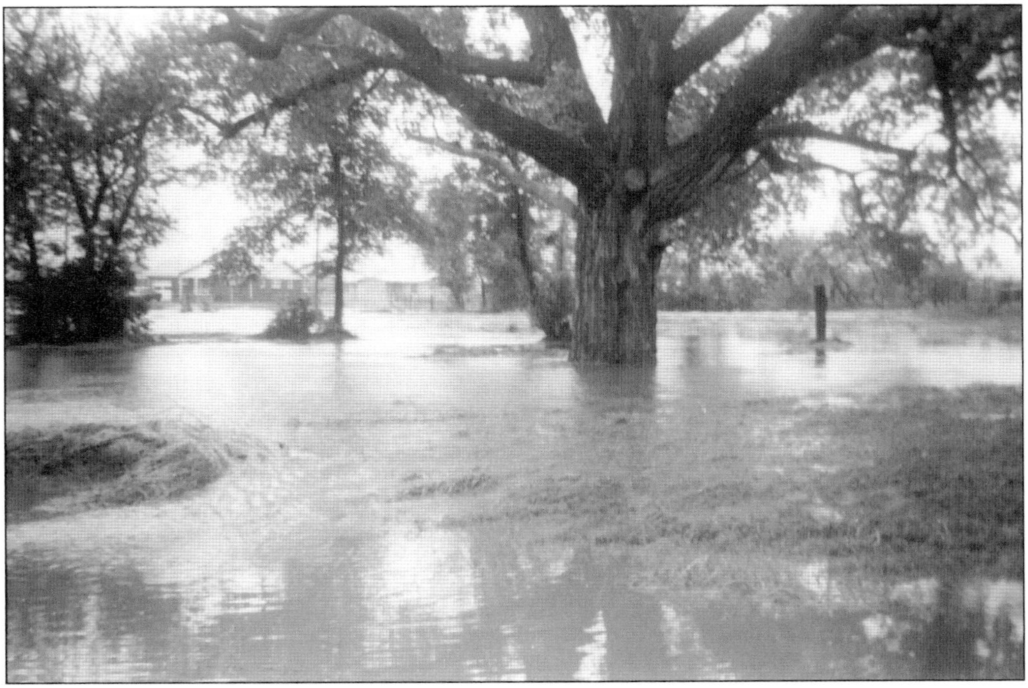

Here are two more images from the flood of 1957. Above, floodwater covers a pedestrian bridge in the middle of town. Below, water rushes through a drainage ditch. The ditch is filled to capacity, and the water is forming rapids in the park that has the town swimming pool. The water made it into at least one house in this part of town. (Both, courtesy of the Mulvane Historical Museum.)

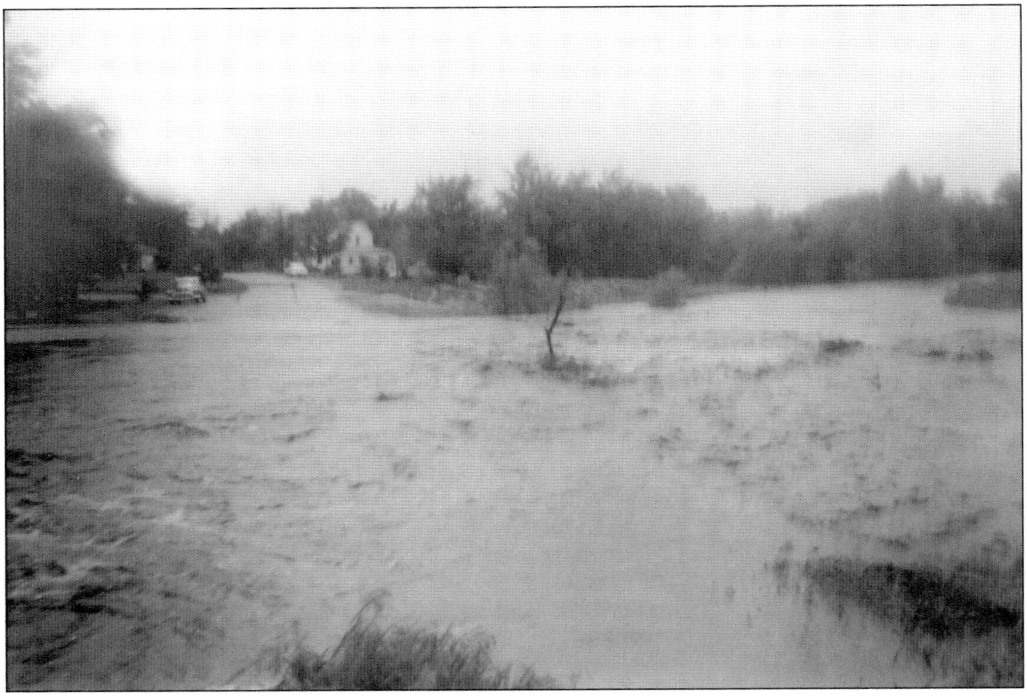

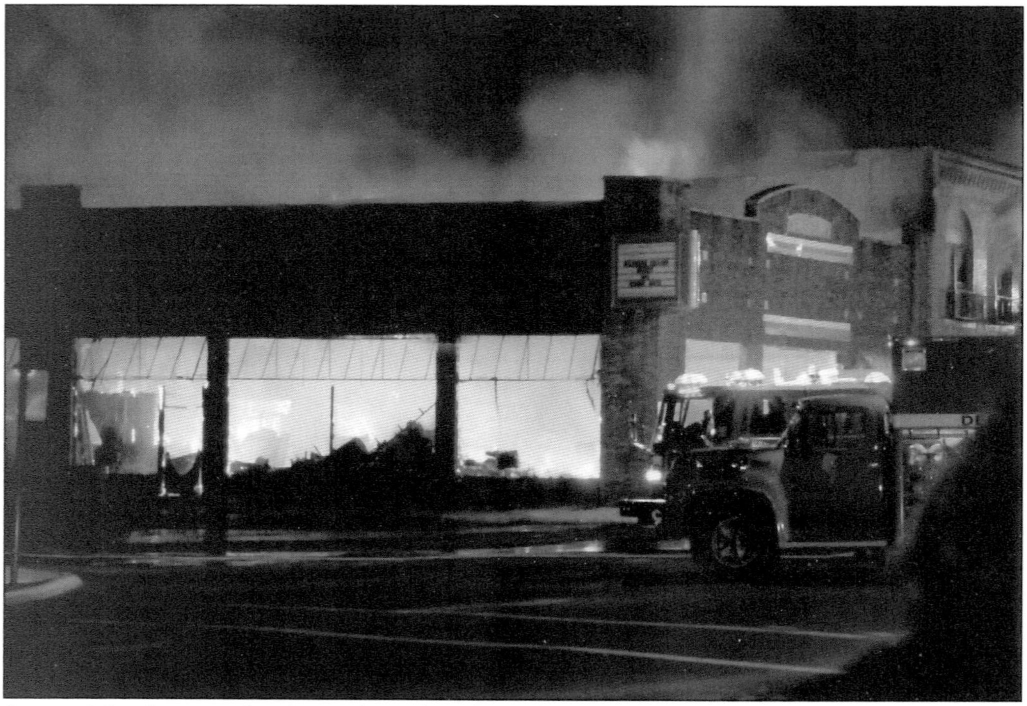

Some of the disasters that have plagued Mulvane have been man-made. On January 29, 1999, a fire erupted in downtown Mulvane. It destroyed the Nessley Building, which was the home of Wyldewood Cellars (a local winery), and the adjacent building, housing Rowan's Flower Shop. Firefighters from Sedgwick and Sumner Counties fought the blaze until after dawn the next day. (Both, courtesy of the Mulvane Historical Museum.)

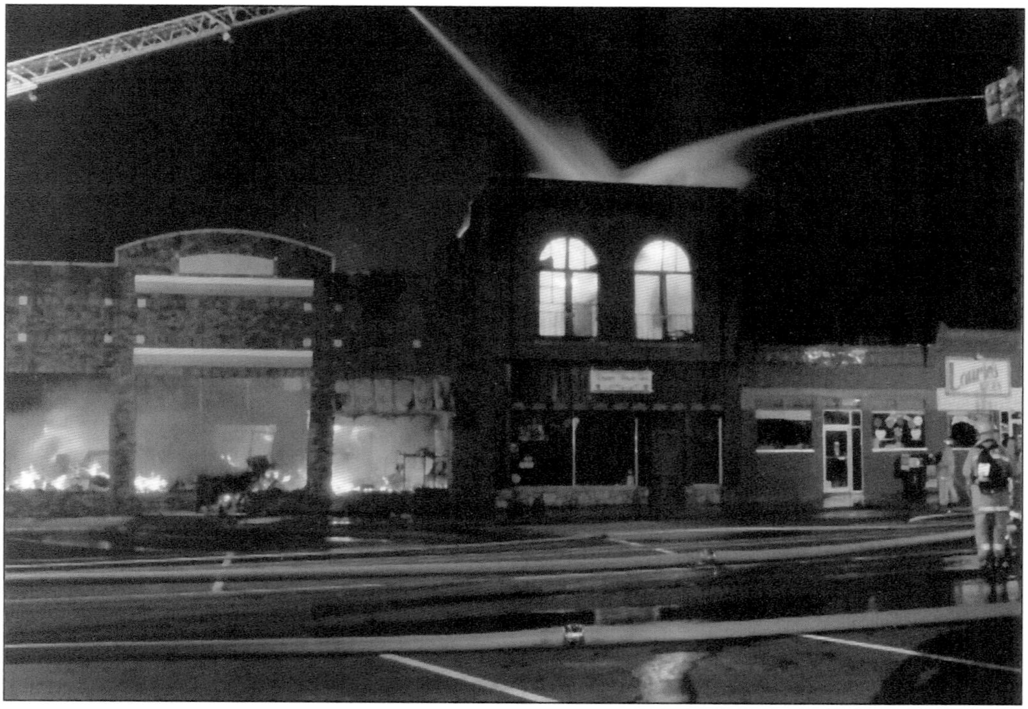

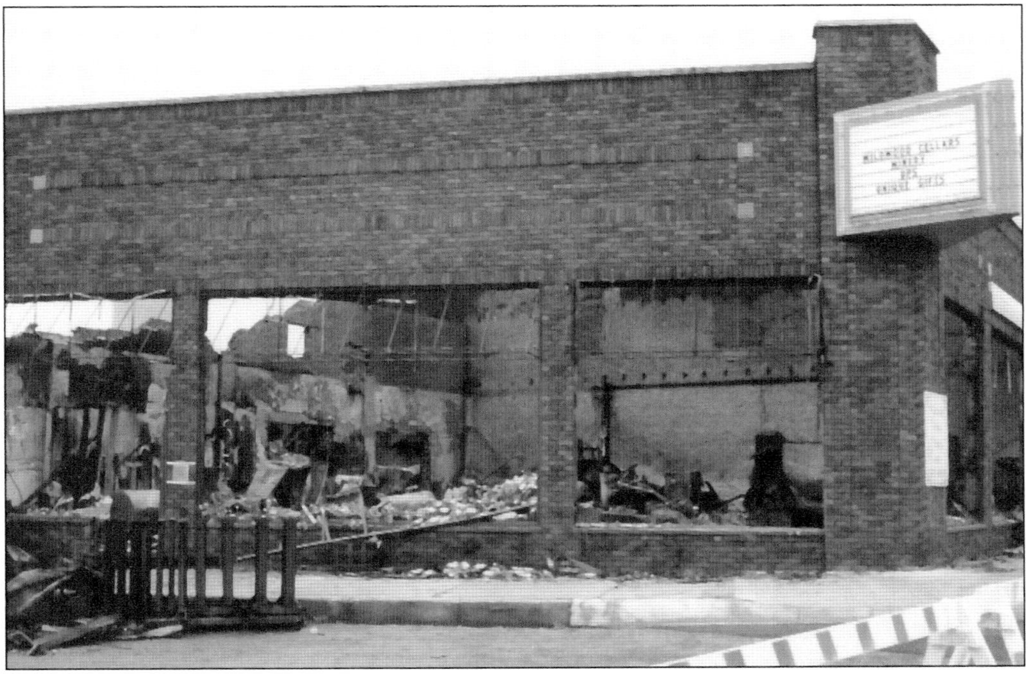

After sunrise the next day, the full extent of the destruction could be seen. Both buildings were a total loss. The fact that more buildings weren't lost is a testimonial to the work of the firefighters who answered the call that night. Today, the winery has a new home near the Mulvane exit on the Kansas Turnpike. Rowan's Flowers is located in another building on Main Street. (Both, courtesy of the Mulvane Historical Museum.)

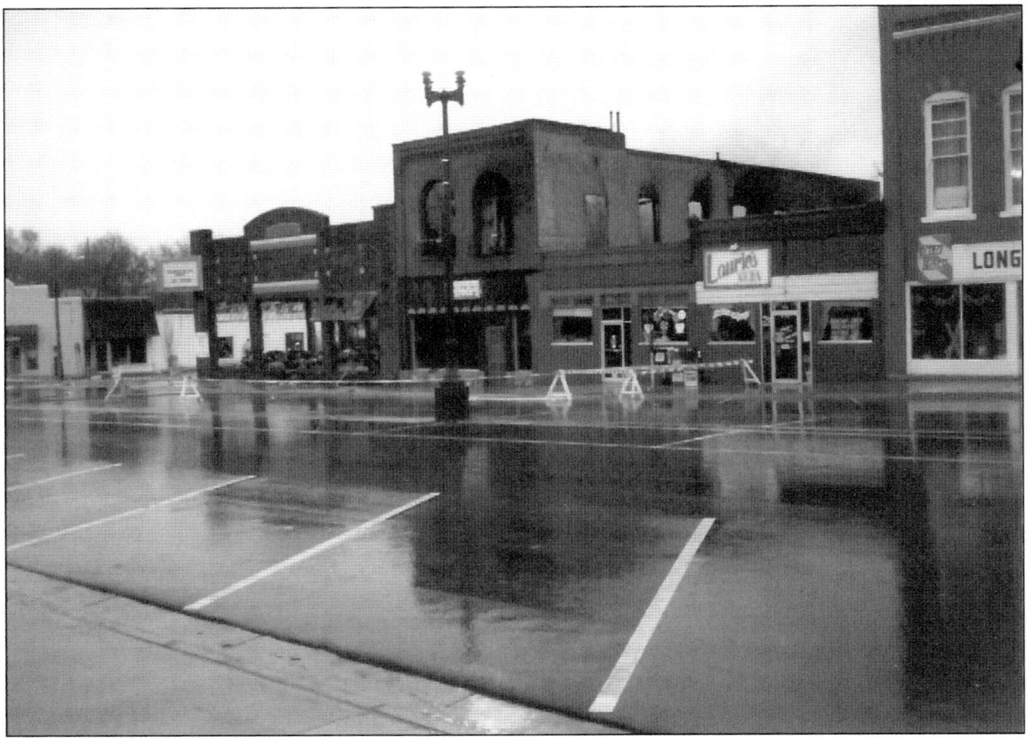

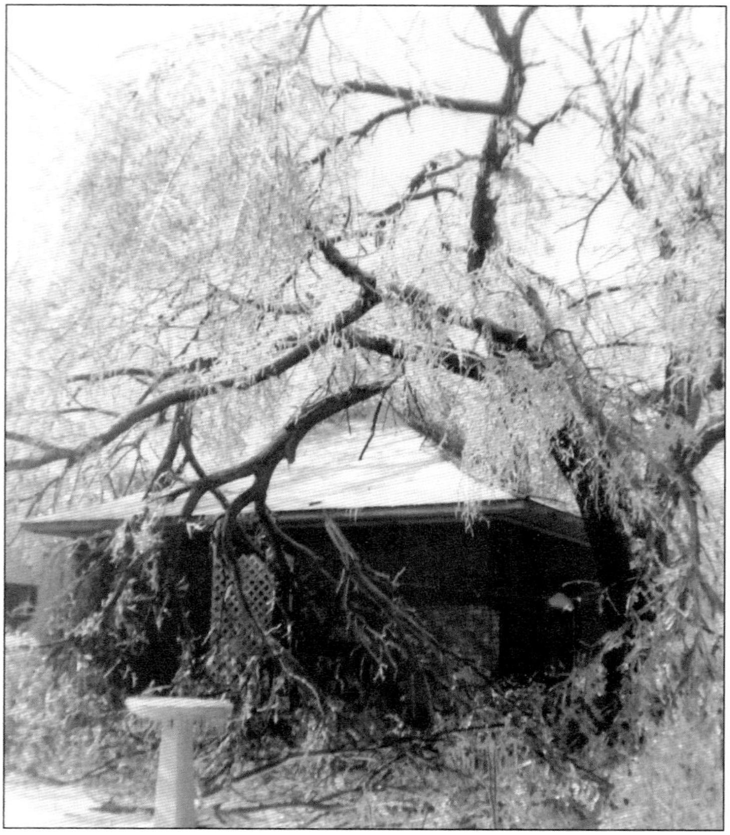

Mulvane has also experienced major ice storms. Not only do ice storms cause hazardous driving conditions, they can destroy trees and down power lines. A 1955 ice storm was particularly serious. Several trees were significantly damaged, and many people were without power. The cleanup of tree limbs took weeks. (Both, courtesy of the Mulvane Historical Museum.)

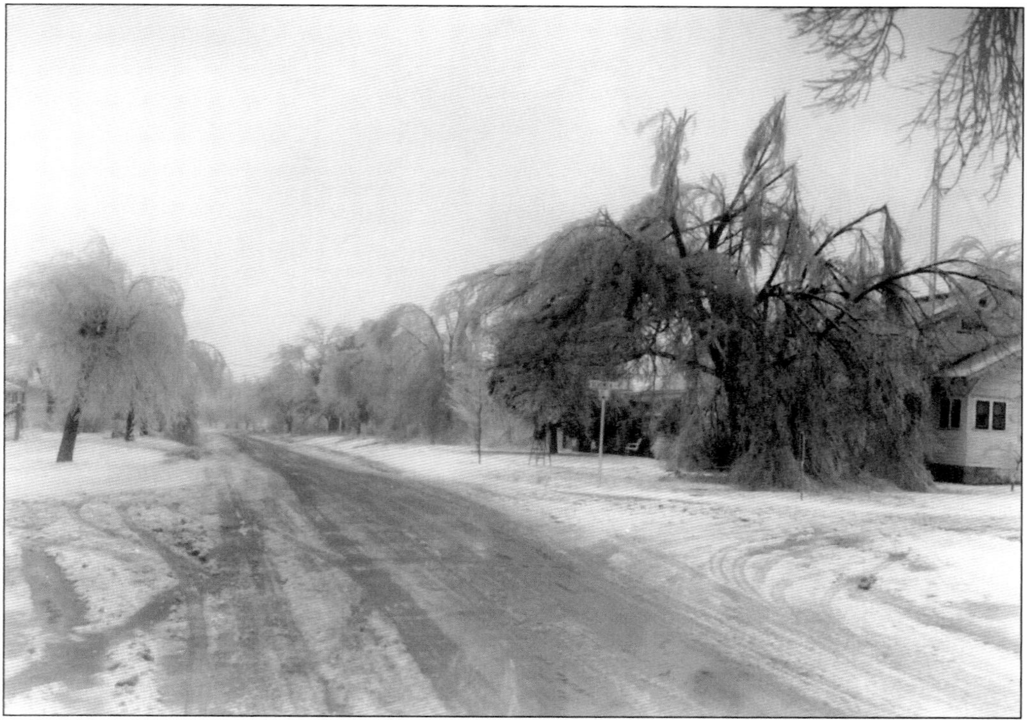

Seven

Good Days

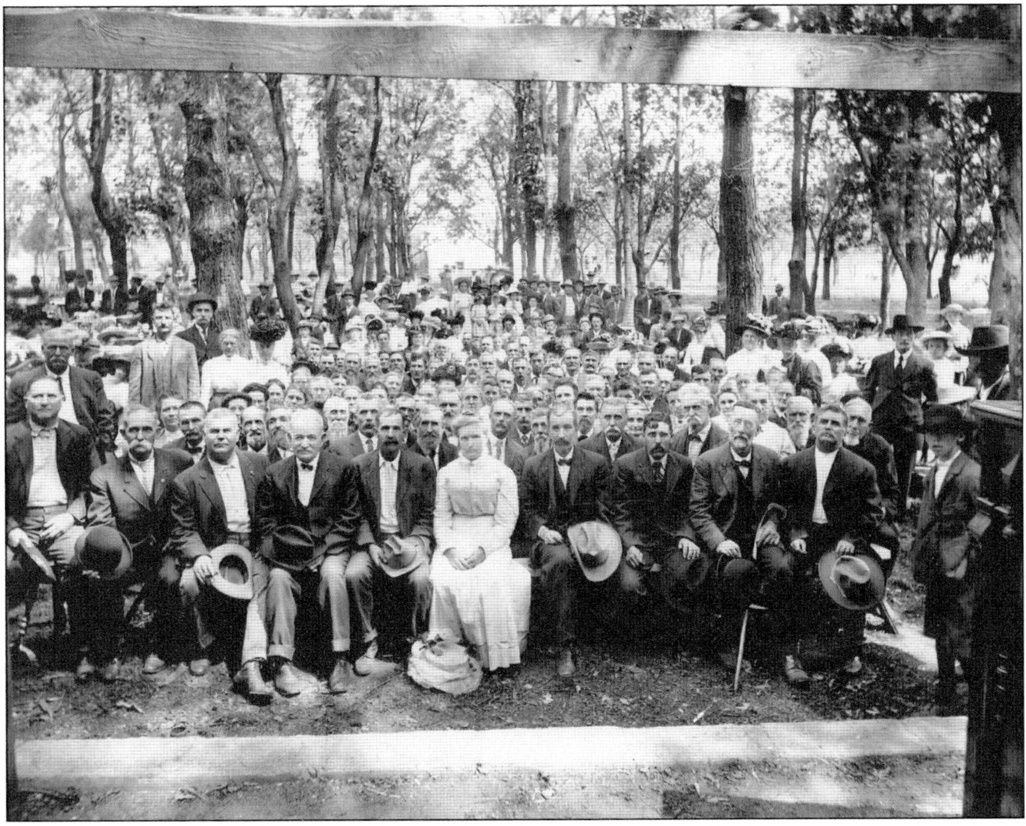

Residents gather at an Old Settlers Days picnic in the early 20th century. The Old Settlers Days celebration was launched in 1873, six years before Mulvane was founded. Today, it is an annual event held during the third weekend of August. The woman in the front row wearing the white dress is Mrs. Sanford Burnell, the first white child born in Sedgwick County. (Courtesy of the Mulvane Historical Museum.)

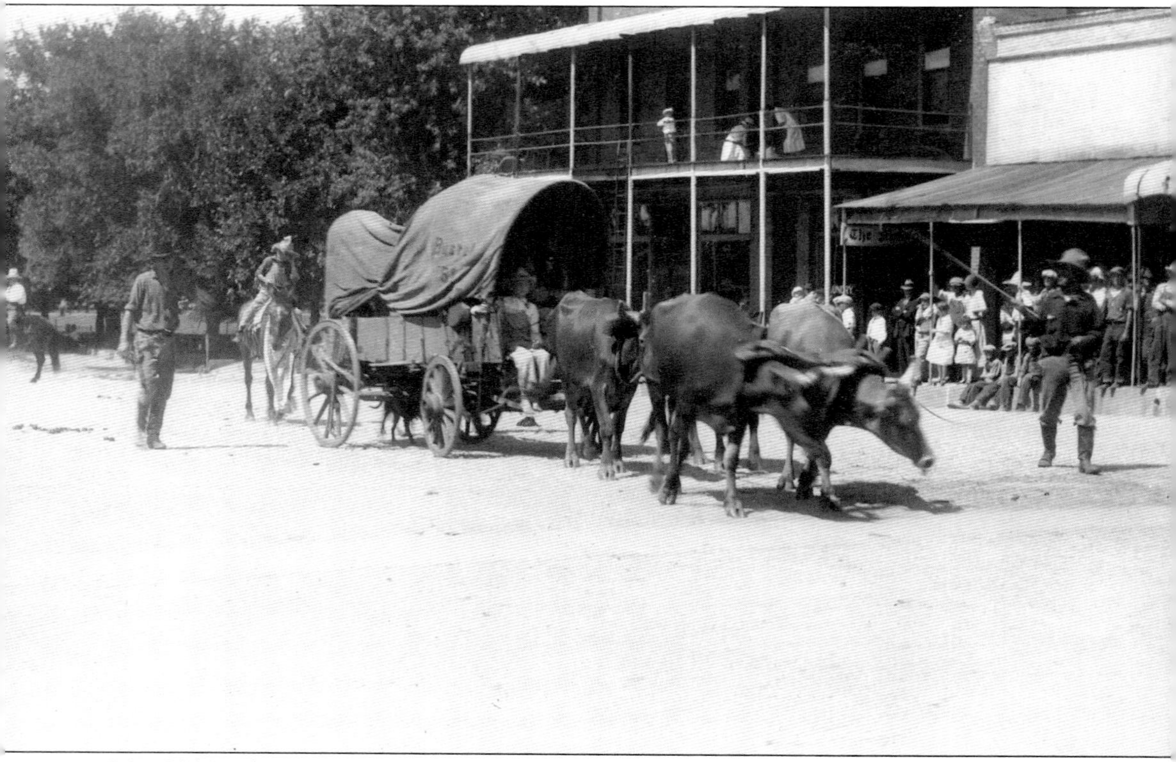

The Old Settlers Days Parade was launched in 1915. The organizer of the first parade was George Blair. In this photograph of an early parade, Fred Logan uses a team of four oxen to pull his covered wagon. Logan farmed in the area, and he and his oxen were fixtures at Old Settlers Days activities for years. (Courtesy of the Mulvane Historical Museum.)

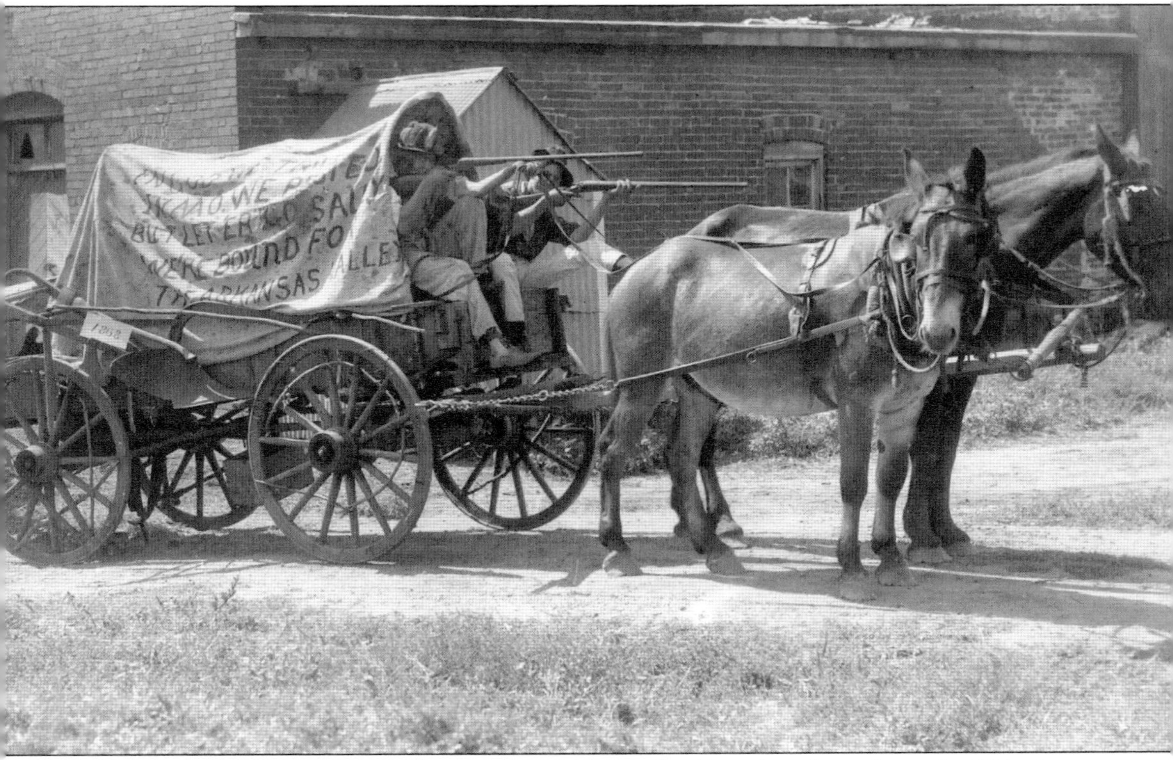

George Seaman drives his covered wagon in an Old Settlers Days Parade in the early 1920s. It is the same wagon that his father used to bring him to Kansas from Missouri in 1871. (Courtesy of the Mulvane Historical Museum.)

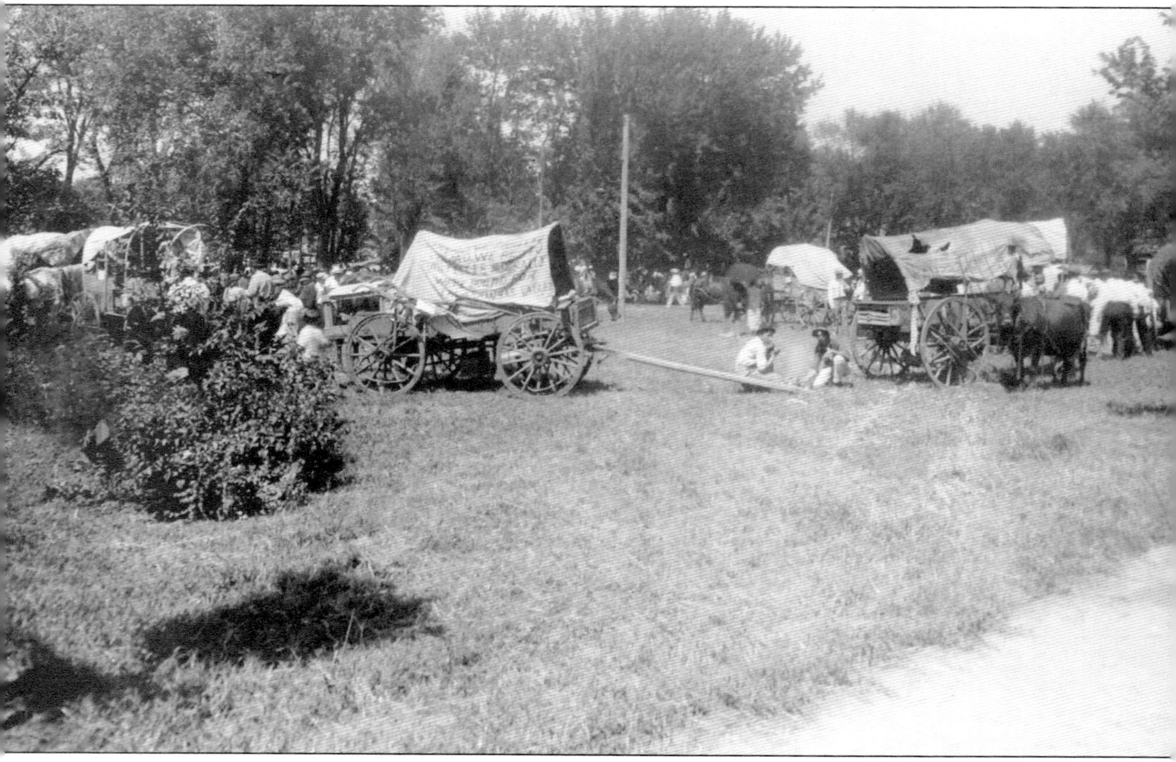

A group of wagon masters has camped during the Old Settlers Days weekend. For many of these old settlers, camping out with a wagon was a fairly fresh memory. George Seaman's wagon is clearly visible in the middle of the photograph. (Courtesy of the Mulvane Historical Museum.)

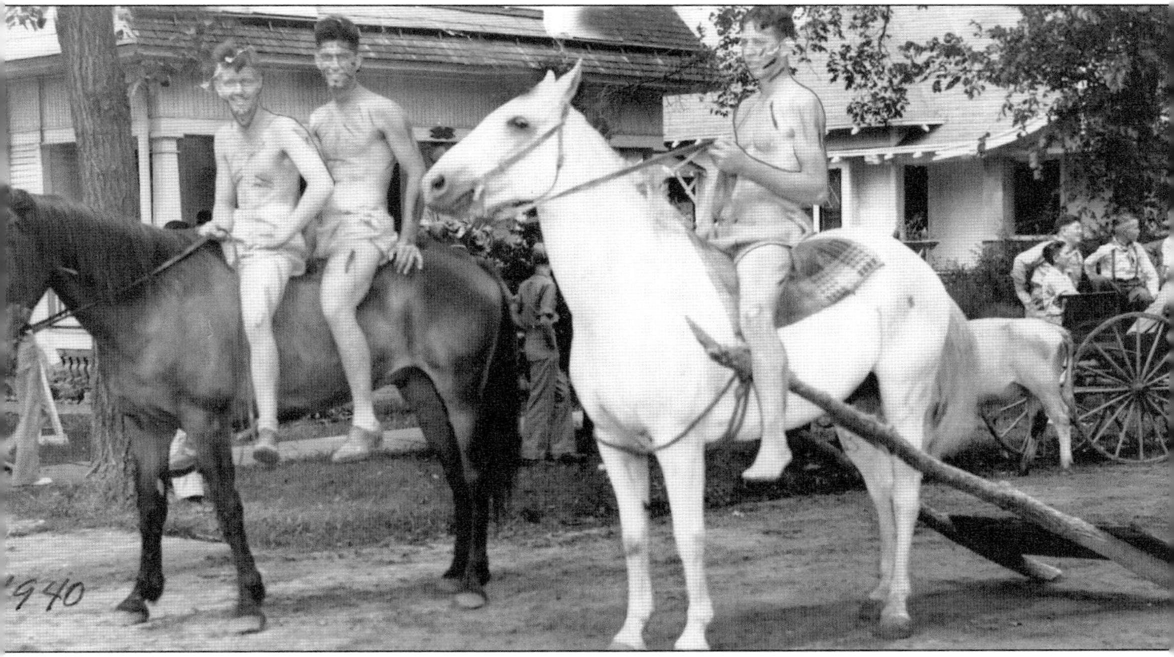

Native American culture has always been a key part of the history of the Great Plains. In the 1940 parade, these unidentified young men paid tribute to the people who inhabited this land before white settlers arrived. Osage Indians primarily inhabited this part of Kansas when white settlers began arriving. West of the Arkansas River was home to the Comanche, the Apache, the Cheyenne, the Kiowa, and the Arapaho. As these were warrior tribes, neither the Plains Indians nor the white settlers would cross the river. (Courtesy of the Mulvane Historical Museum.)

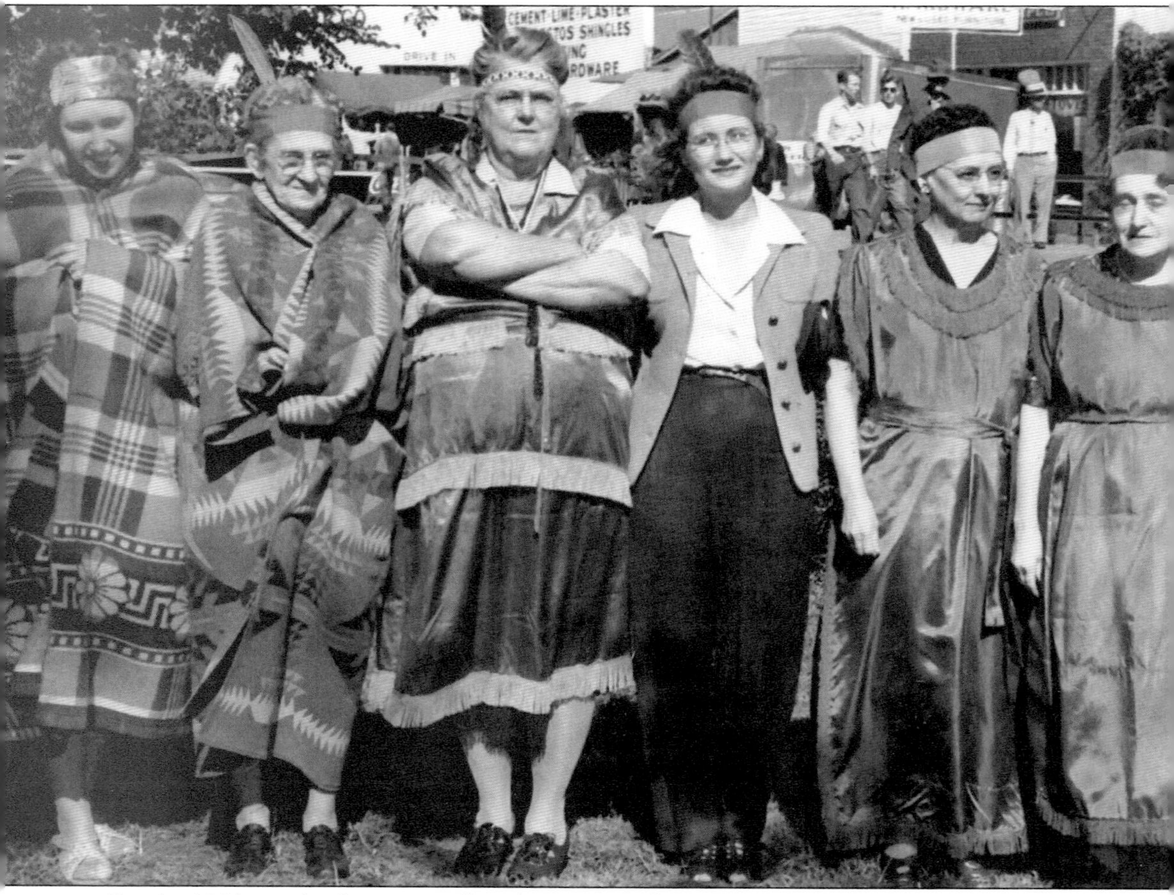

For the 1946 parade, this group of Wichita women from Hontias Lodge No. 68 dressed as Native Americans. The settlers of this area had very good relations with Native Americans. In addition to the Osage Indians, the area was home to Kanza and Wichita Indians, among other tribes. These tribes were peaceful and readily traded with early settlers. The best-known Native American in the area was Jesse Chisholm, who established the cattle trail that bears his name. The ladies here include Sue Samuel, Anna Parker, Lucille Caboone, Pearl Scarth, and Dorothy Lorsong. (Courtesy of the Mulvane Historical Museum.)

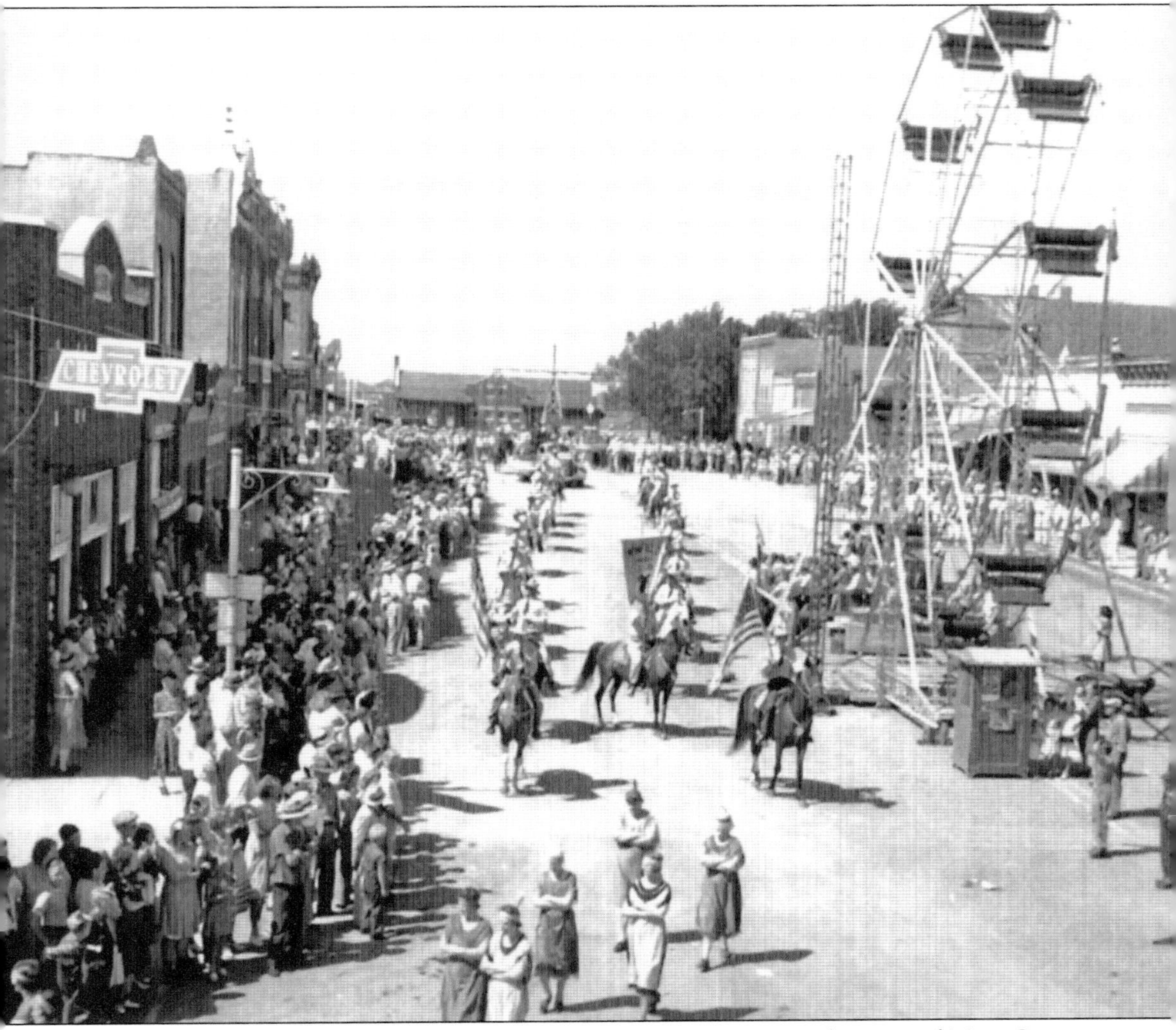

This photograph shows an Old Settlers Days Parade from the 1930s. The view of Main Street looks to the west, in the direction of the railroad depot. A uniformed equestrian unit is riding down the street. The area of Sedgwick and Sumner Counties has been the home of horse breeders since it was first settled, and equestrian units have been a staple of the Old Settlers Days Parade from the very beginning. Also, by the time of this photograph, the street carnival had become a part of the weekend celebration. (Courtesy of the Mulvane Historical Museum.)

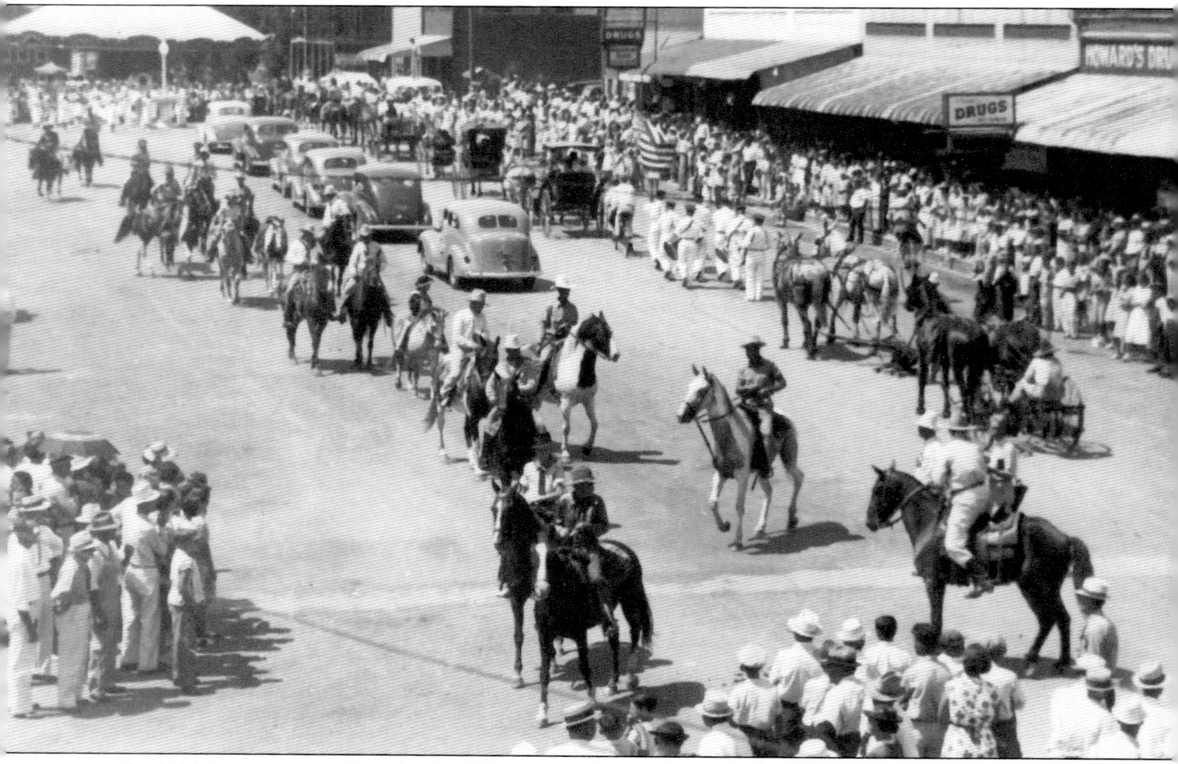

The Old Settlers Days Parade of 1938 is shown here. The parade route would pass by the spectators on the one side of Main Street and then make a U-turn and pass by the spectators on the other side of the street. Here, horse-drawn buggies and horseback riders parade while cars utilize the center-street parking. The view shows the north side of Main Street from the intersection at First Street until it reaches the intersection at Second Street. The sidewalk-covering canopies offered protection from the August sun. (Courtesy of the Mulvane Historical Museum.)

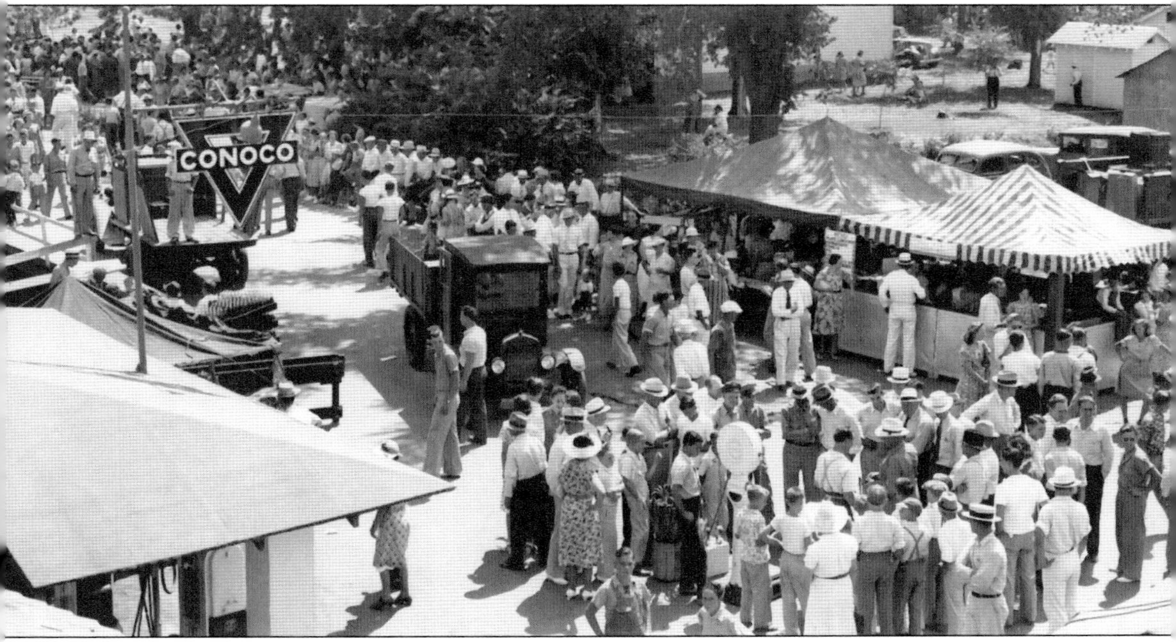

The Old Settlers Days picnic of 1939 is shown here. Food vendors would set up booths all along Main Street, and customers would sample treats from a wide variety of menus. People would then take the food to Old Settlers Park, directly behind the vendors, and enjoy a picnic lunch. The delicious aromas could be smelled all over downtown. The menu under the striped tent includes hamburgers, hot dogs, and fresh pie. Any of the individual items on the menu could be purchased for less than a dollar. The menu items are much the same today, but the prices are a little different. (Courtesy of the Mulvane Historical Museum.)

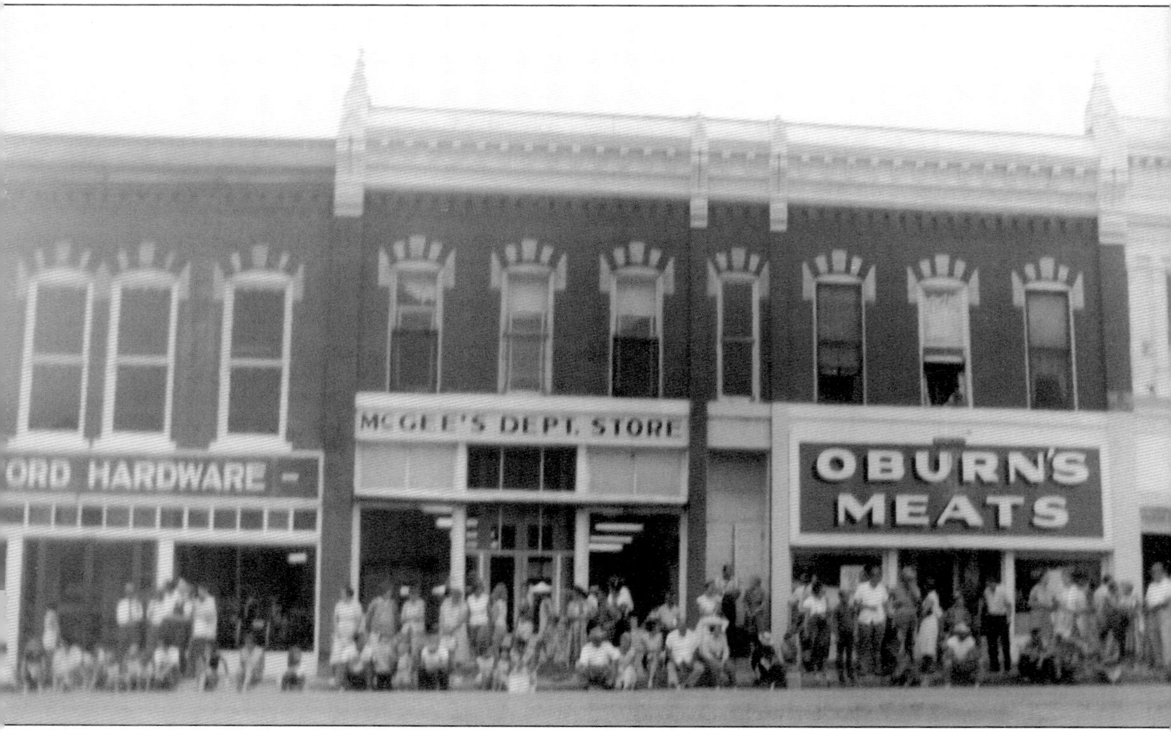

People are starting to gather on the south side of Main Street as the 1960 Old Settlers Days Parade is about to commence. Like the other downtown merchants, the hardware store, the department store, and the meat market would close during the parade. (Courtesy of the Mulvane Historical Museum.)

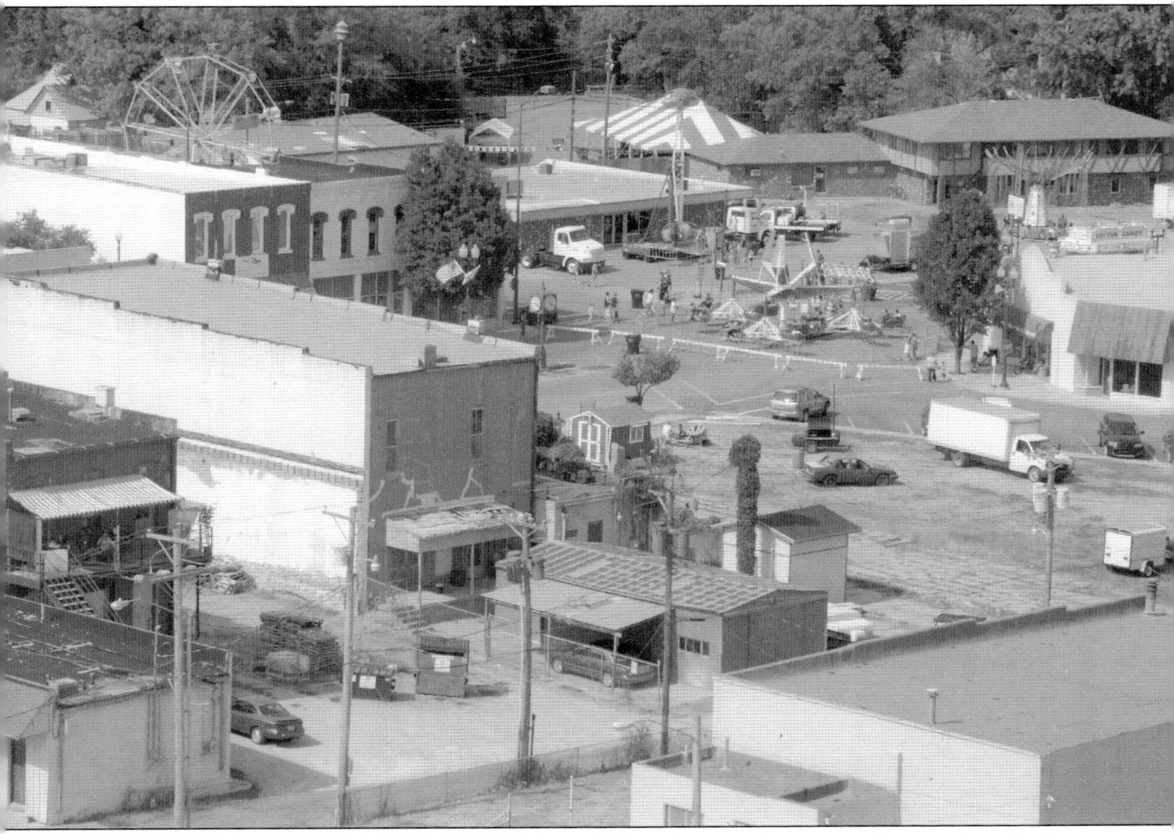

This photograph, taken from the top of the Mulvane Co-op, shows people spending Friday afternoon preparing to launch the 2012 Old Settlers Days weekend. The street carnival and food vendors will be open for business by sundown, and the streets will be packed with people of all ages. (Photograph by Gerald McCoy.)

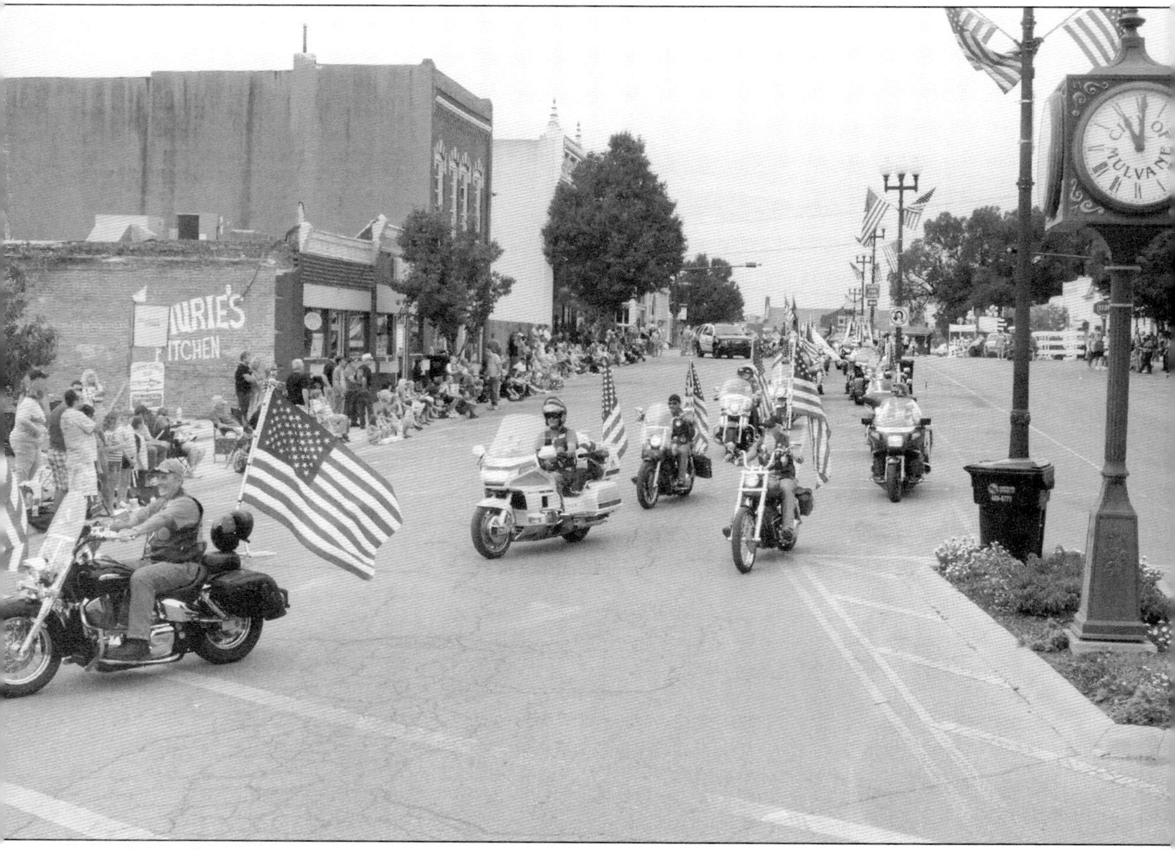

The Mulvane chapter of the Patriot Guard leads the 2012 Old Settlers Days Parade. Mulvane is the birthplace of the Patriot Guard Motorcycle Club. Military veterans at Mulvane American Legion Post 136 created it in 2005. The original mission of the group was to serve as a funeral escort for American servicemen and servicewomen who died in battle in the Persian Gulf wars. It has since grown to include the funerals of law enforcement officers, fire department personnel, first responders, and any active duty member or veteran of the US Armed Forces. (Photograph by Gerald McCoy.)

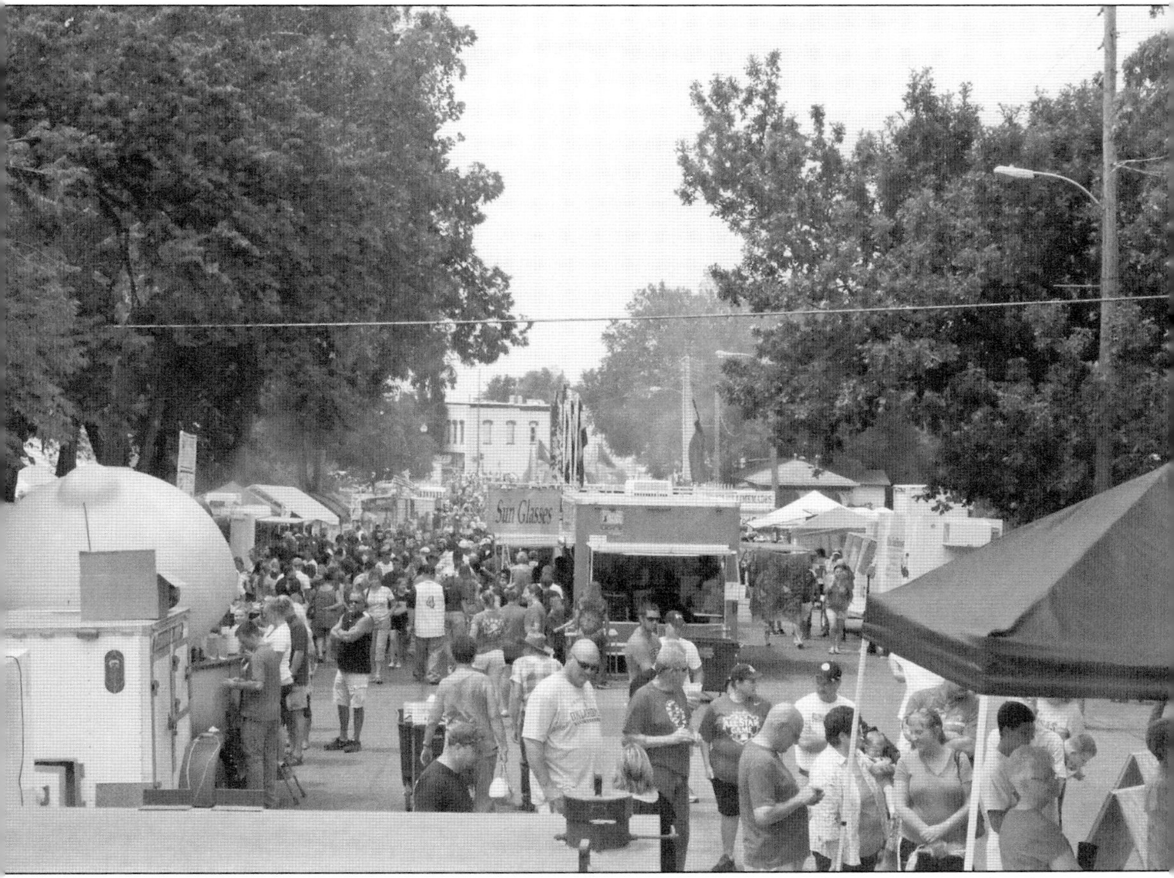

This view of the 2012 Old Settlers Days is looking west, in the direction of downtown. As has been the custom for decades, food vendors and carnival rides fill Main Street during the celebration. Thousands of people of all ages attend the family-friendly event to enjoy the food, carnival rides, and antique car show. On the left side of the street is Old Settlers Park, a gathering place for people to enjoy their lunch while they listen to live music. (Photograph by Gerald McCoy.)

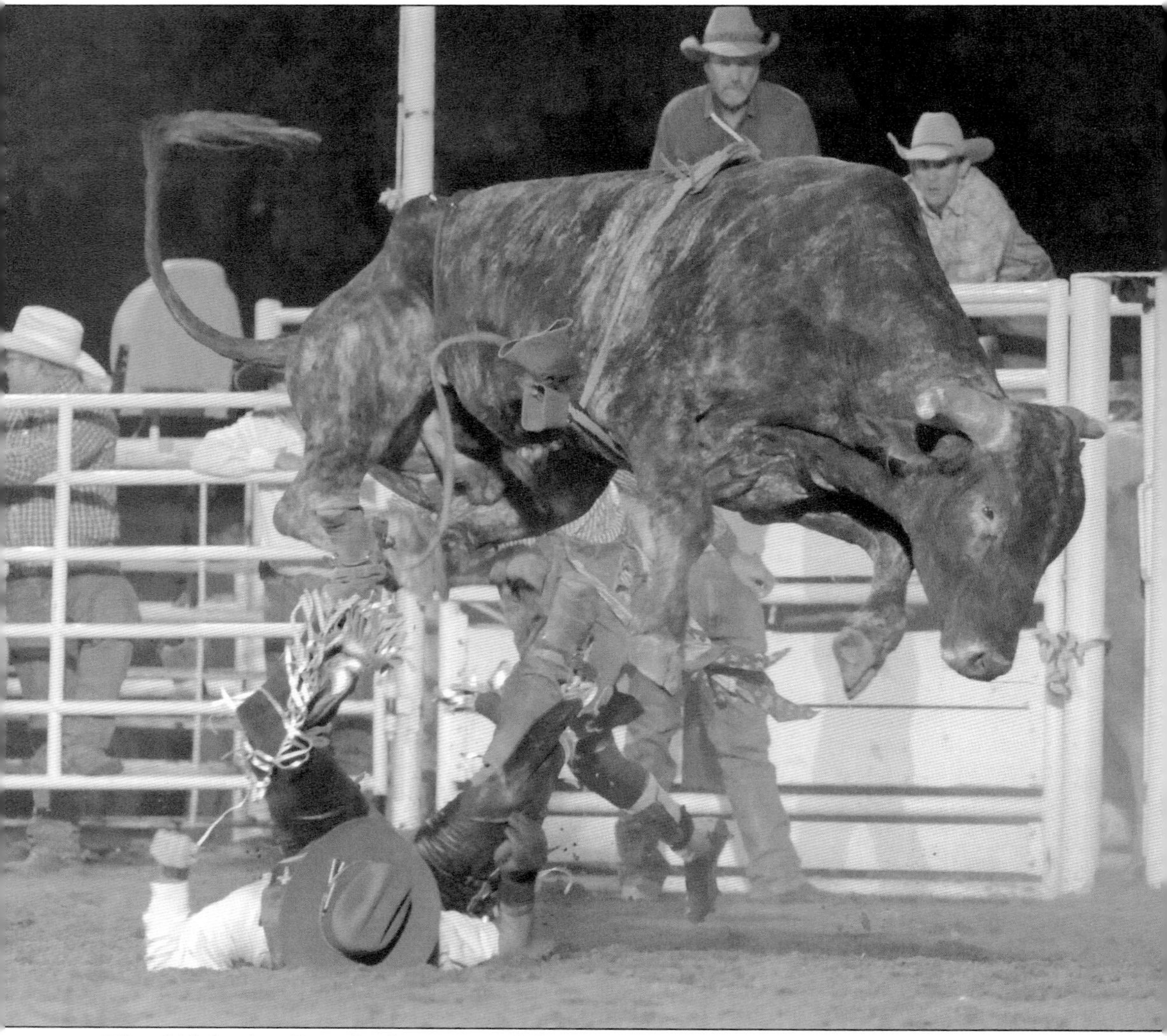

The Old Settlers Days Rodeo is one of the highlights of the weekend. There are performances Friday night and Saturday night. Cowboys and cowgirls from Kansas, Oklahoma, and beyond come to Mulvane to compete in the rodeo. Events include bronc riding, calf roping, steer wrestling, ladies' barrel racing, and bull riding. There are events for the youngsters, such as a shoe scramble and mutton busting. Local merchants support the rodeo by sponsoring championship awards in each event. In this photograph from the 2012 competition, a bull rider finds himself in a bad spot. (Photograph by Gerald McCoy.)

Eight

NOWADAYS

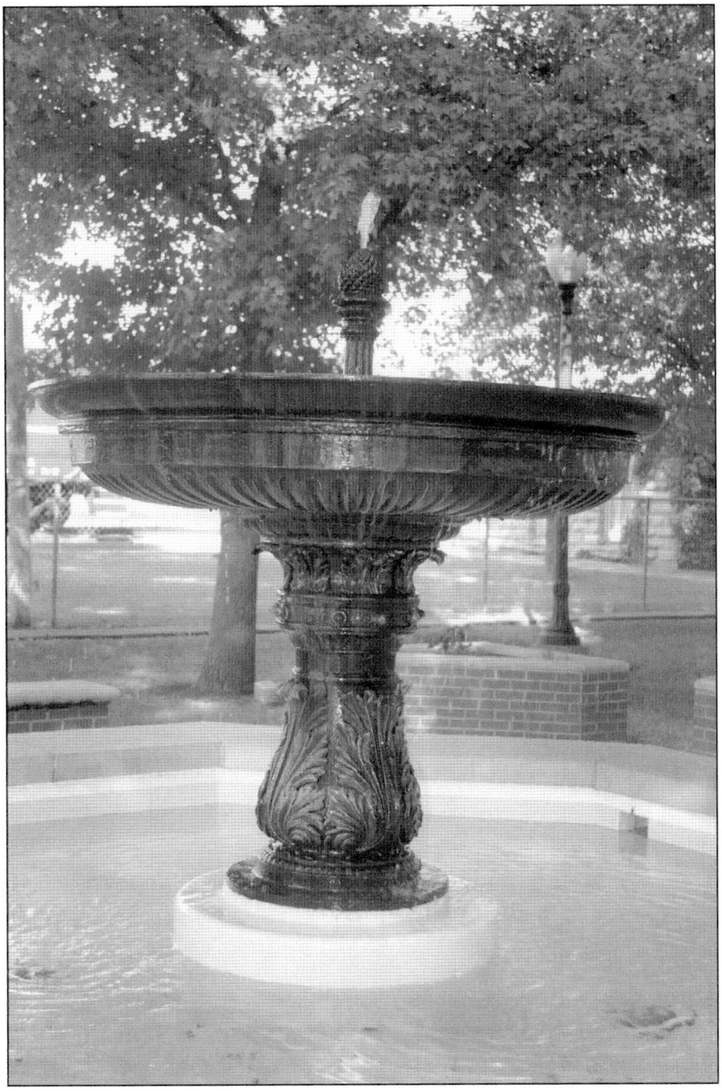

For decades, a large water fountain in the intersection of First and Main Streets was used to water horses when people would visit downtown. The water fountain remained there well into the automobile era before it was removed. The fate of the original water fountain is unknown, but a replica stands in Cobb Park, which is adjacent to the Mulvane Historical Museum. It stands in a small pool that serves as a wishing well. Today, people drop coins in the fountain in the hopes of receiving good luck. (Photograph by Gerald McCoy.)

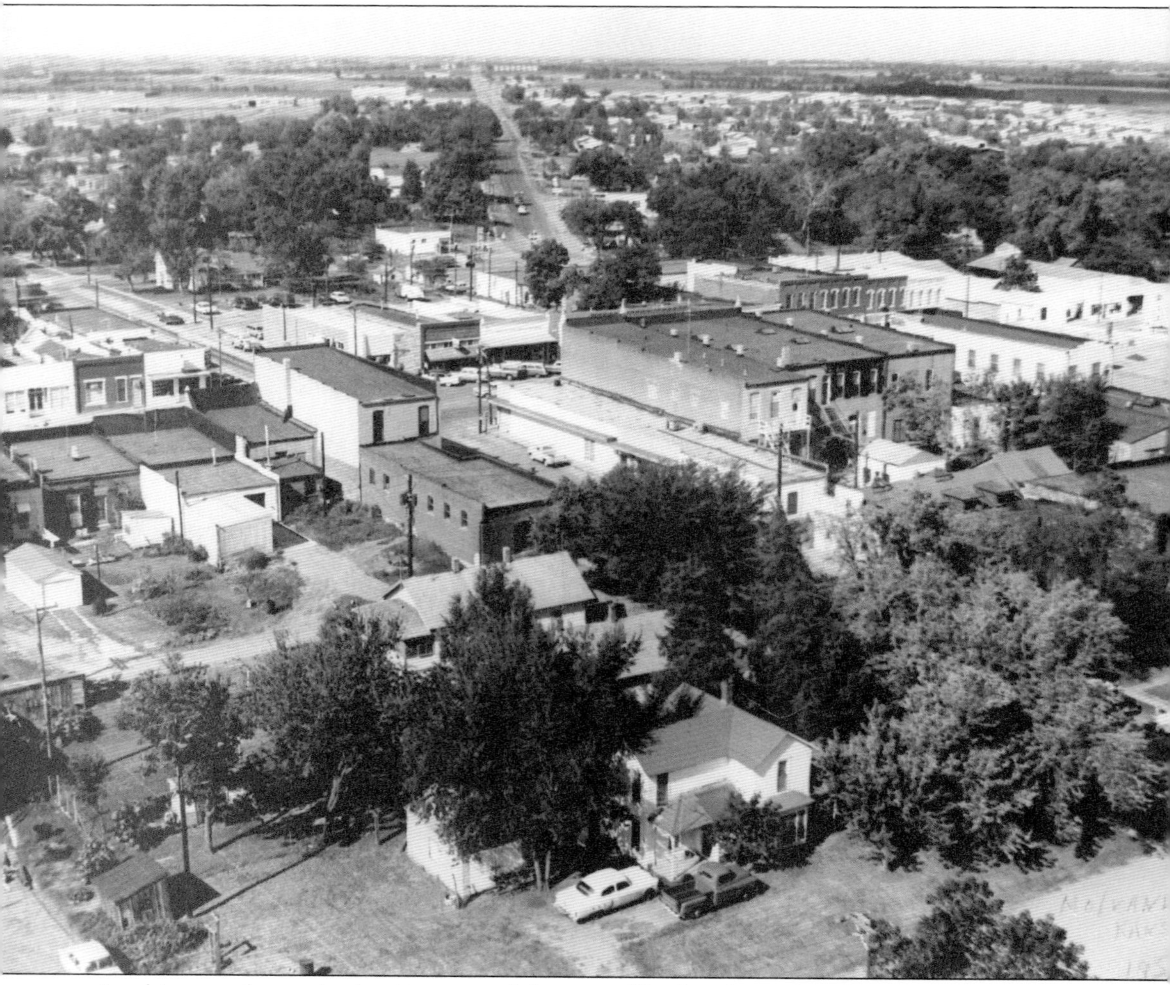

Looking northeast, in the direction of the city of Derby, this 1950s photograph reveals Second Street, the main north-south route through Mulvane, as a two-lane road. The downtown area is active with shoppers and merchants. A fire that would dramatically change the look of downtown Mulvane has not yet touched the south side of Main Street. From the 1920s until the time of this photograph, there were relatively few changes in the way the town looked. (Courtesy of the Mulvane Historical Museum.)

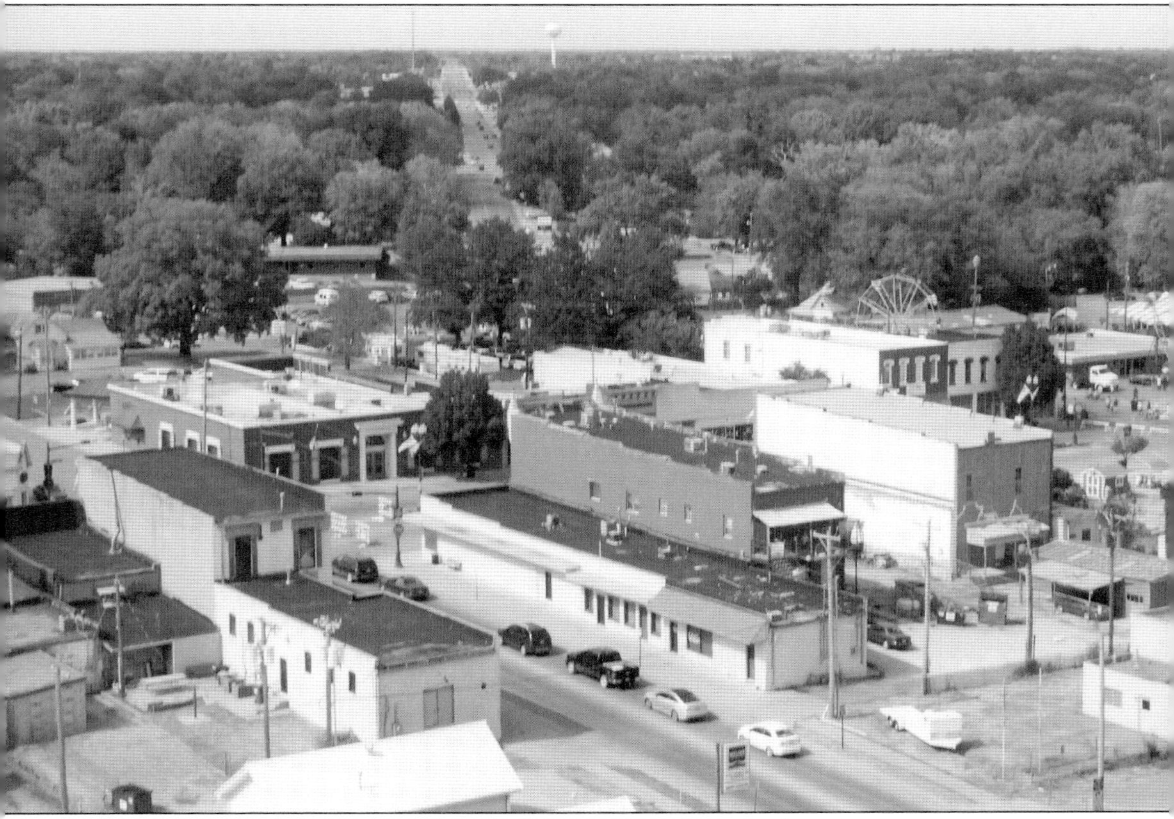

This 2012 photograph, taken from the top of the Mulvane Co-op, is from the same perspective as that on the previous page. The downtown area has been blocked to car traffic as the town prepares for Old Settlers Days. Significant differences from the previous photograph can be seen. Note that Second Street is a four-lane boulevard rather than a two-lane street, and, on the horizon, a modern water tower serves the community. The loss of buildings on the south side of Main Street is apparent, while the Carson Bank building has expanded. (Photograph by Gerald McCoy.)

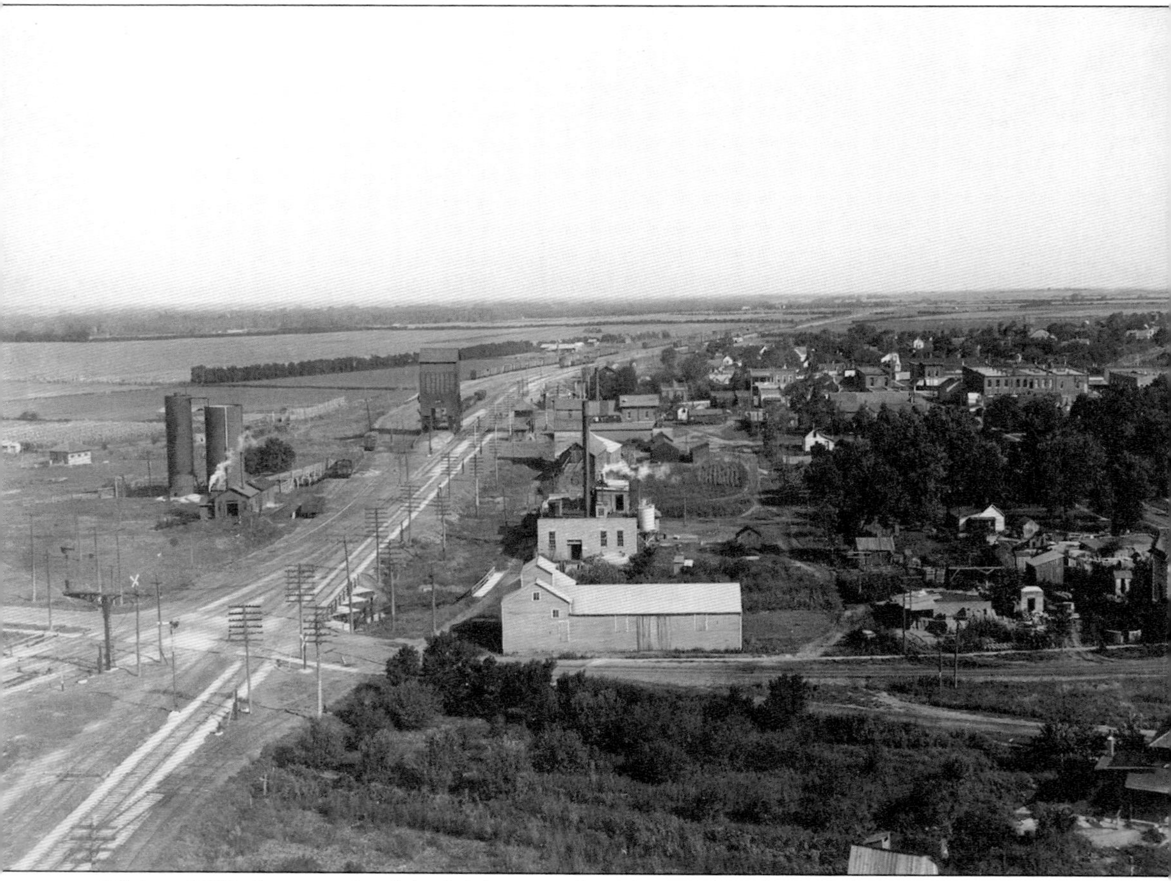

This c. 1920 photograph of the Mulvane rail yard was taken from the south, looking north. At this time, Mulvane was very much a small Kansas town. The coal bin can be seen in the distance, and a close look reveals the downtown area on the right side of the photograph. Only a few houses are sprinkled around town, and farms and fields dominate the landscape. At this time, passenger train service shuttled people north to Wichita and south to Oklahoma. Horse-drawn wagons were still a common mode of transportation for local trips. (Courtesy of the Mulvane Historical Museum.)

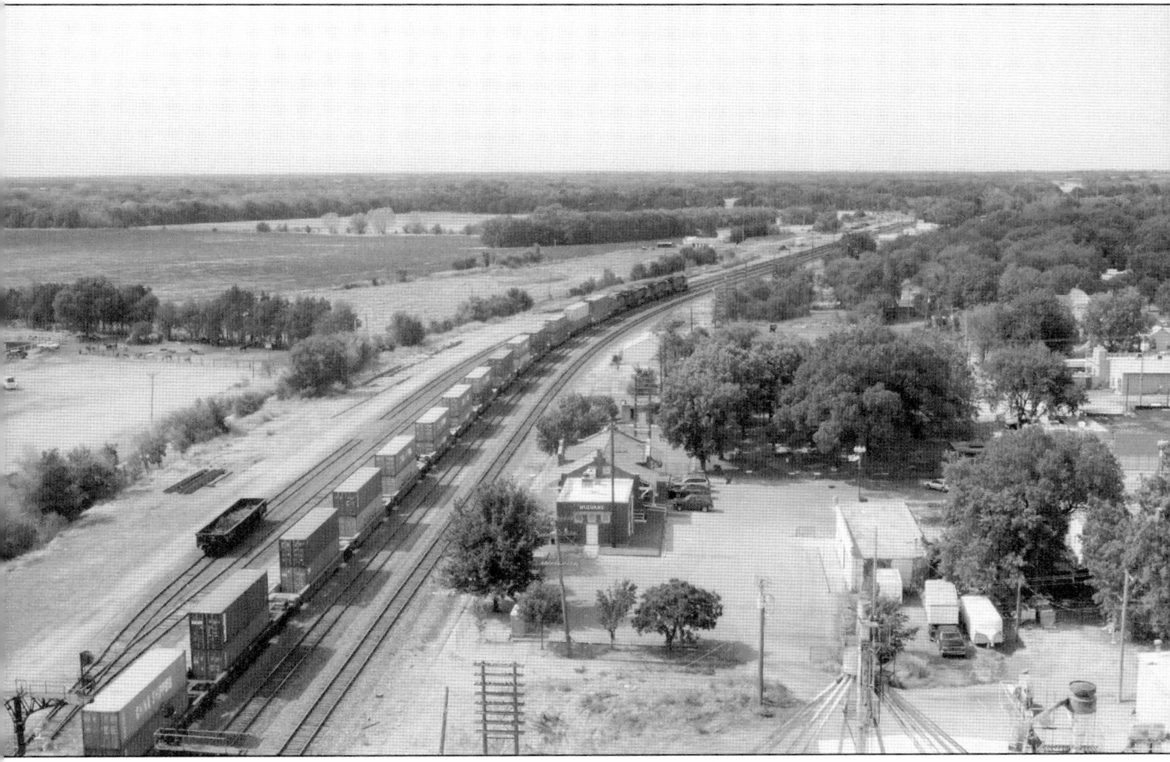

This 2012 photograph shows the same view as that on the previous page. Again, the photograph was taken from the top of the Mulvane Co-op during Old Settlers Days. The view is north toward Wichita. The trains that now pass through Mulvane carry freight rather than people, and the town has grown and matured. The coal bin is gone; locomotives with diesel engines now pull the trains. On the left side of the photograph, the town has expanded west of the train tracks, but farms and fields still dominate the landscape just beyond the edge of town. (Photograph by Gerald McCoy.)

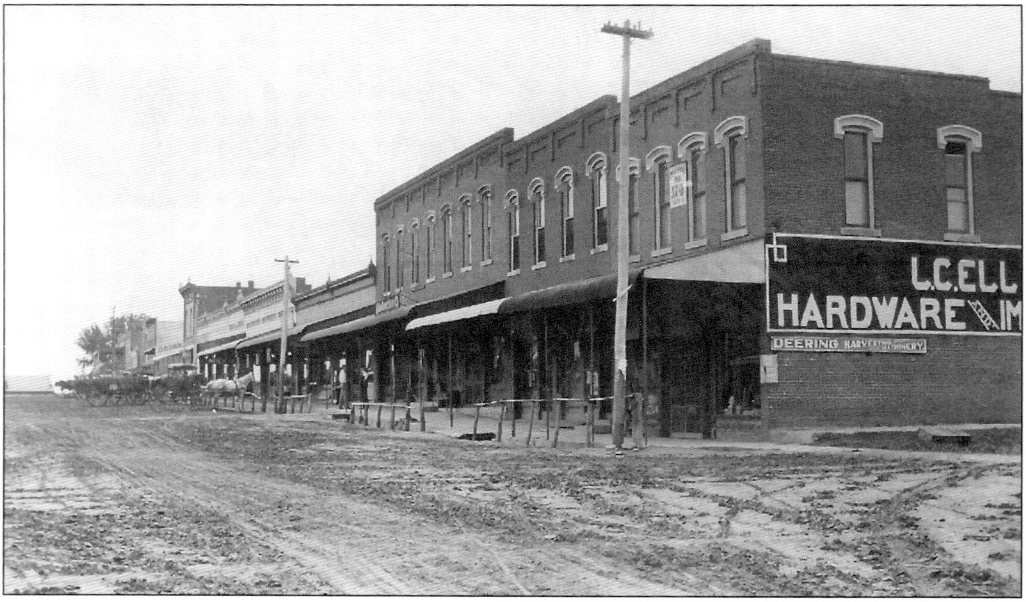

Above, the northwest corner of Second and Main Streets is seen around 1915, before Mulvane's streets were paved. This is the north side of Main Street between First and Second Streets. The below photograph shows how that intersection appears today. The building that housed the hardware store is now the Mulvane Care and Share, a store that sells gently used merchandise. That building looks much the same, but the rest of the block has undergone several changes through the years. (Above, courtesy of the Mulvane Historical Museum; below, courtesy of the author.)

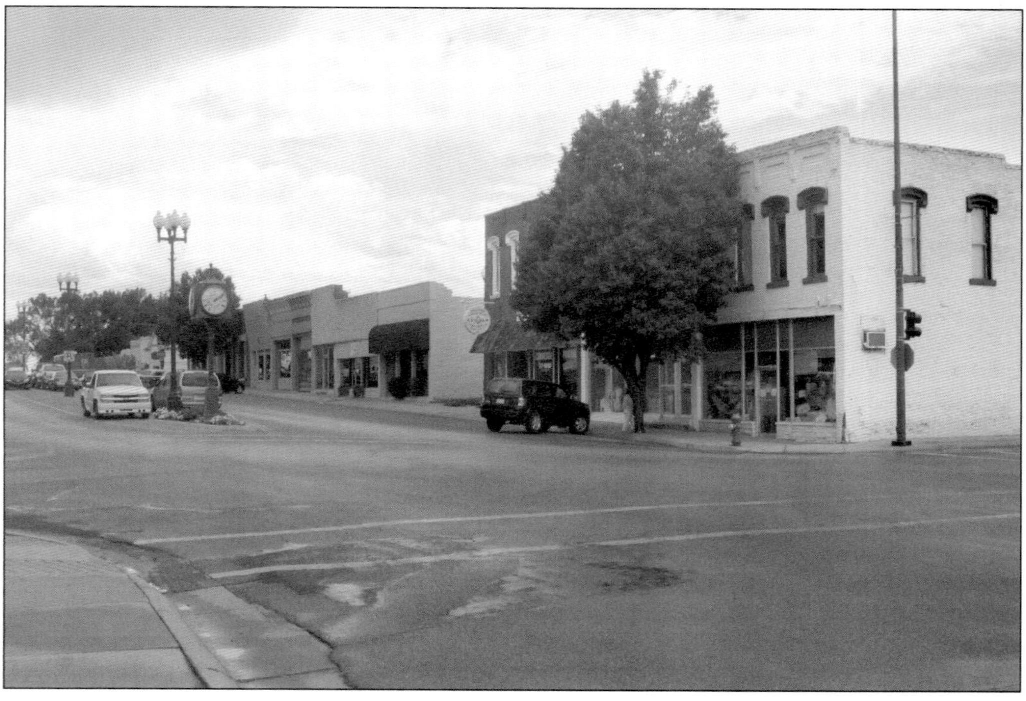

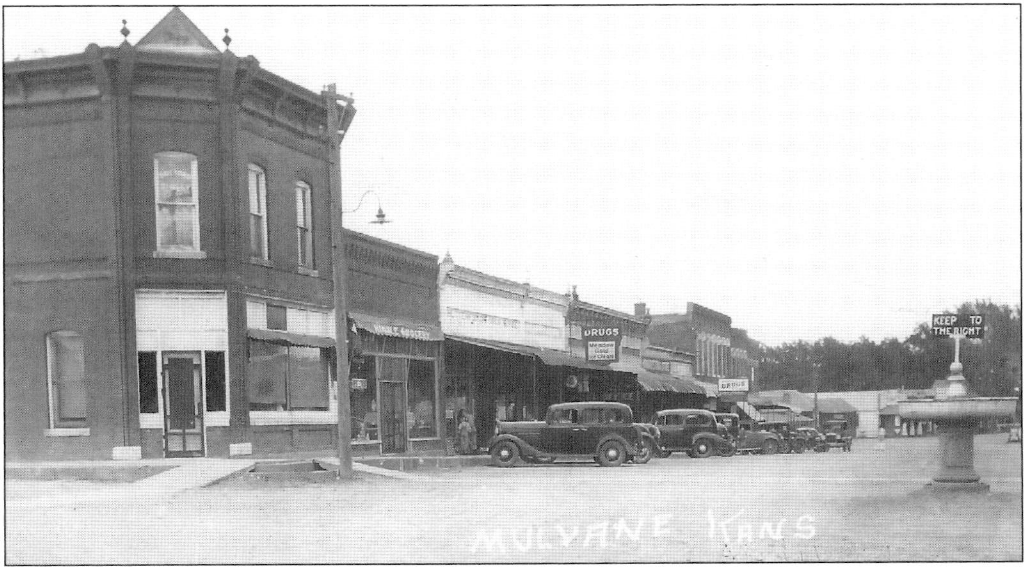

This 1930s photograph shows the northeast corner of First and Main Streets. The bank stands on the corner, and the grocery store is next door. The water fountain is still in the intersection, even though horse-drawn wagons have long since gone by the wayside. The second floor of the bank building houses the medical practice of Dr. Shelly. Two boys can be seen peering into the window of Butterfield's Drug Store, one of two drugstores on the block. Perhaps they are craving a serving of the Meadow Gold Ice Cream that is sold inside. (Courtesy of the Mulvane Historical Museum.)

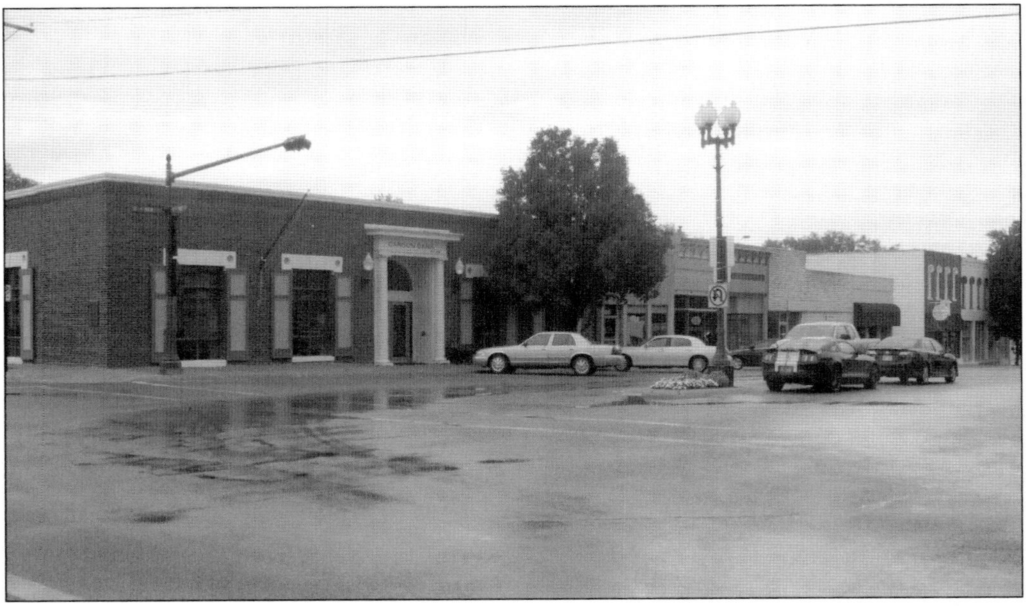

The same part of town looks very different today. The bank is still on the corner of First and Main Streets, but the grocery store is gone and the bank has grown to fill its space. Neither drugstore is still in business, and many of the buildings have been replaced by smaller structures. Nostalgic streetlamps provide light at night, and the water fountain for horses is a thing of the past. On the right side of the photograph is the hardware store building. This holdover structure from an earlier time houses the Mulvane Care and Share. (Photograph by Gerald McCoy.)

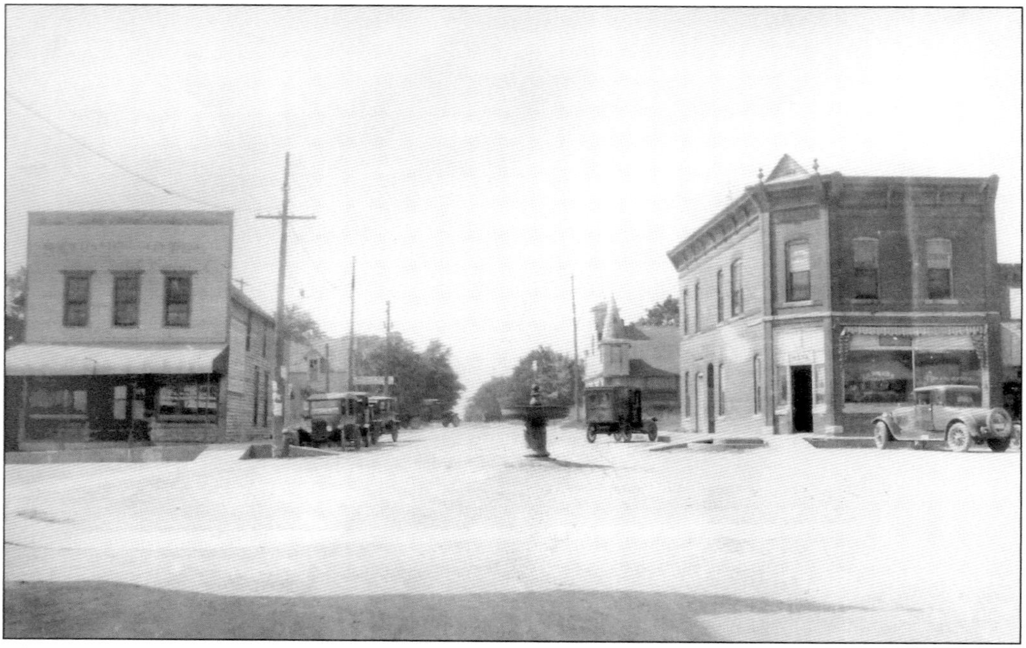

This is a photograph of First Street as it intersects with Main Street. The view is from the south, looking north. Even though cars have replaced horses, the water fountain is still at the intersection. The castle-like building to the north of the bank is Mulvane's original opera house. During its lifetime, this building also housed a grocery store and a small, but popular, roller-skating rink. On the left side of the intersection, at the northwest corner, is the laundry. (Courtesy of the Mulvane Historical Museum.)

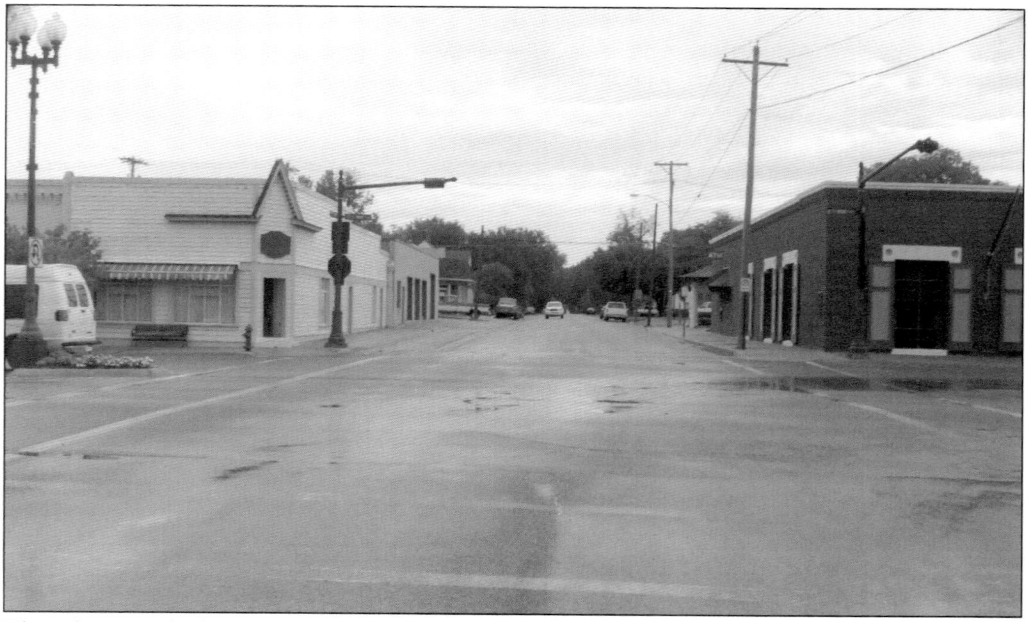

This photograph shows the same part of town as it appears today. The water fountain is gone, and the bank building is new. The old opera house building has been torn down. The building on the northwest corner of the intersection was used as a dealers' school for employees of the Kansas Star Casino. (Photograph by Gerald McCoy.)

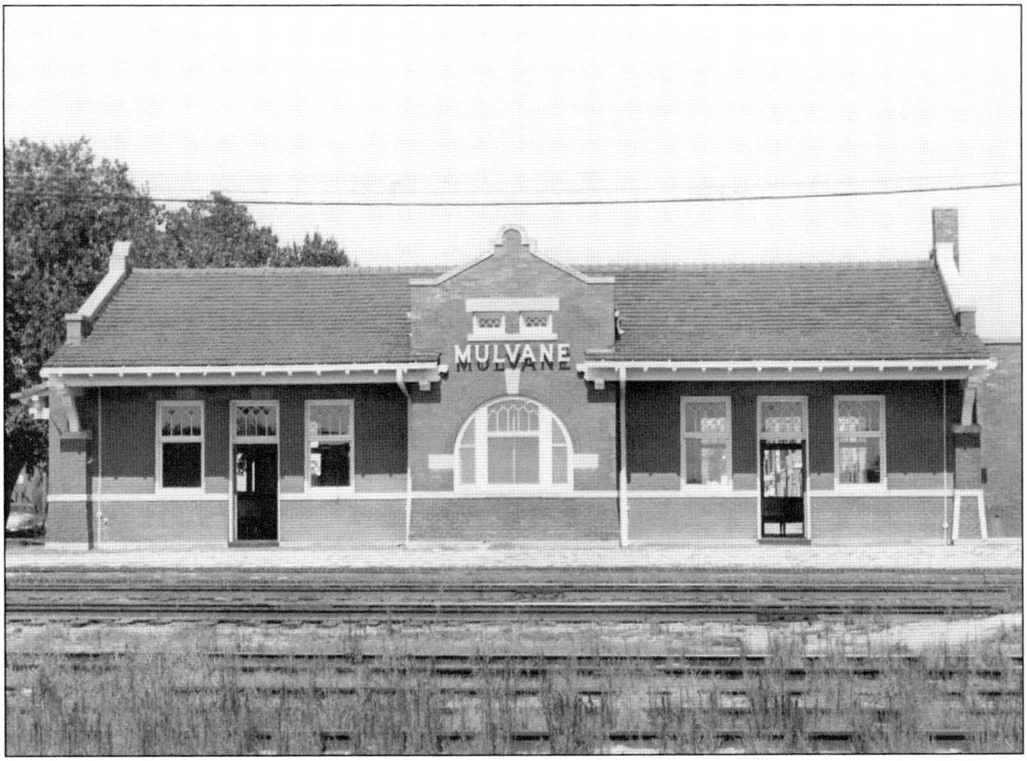

The above photograph, from approximately the 1950s, shows the west side of the railroad depot. On this side of the depot, passengers got on and got off the train. The station is no longer used for passenger service. The below photograph shows the east side of the railroad depot today. The depot is now the home of the Mulvane Historical Museum and the Mulvane Historical Society. The exterior of the building has changed very little since it was built in 1910. (Above, courtesy of the Mulvane Historical Museum; below, courtesy of the author.)

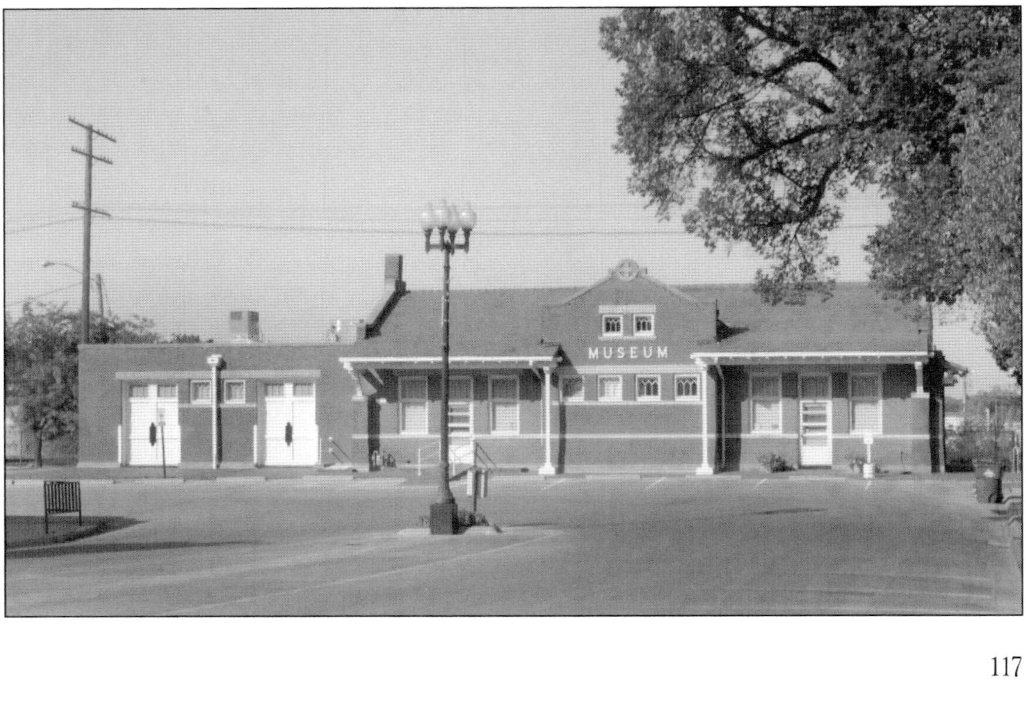

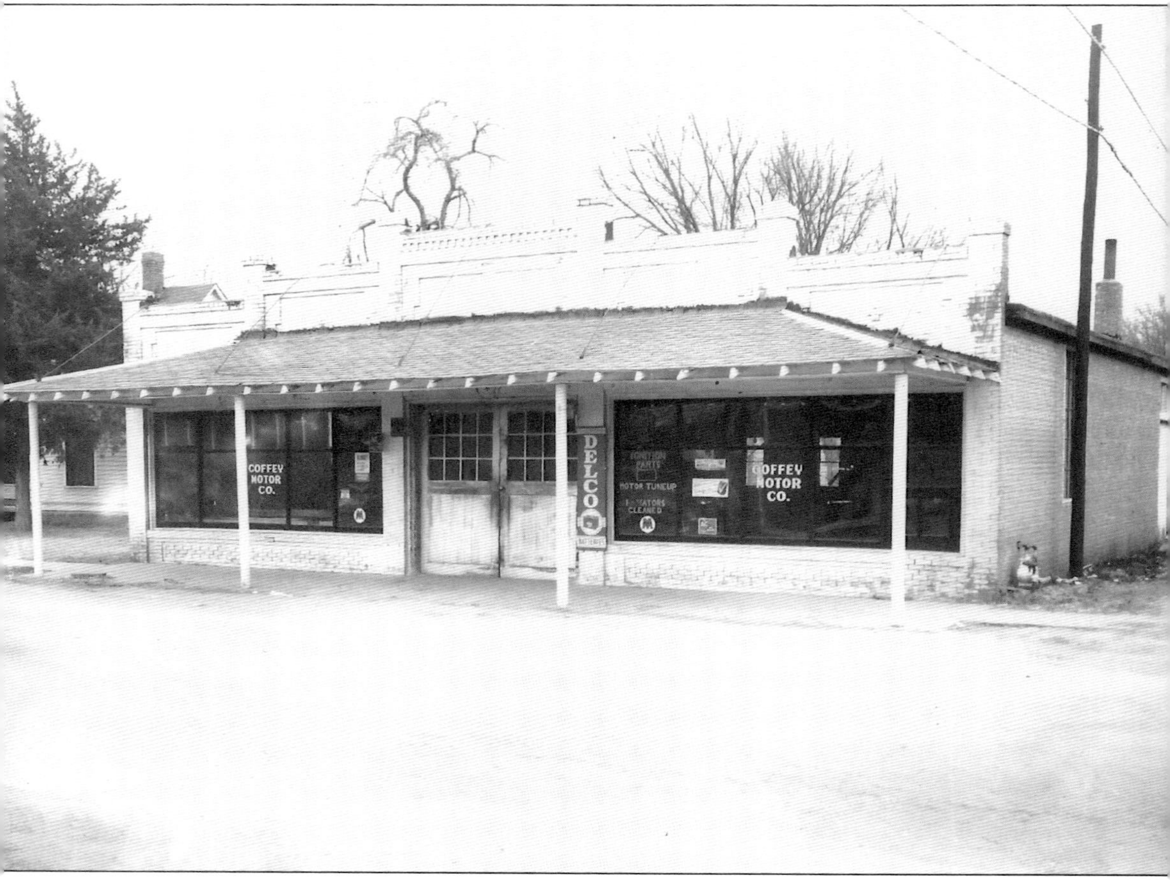

This building is located on Second Street in Mulvane. It has had several tenants. Originally, it was an auto parts store, and it has also been a pool hall. The building straddles the Sedgwick-Sumner County Line. In this photograph, it houses the Coffey Motor Company, an auto parts dealer. At one time, a wall divided the building into two halves. Two individual doors, one for each half of the building, replaced the large double doors, allowing two separate businesses to operate. (Courtesy of the Mulvane Historical Museum.)

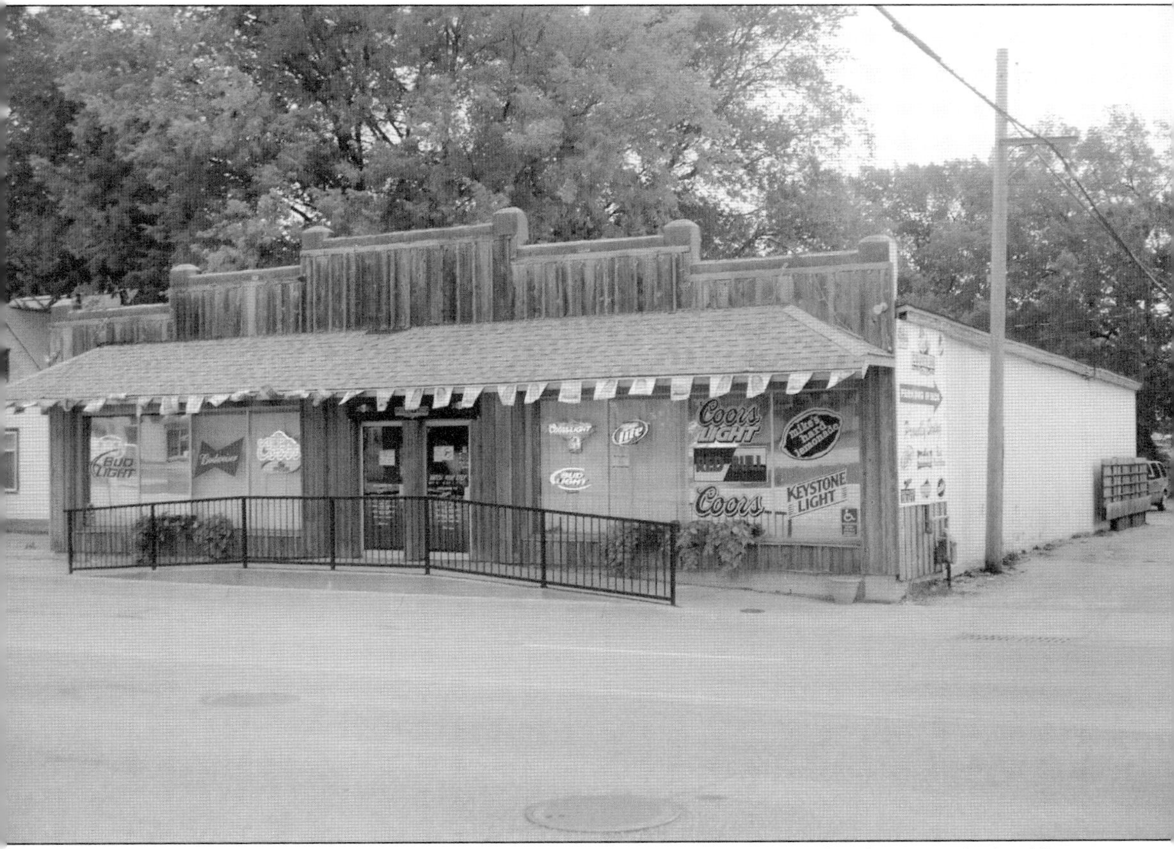

Today, the Second Street building is home to R.D.'s County Line, named so because the building straddles Sedgwick and Sumner Counties. The advertising accurately states that meals are prepared in Sedgwick County but eaten in Sumner County. It offers sandwiches, pool, and live music. It features a relaxed atmosphere in a friendly environment where neighbors get together to celebrate birthdays, anniversaries, or just a nice conversation after work. The live music showcases some of the area's top singers and musicians. On any given weekend, one can hear country, rock, or the blues. (Photograph by Gerald McCoy.)

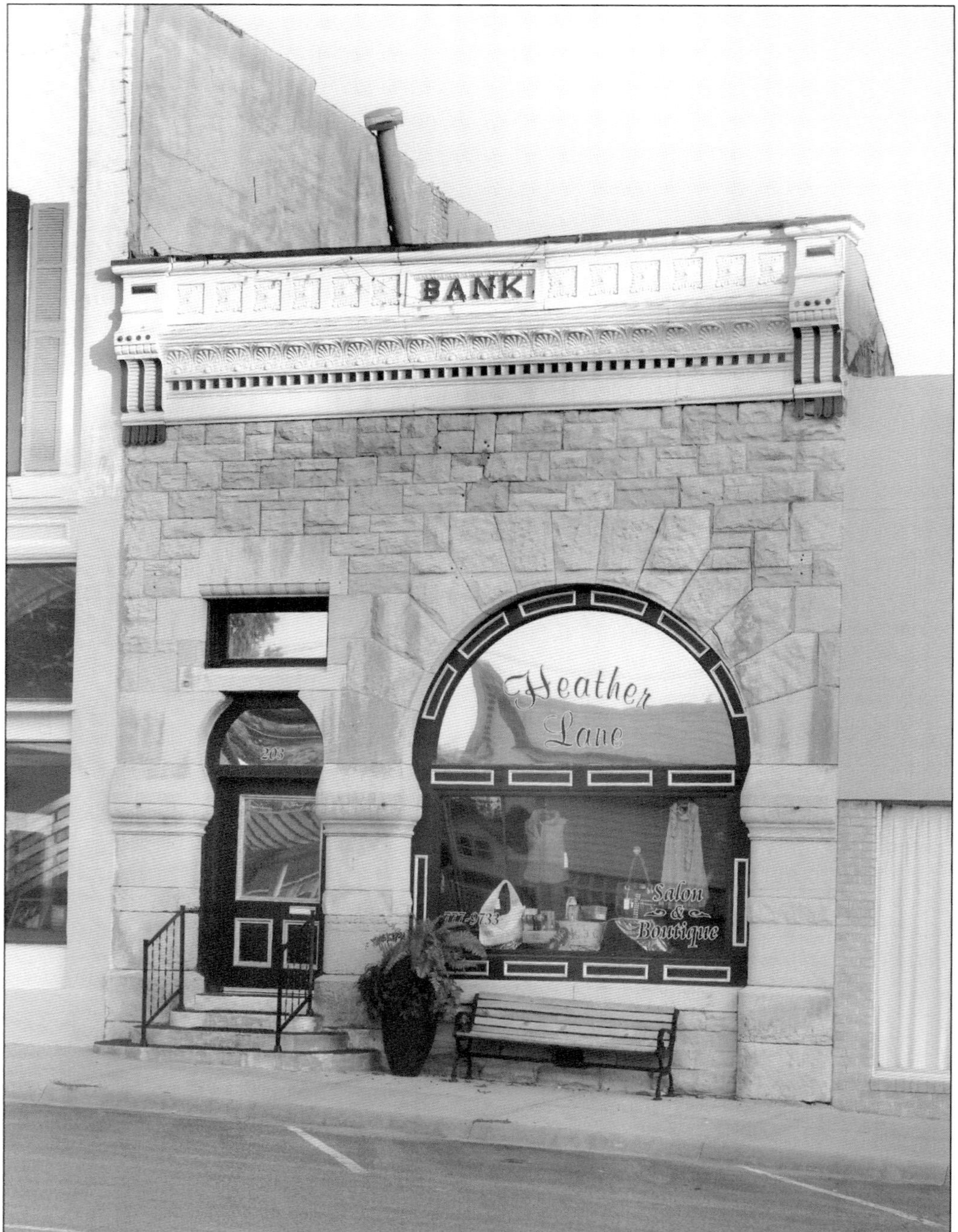

This building, on the south side of Main Street just west of First Street, is the original site of the Mulvane State Bank, which was founded in 1886. The original bank building was destroyed by fire in 1893 and was rebuilt at the same location. In 1954, the bank moved to its present location across the street. The building is now the home of Heather Lane, a hair salon and gift shop. The establishment offers hair-styling services, manicures, pedicures, and fashion accessories. When the building was restored, the word "Bank" was retained as part of the exterior. (Photograph by Gerald McCoy.)

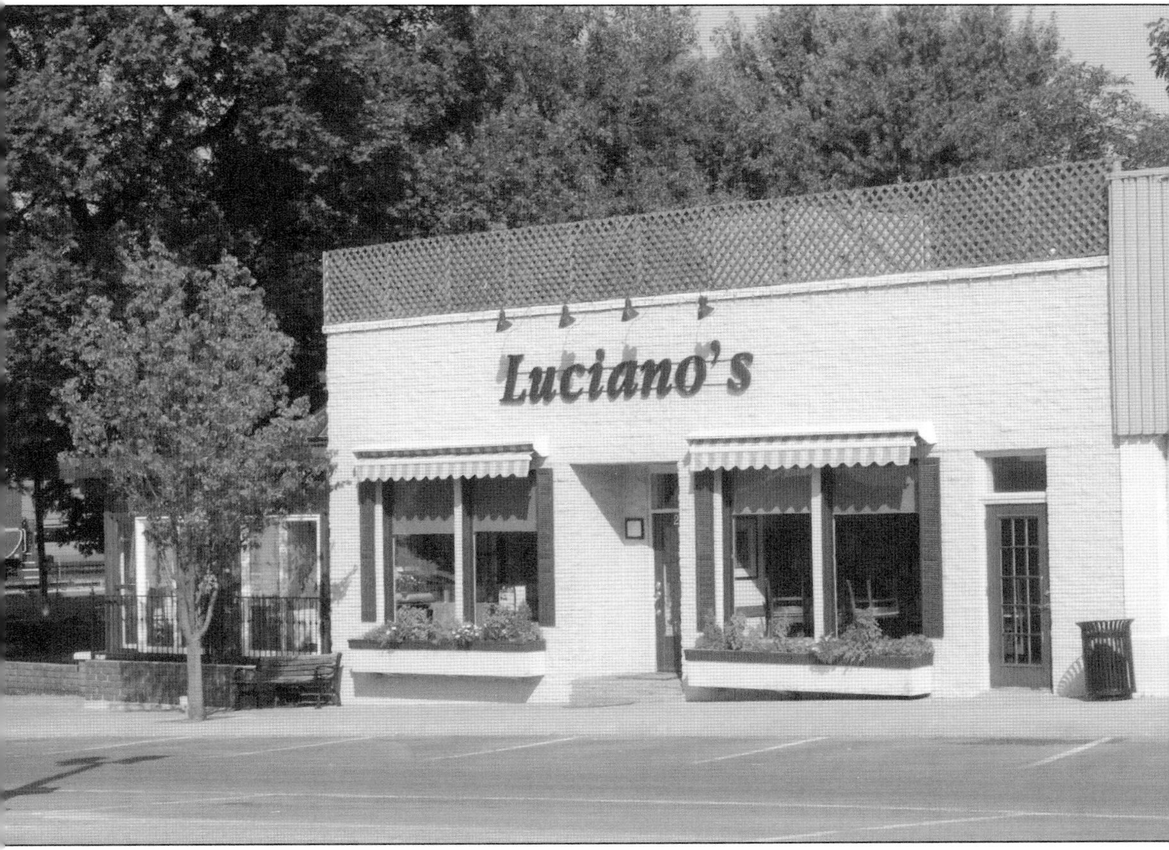

Luciano's Italian Restaurant is on the north side of Main Street, where the Canaday Lumber Yard once stood. Luciano Mottola was born in Italy and grew up in Viareggio, but he selected Mulvane as the place to open his restaurant. The wheat fields and sunflowers reminded him of his Tuscan homeland. Luciano's features authentic Italian cuisine, including salads, pasta, and fine wines. The restaurant, located in a historic part of town, possesses a special ambiance. It is considered to be one of the best dining experiences in this part of Kansas. (Photograph by Gerald McCoy.)

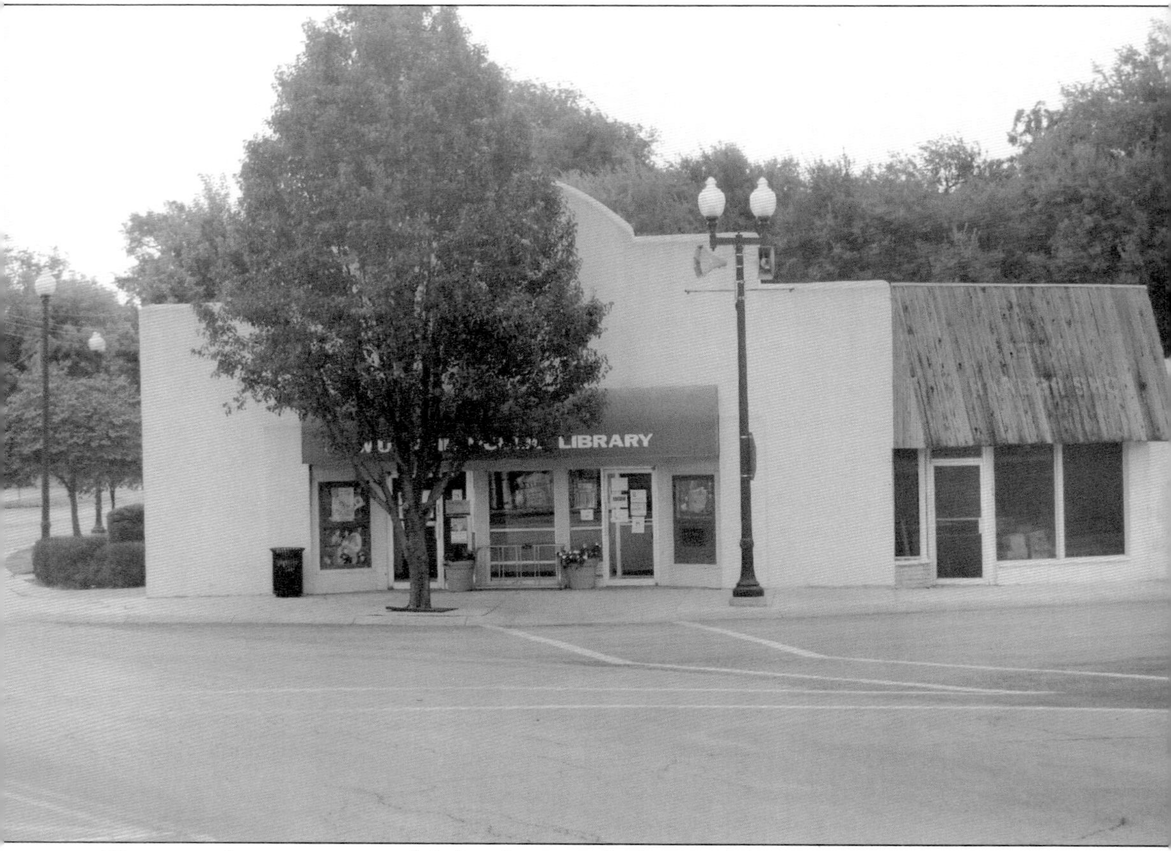

The town theater was remodeled and is now the home of the Mulvane Public Library. Where once the likes of Errol Flynn and Douglas Fairbanks were seen on the silver screen, a different kind of storytelling takes place. Children gather for reading, students come to do research, and residents check out books from best-selling authors. The library loan system gives people access to materials from all over Kansas. The building offers the library much more space than it had in its previous building on Main Street, and it preserves one of Mulvane's landmark structures. (Photograph by Gerald McCoy.)

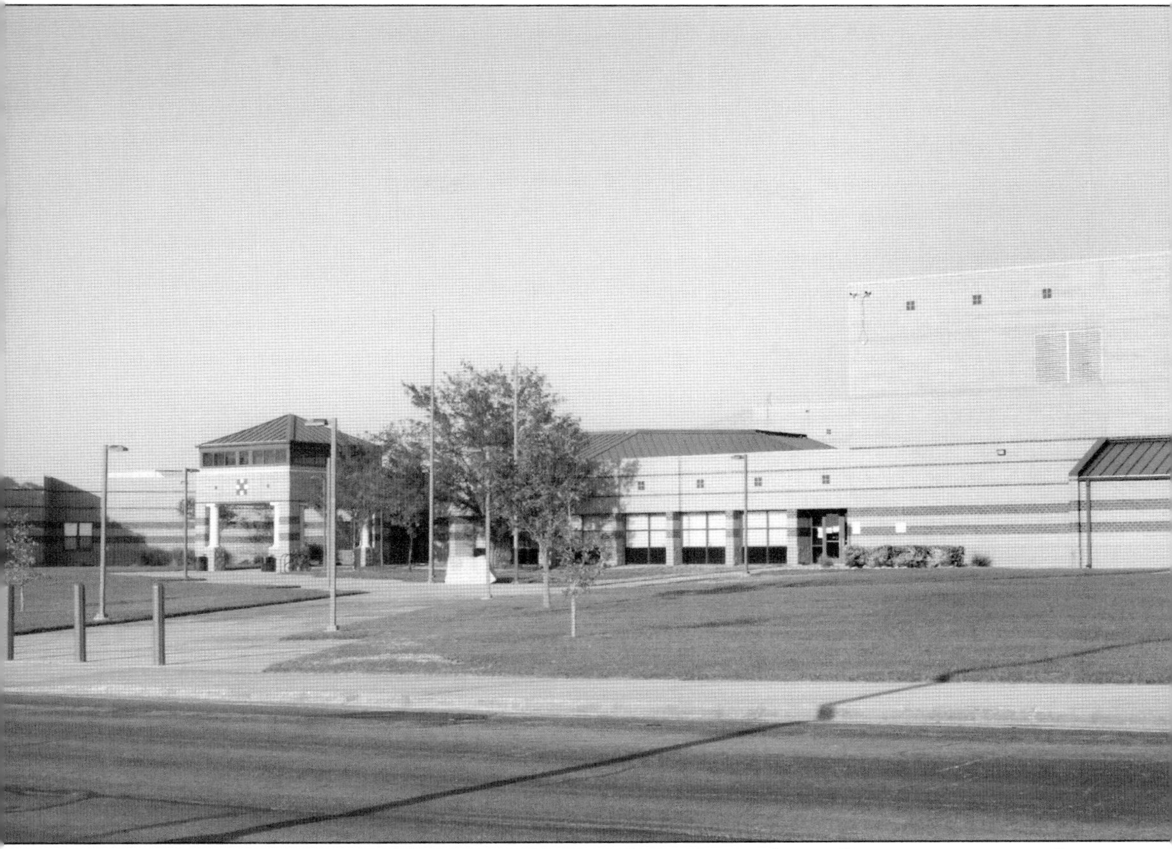

The new Mulvane High School has an enrollment of over 600 students. On a monument at the front of the building is a quote from Winston Churchill. The British prime minister was talking about the D-Day invasion and its relationship to World War II, but the idea also applies to education and graduation from high school. "Now this is not the end. It is not even the beginning of the end. But it is perhaps the end of the beginning." (Photograph by Gerald McCoy.)

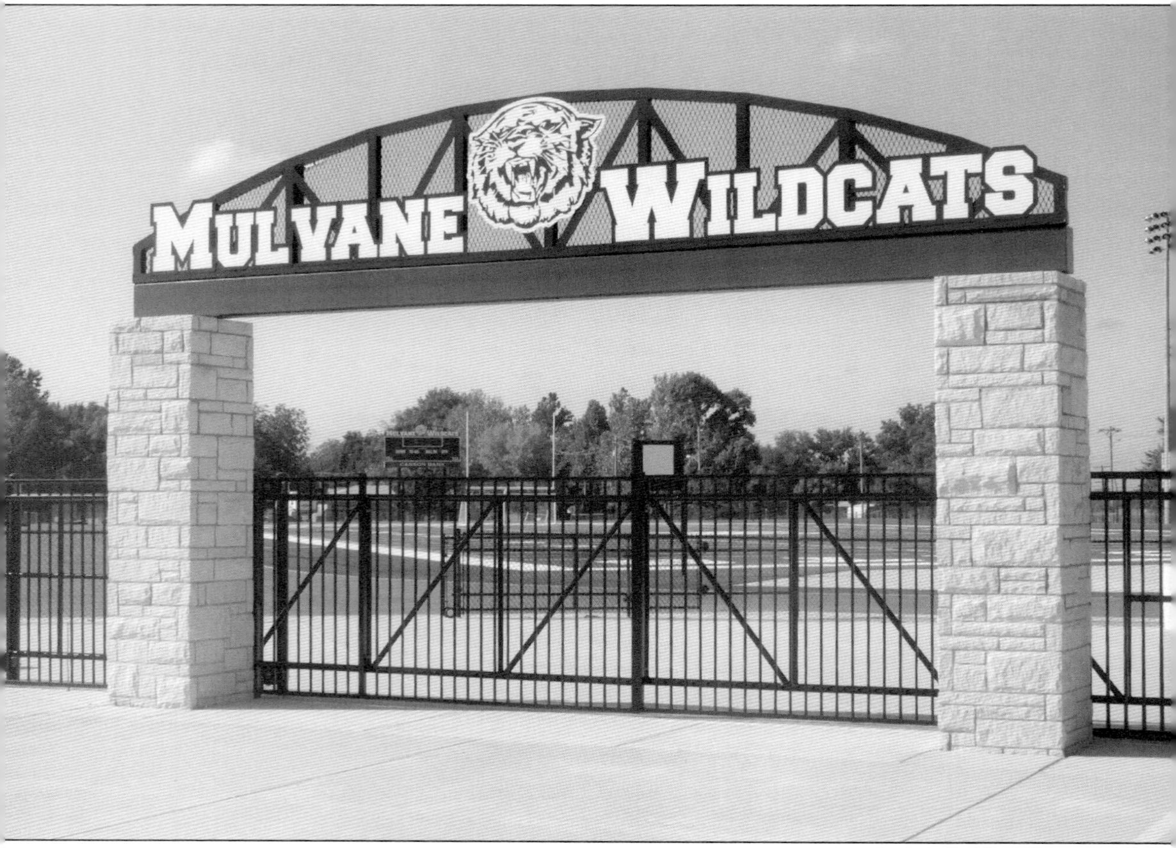

Lyle Couch Field has been the home of the Wildcats football team since 1955. In 2012, it underwent renovation that included a new entrance to the seating area. Couch was the principal of Mulvane High School for eight years, joining the staff in 1963. He was highly regarded by his peers, students, and the community. He played a vital part in the school's administration, and his knowledge, capability, and interest in education and the community helped establish an outstanding educational program. In the fall of 1970, Couch was diagnosed with a brain tumor, and he passed away on November 23, 1971. The school board, led by Superintendent Dean Parks, honored Lyle Couch by naming the football stadium after him. (Photograph by Gerald McCoy.)

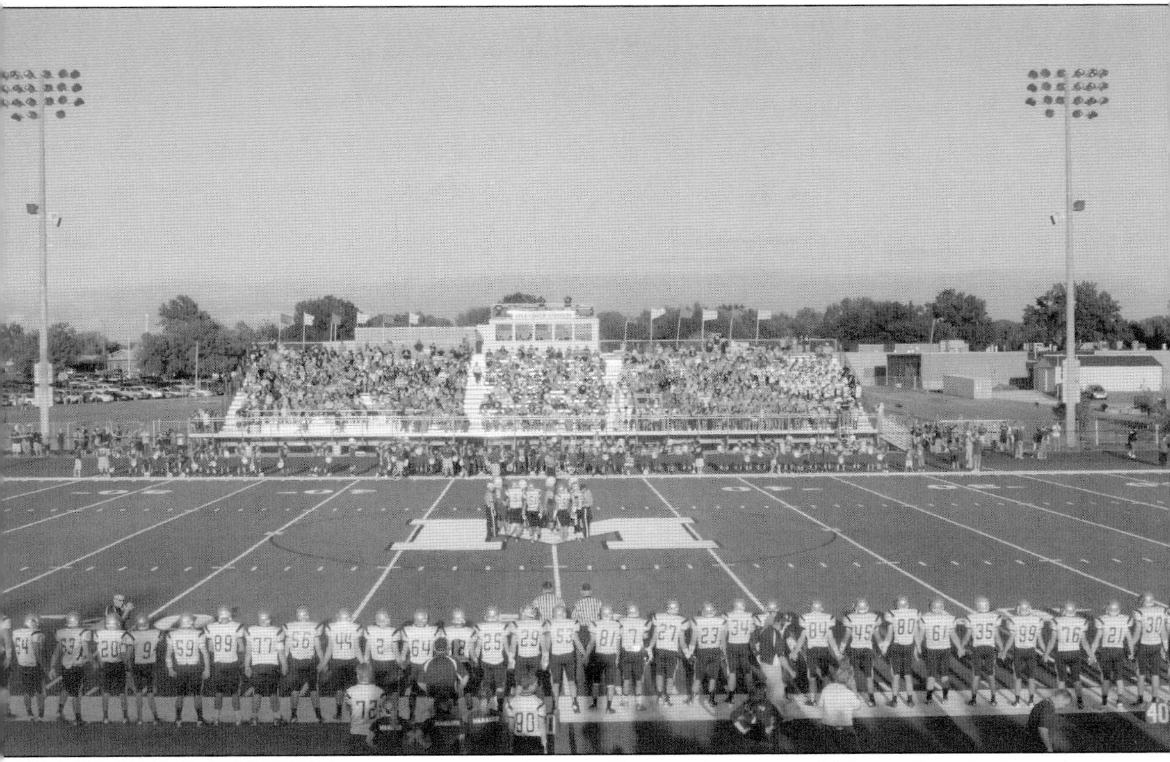

Another part of the field's renovation was the installation of a new turf. Shown here is the coin toss for the first game played on the new surface. Mulvane went on to defeat Chanute High School 30-9 on August 31, 2012. The first game played here was held on September 23, 1955, when Derby blanked Mulvane 6-0. Prior to this field, games were played at the site of the old high school. That field was distinctive because it was built on uneven ground. One team or the other was always moving the ball uphill. (Photograph by Gerald McCoy.)

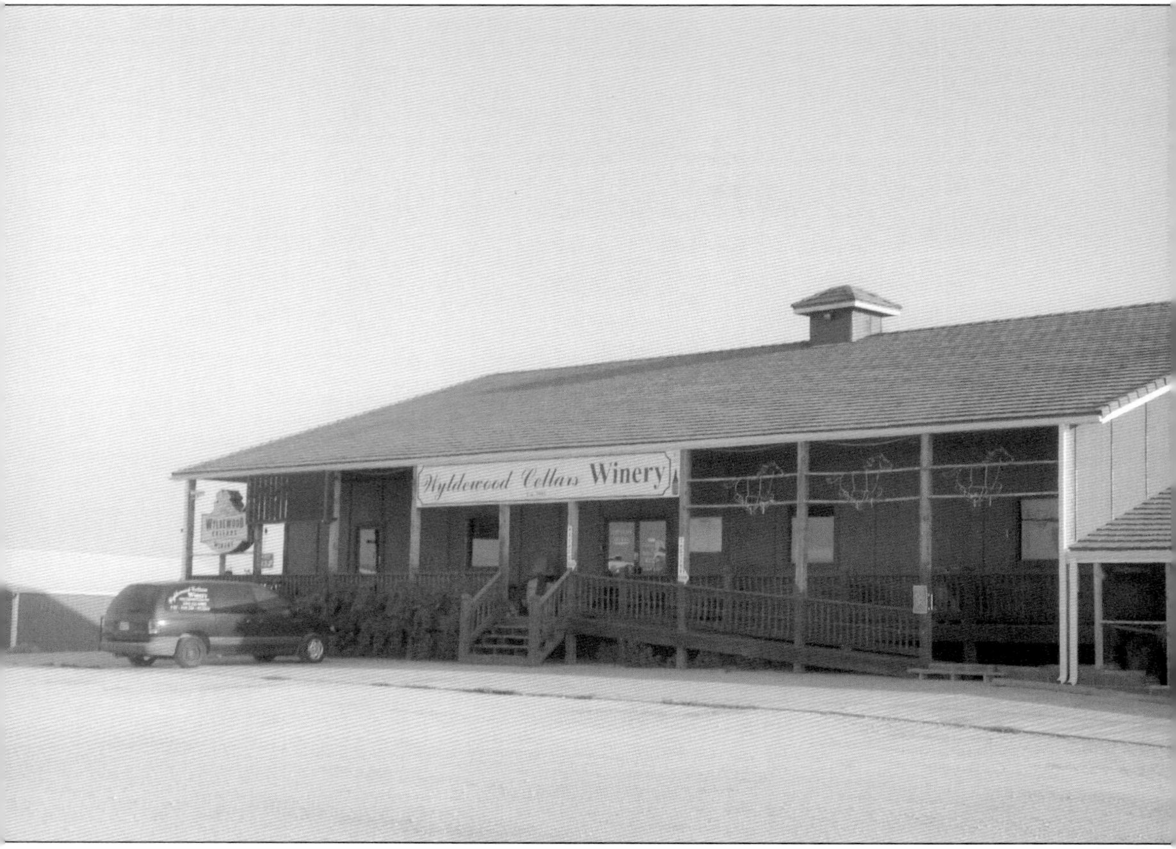

Wyldewood Cellars was launched in December 1994 by the brother-and-sister team of John and Merry Brewer. Since a 1999 fire, the winery has been at the location shown here, just outside of Mulvane. Wyldewood Cellars now produces over 40 different types of Kansas wine. What began as a small elderberry winery has blossomed into an internationally recognized winery, the winner of over 400 international awards. Wyldewood Cellars' Spiced Elderberry Wine was served at the 2002 Winter Olympics in Utah and was awarded the Best Non-Grape Wine in North and Latin America, among many other gold medals. (Photograph by Gerald McCoy.)

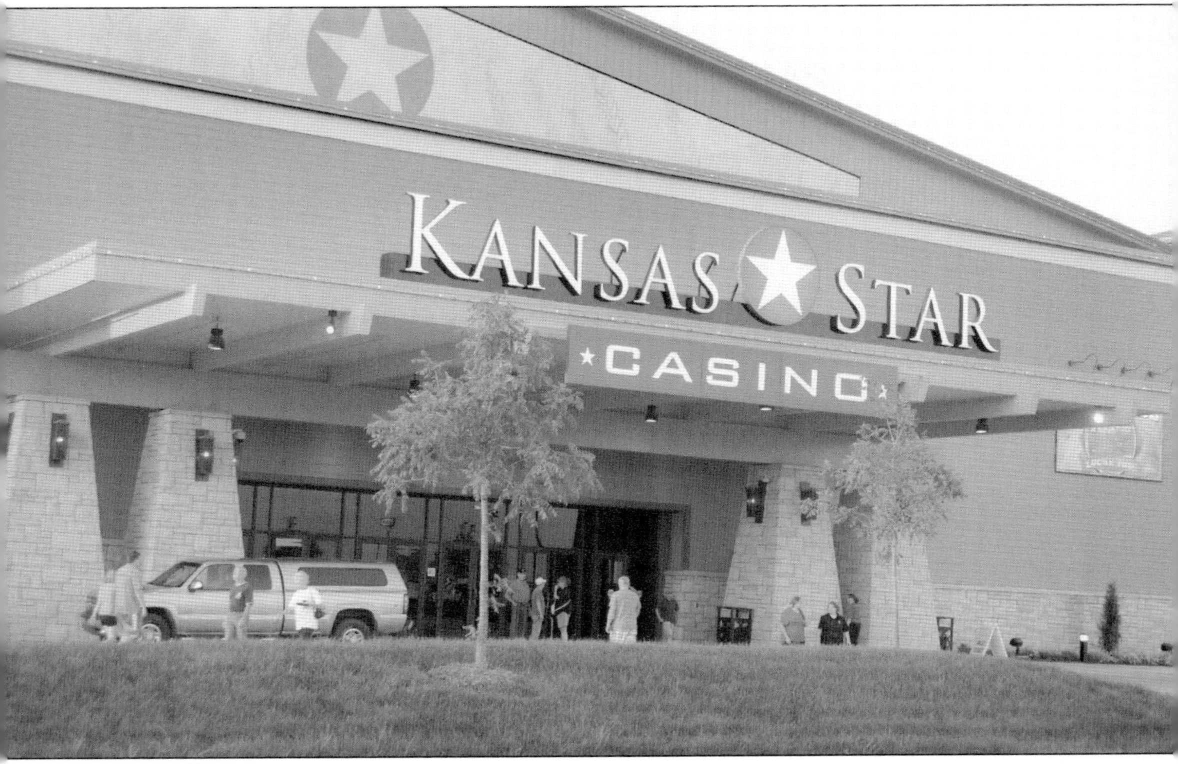

The Kansas Star Casino opened for business on December 26, 2011. It offers gaming activities for those who want to come to Mulvane and sample a little bit of Las Vegas–style excitement The second phase of construction will offer 1,750 slots, 50 table games, and a five-table poker room. The Kansas Star hotel will feature 300 deluxe rooms and suites as well as dining options that include a 250-seat buffet, a steak house showcasing steaks and fresh seafood, a sports bar, and a food court. There will also be an event center with over 4,000 seats, an RV park, and a 24-acre equine center. (Photograph by Gerald McCoy.)

Consistent with our mission to preserve history on a local level, this book was printed in South Carolina on American-made paper and manufactured entirely in the United States. Products carrying the accredited Forest Stewardship Council (FSC) label are printed on 100 percent FSC-certified paper.